The Soul in the Brain

The Soul in the Brain

The Cerebral Basis of Language, Art, and Belief

MICHAEL R. TRIMBLE, M.D., F.R.C.P.,
F.R.C.PSYCH.

Professor of Behavioral Neurology
Institute of Neurology
University of London
London, United Kingdom

The Johns Hopkins University Press
Baltimore

The Johns Hopkins University Press
2715 North Charles Street
Baltimore, Maryland 21218-4363
www.press.jhu.edu

Library of Congress Cataloging-in-Publication Data

Trimble, Michael R.
The soul in the brain : the cerebral basis of language, art, and belief /
Michael R. Trimble.
p. ; cm.
Includes bibliographical references and index.
ISBN 0-8018-8481-0 (hardcover : alk. paper)
1. Brain—Miscellanea. 2. Neuropsychology. 3. Language and culture.
4. Neurobiology. 5. Art. I. Title.
[DNLM: 1. Neuropsychology. 2. Brain Diseases—physiopathology.
3. Language Disorders—psychology. 4. Language. 5. Religion and medicine.
WL 103.5 T831s 2006]
QP376.T75 2006
612.8—dc22   2006012325

A catalog record for this book is available from the British Library.

To Graham, who has the gift of laughter
which he has shared with so many of us over the years,
as a reminder of the important things in life

Gods withdraw, but their rituals live on, and no one except a few intellectuals notices that they have ceased to mean anything

—E. R. Dodds, *The Greeks and the Irrational*

CONTENTS

The author is grateful to several people who have viewed parts or the whole of various portions of the final manuscript. He is especially grateful to Andrea Cavanna, John Cutting, Tim Griffiths, Lennart Heimer, Lisa Hughes, Gavin Selerei, John Smythies, Liane Strauss, Shakti Temple-Smith, Jason Warren, Jenifer Wilson-Barnett, and Adam Zeman.

If you fear that opening your mind will cause your brain to fall out, then this book is not for you. If you are unhappy discussing neuroscience in the context of poetry, music, and, above all, religion, then again this text cannot be recommended. For what I have attempted to do is to understand how it is that the human species, so enamored with its own logical and critical facilities, has held strong religious beliefs and a reverence for the arts, apparently since the dawn of what we call civilization. The period of the Enlightenment, with its lifting of the veils on so many mysteries; the conceptual revolutions of Copernicus, Darwin, and Freud; and the past hundred years of astonishing development in all the sciences has seemingly not shifted the overall tone of human thought and behavior on these matters one iota. How did such faithful knowledge arise, and what might neuroscience have to contribute to such a question?

I was first driven to think on these matters by my patients, many of whom have epilepsy, mood disorders, or combinations of the neurological and the psychopathological, who would often either bring me some of their writings or regale me with their religious experiences. I should make it clear that epilepsy, bipolar disorder, and schizophrenia can be devastating human conditions, but we now accept them to be related to disturbed brain structure or function, as opposed to being the wages of sin, and in the past few years many people have benefited from treatments that have arisen from our understanding of how the brain works and how it may be disordered in such illnesses.

The path of knowledge over the past three hundred years has extended toward a deeper and more coherent picture of the nature of humankind and of the natural forces that drive behavior. The human brain has been central to this endeavor, but only in the past thirty years or so have newer techniques of investigation of brain structure and function become available, allowing further penetration of the mysteries of human feelings, thoughts, and emotions. Alongside these methods, in medical practice, much more attention has been given to understanding what happens when the mind goes wrong as a consequence of either neurological or psychiatric illness. This has established the somatic nature of much mental illness, as a profusion of neural systems, neurotransmitters, and neuromodulators have become implicated in pathogeneses.

Religion, in a more general sense, has not generated much scientific interest until recently. The well-known Cartesian dualism idealized the split between *res cogitans*, things of the mind, including the soul, and *res extensa*, dimensional objects, extended in space, which could be measured. Science became a matter of measurement; the soul could rest peacefully, protected from the prying intrusion of progress.

An interest in religious practices and the meaning of, for example, religious rituals stems to a large extent from the anthropological studies of the nineteenth and twentieth centuries, when the predominant Judeo-Christian beliefs of the Western world became subject to comparison with a multitude of religious practices from around the world. Attempts to usurp the concepts of religion altogether, atheism by any other name, have an even longer history, although a careful line was drawn between skepticism, such as that promoted by the interesting Scottish philosopher David Hume (1711–76), and atheism, which was against the law, at least in England. However, these and related concepts should not be confused with a desire by scientists to understand human behavior and its meaning, in its complexity and entirety. Any question about the existence of God or the gods should be an empirical issue, seen in the same context as, for example, questions about the spherical nature of the world or the composition of the moon. In the same way that the seventeenth century gave the inquisitive investigator the appropriate methods with which to test hypotheses about the nature of the world, the twenty-first century allows for the study of human feelings and experiences in ways never before imagined. This book explores the ground of some of those feelings.

I have taken clinical observations and investigations of several neuropsychiatric disorders to launch an investigation into some aspects of the way the human brain modulates artistic and religious experiences. Many of the symptoms of people with the disorders I describe are not universal and, especially in the case of epilepsy, affect a minority of patients. Furthermore, although I am fascinated by the phenomena I am writing about, I hope my interest has never been intrusive for such patients, especially by my inquiries about their deeply held personal beliefs and practices.

The ideas in this book originated with a simple observation that, in the growing literature on the literary talents of people with epilepsy (from Dostoevsky on), few poets seem to be included. In fact, I came to the conclusion that writing effective poetry is probably incompatible with certain disorders, schizophrenia being one, and seems highly restrained by epilepsy. In contrast, there seem to be legions of poets with what used to be called manic-depressive illness, or cyclothymia. I agree with the sentiments of the neuroscientist J. Z. Young who noted that poets teach us to use words with special force. We may need their help finding new ways to talk about brains.[1]

My neuroscientific interests have straddled the borders between neuropsychiatry, behavioral neurology, and biological psychiatry, and in the past few decades a wealth of information has become available about brain function and dysfunction in the kinds of disorder mentioned above. A central question then became whether a study of the alterations of language in these conditions might lead to an understanding of the cerebral representations and anatomical circuitry associated with poetry as opposed to, say, prose. The studies bearing on these issues are reviewed, and certain conclusions emerge, especially about the brain hemisphere contributions that relate to poetic expression.

Other fascinating features of some of the neuropsychiatric disorders discussed in the text are the associated change of religious behaviors and the often profound religious experiences reported in subgroups of patients. The term *hyperreligiosity* is often used to describe this phenomenon, and it has been the subject now of several investigations, which also hint at its possible relationship with neuroanatomical circuits, giving us a handle on yet another distinctly human capacity that simply has to have cerebral counterparts.

A linking theme between poetry and religion is music. Many have argued that music is different from the other arts, especially in not having a representational capacity in the way that, for example, a painting of an apple has. Others maintain that music could or should be treated as a language in its own right. This is a controversial issue, but following on such lines of thought, my review of the literature suggests that areas of the brain that are involved in mediating poetry and religious experiences may also link, in part, to our capacity to respond to music.

Why do we cry when we listen to music? I suspect that music brings tears to people's eyes more often than any other art form, followed by poetry, with novels and the visual arts farther down the list. In one survey of emotional experiences to paintings, James Elkins, who admits never having cried before a painting, has found few people who did and notes that neither the art historian Sir Ernst Gombrich nor Leonardo da Vinci were so moved.[2] These observations take me into some speculations about the meaning of tragedy and lead me to ask, as have others, Why do we go to the theater to cry? Tragedy, poetry, music, religious feelings, and tears are all intertwined, but I would suggest that this coalescence reflects our biological heritage, starting with an evolutionary development of the brains of primates and leading up to *Homo sapiens,* where such behaviors become manifest.

The study of disorders of the brain can shed light on how the brain works, and clinical observation followed by attempts to reveal underlying anatomy, physiology, and pathology is a time-honored methodology. The path less taken has been to study the influence of disorders, especially neuropsychiatric disorders, on behaviors that relate to artistic expression or religiosity. This neglect has occurred in spite of a well-trod history of observations, which I suggest form solid enough stepping stones on which to venture forth. In part, this relates to a lack of interest in such topics on the part of practitioners and neuroscientists and an even greater lack of interest among those who fund research. It also reflects on the now-closing but still-present gap between neurology and psychiatry as academic disciplines, driven by an irrational attachment to a Cartesian dichotomy between mind and brain. Especially from the time of Freud, psychiatry took a psychological as opposed to a neurobiological approach to psychopathology, and it was eclipsed in terms of understanding the brain in relation to psychiatric symptoms by the success of a localizational approach to neurology. This became successful in predicting, in the days before adequate brain scanning, the sites of lesions in the brains of patients and was the basis of neurological clinical practice.

Many things have changed in the past thirty years, some of which are explored in this book. Not the least has been the resurgence of the discipline of neuropsychiatry, a parent of neuroscience, whose practitioners have an interest in the way brain disorders alter behaviors in their wider context. This embraces changes of personality and associations with psychiatric disorders such as depression, mania, and psychoses, in general, but must also embrace changes in a person's approach to cultural phenomena—hence the interest in hyperreligiosity and a related phenomenon, hypergraphia, the tendency toward extensive and often repetitive writing, seen in some neuropsychiatric conditions.

Advances in neuroanatomy, neurophysiology, neurochemistry, and brain-imaging techniques and a greater willingness to accept the primacy of the brain as the organ that controls and modulates our experiences and behavior have spurned new, though barely nascent, disciplines referred to here as neuro-aesthetics and neurotheology. I suggest that explorations of patients with paradigmatic neuropsychiatric conditions, such as epilepsy and bipolar affective disorders, are the key to unraveling some of the mysteries of the cerebral representations of our highest cultural experiences. These, however, like the discipline of neurophilosophy, are jealously guarded fields.

An earlier version of this manuscript was reviewed by an unknown reader, whose comments were helpful in allowing me to anticipate some of the criticisms that will emerge, especially about links between the brain and artistic activities. Sometimes a controversy is not labeled as such, and in medical science generally one can find nine papers that lead to a conclusion and one that does not. There clearly is a controversy, but the data lean in one direction; such leaning is important as long as one does not fall over.

I have taken an evolutionary stance to the whole subject. Anyone who chooses to ignore the fact that we, and our brains, are, at least for now, at the summit of a mountain of evolutionary development that is millions of years old simply has not got a grasp on reality. The paleopsychic processes embedded in the human central nervous system did not simply arrive a few thousand years ago; the drives and cognitions that have brought us this far have millions of years of selection and evolutionary pressure behind them. Furthermore, anyone who cannot work out that, far from our having descended from a golden age, a time before the Fisher King was wounded and when the Grail was here on earth, we have arrived at this point in time through an evolutionary progression from nature itself, red in tooth and claw, again simply has not got it.

In addition to the historical evolutionary context of the book, there is also a historical approach taken to several of the topics. This arises, in part, from a personal interest in the development of ideas that over the past two millennia have been rich and fertile, though in the neurosciences and in neurophilosophy they took off in the eighteenth century. This approach also emphasizes how ideas have accreted over time, giving due credit, I trust, to past masters. If I quote some poetry to enhance a text, it is because this book is, in part, about poetry, but it is also with the hope that those who hold little brief for poetry at present may be stimulated to read a little more.

Naturally, I have a task to maintain a view that poetry is different from prose, an argument developed in chapter 4, but I do not stand alone on such matters and have sought backers for my view. Of course, there is a point at which poetic prose may be referred to as poetry, and, I suppose, prose poetry may be referred to as prose. My point is not that there are always clear-cut differences between the two but that there are different reflections from their surfaces to which we respond differently, and, in spite of the arguments about the borderlands (where all wars are fought), there are many creations that everyone would agree are pieces of poetry and many others that are clearly prose.

Similarly, I do not want to be seen to have adopted a simple right brain–left brain dichotomy in my view of brain function. I do urge investigators to take more interest in the functions of the right hemisphere of the human brain, and I am suggesting that there is something special about the way the right brain modulates language, unifying the languages of poetry, music, and religion. But our brains in health act holistically, in harmony, and only when that harmony is disturbed does one see disorders that clinicians refer to as neurological or psychiatric or neuropsychiatric.

In the final chapter the ideas developed in the first eight are summarized, but they spill over into other areas that have to do with our cultural experiences, including a return to considering tragedy and suggesting perhaps a new theory of why we go to the theater to cry. I say return, because some years ago I was awarded a university prize based, in part, on an essay on tragedy (mainly about the works of Thomas Hardy), which I turned to again while writing this book. I have chosen to quote quite a lot of Nietzsche, again in the hope that those readers unfamiliar with his writings will be stimulated to read more. However, he has so much to say about the topics in the book that I unashamedly quote him liberally.

Of course, having viewed the criticisms, I could have removed some sections of the text that my reviewer found unsatisfactory, but instead I have elaborated on such ideas, in hopes of making them clearer. If I have made a slip in my references to the structure or function of poetry, I can only apologize. My intention in this book is not to please the too-focused academic but to stimulate ideas.

No doubt many will take me to task for really believing that the brain is it—no brain, no sensations, no feelings, no movements, and no philosophy. Most neuroscientists now take such a view (there have been notable exceptions, such as the neurosurgeon Wilder Penfield or the neurophysiologist Sir John Eccles), but many writers, especially those wedded to folk psychology, including many philosophers, are resistant to it. So be it. But the neuroscientific explorations of human behavior and motives will continue, the conclusions may simply become facts of life (or death), and people will have to come to terms with them in their own perspectives, in the same way that they embrace or ignore Copernicus or Darwin or the ravages of dementia.

This book does not examine the issue of the existence of gods or God; such discussions can be found in countless other books, and they go beyond the neuroscience presented here. However, that question and related ones, such as the basis of truth or morality, usually viewed as questions for theology or philosophy, are not immune from neuroscientific enquiry. I would venture to speculate that they cannot advance (beyond the speculations of the past two thousand or so years) without the implantation of a neuroscientific perspective. What we know and how we know it are topics that firmly cross the horizon of neurobiology, and only the naïve will continue to ignore that eventuality.

My first degree was in neuroanatomy, and it is still with a sense of awe and wonder that I view the human brain, when seen in vivo during anatomical dissection or reconstructed through one of the wonderful high-resolution brain scanners that we now have at our disposal. Dissect a brain and you will alter your perspective on the world and your place in it. If you open up a brain, the mind will, eventually, fall out.

CHAPTER ONE

Where Did It All Begin?

William Blake (1757–1827), visionary poet and poet of visions, possible madman but considered genius, beheld a world in a grain of sand, and God in anyone who could see the Infinite in all things.[1] And yet there are more stars in our galaxy than there are grains of sand on all the beaches of our world, and perhaps more galaxies in the universe than the number of those stars. Cosmologists study the fossils of the stars, those imprints of universal history, taking snapshots from the past as the first billions-years-old starlight echoes back to us the inchoate reverberations of that time when everything emerged from its dense beginning. We are told that the expansion of the universe, unfolding with the big bang from condensed gas, far hotter and denser than our sun's core, some 18 billion years ago spun those tiny fragments that were to become our earth into orbit, with its nearest sun to ours some 25 trillion miles away. Atoms, which developed from primordial material, coalesced and conjoined to condense into these planets, stars, and galaxies, forming, in our small microcosm, the intricate structure and nature of our solar system with its surrounding universe. We now know that planets are common and that ours is not unique. Our sun is a star in a galaxy that contains billions of stars. Many planets surround those stars—worlds, some like ours, fertile for life, in orbit around other suns as life enhancing as ours. The very hugeness of the universe is unimaginable, unless we revert to metaphor and, like Blake, can salvage a world in a grain of sand.

Poised between the atoms and the stars is our humble human scale. We are but one stage in the emergence of life on this planet, a process that has taken some 4.5 billion years. We simply do not know how or when life got started here, whether underground or in space, as part of a natural process or by accident, and we do not know whether the galaxy that enfolds us is teeming with life, similar to or unlike ours. Oxygen exhaled by primitive organisms for a billion years led to the development of multicellular life. The 550 million years of the Cambrian era saw the greening of the land and the explosion of life before mammalian descent ushered in human development. The first mammals appeared about 50 million years ago; the earliest hominids, some 4 million to 4.5 million. With *Australopithicus, Homo habilis, H. erectus,*[2] and then *H. sapiens,* perhaps 50,000 to 150,000 years ago, evolution saw the rise of human culture, religion, myth, music, and madness.[3]

Myth

An appropriate starting point is myth. Myths, masquerading as the revealed truth of a religion or enjoyed as psychologically symbolic narratives, are to be read as metaphors, our inner world transformations of the outer world. We do not know where and when myths originated on our cultural time scale, but their purpose may be guessed. Myths frame for a group of people the intuited order of nature and help individuals navigate their way through the stages of life from birth to death and perhaps beyond. The earliest myths, with narrow horizons, were local and tribal and were bound into nature and the natural environment of the group.

Anyone viewing the religions of mankind with an unprejudiced eye must recognize the mythic themes they share, even if differently interpreted by individual societies. Carl Jung's archetypes are one reflection of this underlying structure; Joseph Campbell has called them "universals," albeit locally and socially conditioned. These were innate, immanent, archetypal creations of the early human psyche, embedded within the structure of the evolving human brain.

The metaphors employed in any mythology may be defined as affect-laden signs and symbols, derived from intuitions of the self and the community. These become revealed through ritual, prayers, poems, meditations, ceremonies, annual festivals, and the like in such a way that all members of the community may be held, both in mind and in sentiment, to a common understanding and thus moved to live in accordance with the structure of the myth. Out of the early individualized and collective myths emerged religion, but what I refer to as religious feelings must have preceded the development of any formal religion and their corresponding institutions.

The Origins of Religion

For little more than perhaps a million years out of the long, glorious evolution of life on this planet has one species, which became *sapiens,* regarded certain things as sacred. These things are set apart, revered, associated with veneration, with ritual, and then with the divine. We have no access to the ancient mind, but we can assume that it was fundamentally different from our own, especially with regard to language.

This theme remains at the heart of the mystery of mankind. Our language not only distinguishes us from all other species of all evolutionary time but also, for each one of us, embeds our individual psychological expression and imprints for us our social and cultural boundaries.

When the concept of gods or a God established itself in the human mind is not known, but religious rituals have been traced back to at least the Neanderthal time, with evidence of the ritualized use of animal parts and human mutilation.[4] The afterworld, or some kind of ancestor abode, was revealed to the individual through dreams, in which the dead were reanimated, the past revived, and the future revealed.

Burying the dead with some afterlife in mind implies a ceremony, which itself implies an emotional aura, the beginnings of grief and the contrasting joy of the wake.[5] The dating of such epochal events will forever be only speculation. Some say that some kind of religious ceremonies have been practiced for more than a million years. Like everything in evolution however, things could only have graduated; there was no sudden enlightenment of the world's primates, only a progressive apprehension of the sacred.

The earliest rituals provide some clues. It is known that in Paleolithic times, some 100,000 years ago, the dead were buried with objects, presumably to help them on a journey or in some kind of afterlife existence. Tools and hunting weapons, food and flowers aided the preliterate Neanderthal on an ethereal way to a world that, if not known, was at least imagined. Later, the dead were buried with ornaments, necklaces, and beads, and the early semblances of religious art were observed. Cave art reveals a world perhaps haunted by spirits. The shaman appeared, and religious symbolism flourished.[6]

Cro-Magnon, an early modern human, handsome with a high, rounded forehead,[7] swarmed over the planet in the middle Stone Age, some hundred thousand years ago. The genus *Homo,* by now *sapiens* and language fluent, provided the first examples of prehistoric art and developed a complexity of spiritual beliefs, which included some idea of the gods. They made fire from flint and fashioned clay figures of animals and humans, especially women with bulging breasts and backsides—so-called Venus figurines. The era saw a symbolic explosion. Cro-Magnon also made the first musical instruments.[8]

The Fragmented Mind

Sometime in the fourth millennium BC, writing and mathematical measurement emerged in human culture and with it the idea of cosmic order. With this magnificent intellectual achievement, ultimately leading to our twenty-first-century ability to use computers and at least try for the stars, came the rise of concepts of civil order, and allegorical identifications began to be taken seriously. Probably for the first time, mythology, which had coalesced with reality yet was immediate in its individual and communal interpretation, became codified with institutional agendas. A system was formed that took advantage of and enslaved the primitive by attempting to abstract the mental deities from their objects; as Blake has observed, "Men forgot that all deities reside in the human breast."[9] Thus began the priesthood. Metaphors were misread and misplaced, denotation trumped connotation, the messenger was mistaken for the message, and life and thought were thrown off balance.[10]

A further sundering of the cognitive structure of myth, as culturally divisive as the division itself, emerged with Zarathustra (628–551 BC), also known as Zoroaster, whose writings date back to the sixth century BC. With Zarathustra, the sacred also bore the profane. After receiving a vision from the Wise Lord, Zarathustra preached his monotheistic teachings to an essentially polytheistic Iranian society. The Wise, all-good Lord had an adversary, the principle of evil, and it was up to man to decide, out of free choice, whether to follow the good or the evil.[11] Thus the conception of an absolute distinction between good and evil emerged, giving birth to the catastrophes that ensued over the next three thousand years. Good gods were contrasted with the bad, and good people and their behaviors and rituals were juxtaposed against evil.[12] Mankind, acting from free will, became fallen; light was contrasted with dark, and life with death. Time became a significant component of eschatology as well, the past progressing to a future, the fall leading to resurrection and the old world to the new.

Dualism

Dualism is a doctrine that posits the existence of two opposing principles. In some versions these work together, bringing harmony, a yin-yang yoyo of cooperation; in others, the two elements at best tolerate and at worst destroy each other. Religious dualism as germinated from the teachings of Zarathustra is but one form of psychological dualism that has permeated the history of human thought and culture. It contrasts with monism, and the religious counterpart of some ideals of monotheism, and with pluralism, the assumption of multiple realities and polytheism. Nevertheless, even monotheistic religions contain within them dualisms and pluralisms, and polytheisms have their dualisms.

The philosophical identification of dualism often distinguishes between two worlds, one knowable to the senses, the other transcendent, ultimately unknowable, as a Platonic ideal or as the *Ding-an-sich*.[13] Whether the opposing elements are Seth and Osiris, matter and spirit, the sacred and the profane, or good and evil, the underlying myths that try to explain the origins and course of the universe also reflect the cognitive dualism of man: masculine and feminine, active and passive, body and soul, love and hate. Blake recognizes the necessity of such opposites for human existence: "Without contraries is no progression . . . From these contraries spring what the religious call Good and Evil. Good is the passive that obeys Reason. Evil is the active springing from Energy. Good is Heaven, Evil is Hell." But he goes on:

> All bibles or sacred codes have been the causes of the following errors:
>
> 1. That man has two real existing principles, Viz: a Body and a Soul
> 2. That Energy, call'd Evil, is alone from the Body, and that Reason, call'd Good, is alone from the soul
> 3. That God will torment Man in Eternity for following his energies."[14]

The theme of dualism also pervades the work of the German philosopher Friedrich Nietzsche (1844–1900). He introduced his own version of Zarathustra in the form of a Rhadamanthine figure who confronts his listeners about their failure to examine their moral codes or faiths. In this celebration of individuality, of joyful self-sufficiency, Zarathustra, after ten years living alone on a mountain, descends to proclaim that God is dead and that man needs to overcome, to become an *Übermensche*.[15] Nietzsche opposed the view that Judeo-Christian morality was a divinely inspired code and emphasized its pagan and secular background. He saw truth as a movable host of metaphors, discussed the arbitrary nature of words, and reoriented philosophy toward the ontological (having to do with the nature of being) as opposed to the epistemological (having to do with the nature of knowledge). Before Nietzsche, the goal of many philosophers was to prove the existence of God, but he shifted the ground of inquiry to ask how beliefs in God or the gods had arisen. His overthrow of metaphysics, especially Platonism, called for a revaluation of all values, since once Platonic values are undermined then everything has to be repositioned, including traditional Christian values and morality, Christianity being referred to by him as Platonism for the people.[16] Zarathustra laments that no one listens to him.

Studies of Religion

Religion has been studied for hundreds of years in one way or another, yet finding a universal definition is difficult. In theory, the term must cover the natural and the supernatural, the theist and the polytheist, the holy texts, rituals, and beliefs of many cultures, the old established orders and the so-called new age cults. In fact, the assumption that religion is a unitary concept is hard to allow; many commentators simply will not be led to a limiting definition, and none is proffered here.

Spirituality has perhaps been segregated from the central concept of religion, the former being the more personal representation of the latter, with individual beliefs and values being contrasted with ritual and tradition. This distinction allows for another component of religion, the experience at the heart of spirituality, to be circumscribed.

The Varieties of Religious Experience

Published just over a hundred years ago, William James's collection of the Gifford lectures remains the most revealing investigation into the psychology of religion ever attempted.[17] James (1842–1910) studied religious experience as he would study other psychological phenomena, accepting their reality but also their vulnerability to scientific enquiry. His definition of religion is pertinent to the theme of this book: "Religion, therefore, as I now ask you arbitrarily to take it, shall mean for us *the feelings, acts, and experiences of individual men in their solitude, so far as they apprehend themselves to stand in relation to whatever they may consider the divine.*"[18]

James was thus concerned with immediate personal experience, which he considered to be universal to humankind and which he placed at the forefront of the psychology of religion. Such experience, he opined, should have natural antecedents. Thus in first lecture, entitled "Religion and Neurology," he explores the potential psychophysical associations of religious feelings.

To understand the nature of religious experience, James emphasizes the need to study those for whom religion was "an acute fever" and not to dwell long on those whose commerce with the deity was "second hand"—religion determined in the believer by others. The ones to study were the geniuses of the religious line, although, he warns, "like many other geniuses that have brought forth fruits effective enough for commemoration in the pages of biography, [they] have often shown symptoms of nervous instability." He points out that "insane conditions" have a considerable advantage for studies of this kind because they isolate specific factors of the mental life, which become available for investigation. This theme is taken up again in a later chapter of this book, but for now it is interesting to note the emphasis that James gave to the melancholic temperament of such people, exemplified by George Fox, the founder of the Quaker religion: "Melancholy," James notes, "constitutes an essential moment in every complete religious evolution."[19]

James refers to the fixed ideas, trances, visions, and auditory hallucinations that accompany states of religiosity as pathological, and he notes that, in the right mind, such ideas and conceptions quickly pass into belief and action. "When a superior intellect and a psychopathic temperament coalesce . . . in the same individual, we have the best possible condition for the kind of effective genius that gets into biographical dictionaries."[20]

James never developed a neurology of religious experiences, in part, because of the rudimentary development of neurology at the time he was working and, perhaps, because he was not a neurologist. He did, however, note the possible epilepsy of St. Paul and touched upon links between déjà vu phenomena, dreamy states, epilepsy, and mysticism.

This book, following James, explores personal religious experience and has nothing to say about the development of any particular religion or about the existence or otherwise of God.[21] It is the primordial sense of the awareness of another, ineffable world that draws my interest and guides the inquiry. The issue of God or gods does not necessarily come into it, in the sense that some religions, such as Buddhism, do not assume a god.

This feeling has been called a sense of the divine; others may prefer alternative expressions. The point is that such feelings, which may become attached to cognitive constructs such as that of a God, seem to be a universal feature of the psychological constitution of humankind and are therefore amenable to scientific enquiry. The concept of basic human instincts, and even of a human nature, has been under attack from various academic and political persuasions for some time. These views have led not only to a devaluation of the exploration of the human psyche (what is it that makes us tick?) but also to countless futile attempts to either suppress knowledge (by academics, who should know better) or to misguidedly try to direct human behavior without understanding the biological imperatives that drive such behavior (by politicians, who will never know better).

As James points out, the extent of religious feelings must be graded: things are seen as more or less divine, states of mind more or less religious. But at the extreme, rather as one knows a poem when one sees one (see chapter 4), there are other states of mind or behavior in which it is quite clear that the experience reported is religious and becomes, when hypertrophied, more than adequate for scientific investigation.

For James, a central characteristic of religious life is the belief in an unseen order, a Platonic reality that lies beyond that given to the senses. "The sentiment of reality can indeed attach itself so strongly to our object of belief that our whole life is polarised through and through, so to speak, by its sense of the existence of the thing believed in, and yet that thing, for purposes of definite description, can hardly be said to be present to our mind at all."[22]

As for the basic psychology underlying the religious sentiment, James considered the normal healthy-minded temperament to be one of optimism, one that espoused goodness and eschewed sin, by confession, absolution, or purgation; evil is minimized. However, another temperament, one he refers to as that of the "sick soul," emphasizes evil as the essential part of the self; such reflections touch on what James refers to as the neurotic constitution, depression, and religious melancholy.[23] James observes that "the completest religions" are those in which pessimism has been best developed, citing especially Buddhism and Christianity. He notes that many saints have possessed the gift of tears, and he describes their moods as "melting" with "exalted affections."[24]

In his attempts to understand the psychological developments of the religious mind, James opens up the theme of the heterogeneous personality and a fundamental dualism at the heart of human nature. In development, the self becomes "straightened out." St. Augustine struggled with two souls in his breast—two wills, as he refers to them—one carnal and one spiritual. For him, as for others, the resolution of the two brings happiness, in addition to some kind of relief. Such resolutions can come about suddenly or slowly, either through some altered action or intellectual insight or through mystical conversion.[25] Conversion, in particular, provokes ecstasies of happiness and indescribable pleasure.

Under his varieties of religious experience James includes the "mystical," and he suggests that religious experiences of the kind being considered in the present book, personal and idiosyncratic, have at their heart "mystical states of consciousness." Such states share several features, including ineffability—a noetic quality, a state of knowledge, transience, and passivity. James considers the power of words to stimulate this sense of mysticism. He refers to Martin Luther's conversion upon hearing a fellow monk repeat the words of the creed: Luther immediately sees the scripture in an entirely new light; the doors of paradise have been opened up for him.

James notes especially the effects of musical sounds, odors, light on the land and the sea, and certain conjunctions of words for their mystical significance:

> Most of us can remember the strangely moving power of passages in certain poems read when we were young, irrational doorways as they were through which the mystery of fact, the wildness and the pangs of life, stole into our hearts and thrilled them. The words have now perhaps become the polished surfaces for us; but lyric poetry and music are alive and significant only in proportion as they fetch these vague vistas of a life continuous with our own, becoming and inviting, yet ever eluding our pursuit. We are alive or dead to the eternal inner message of the arts according as we have kept or lost this mystical susceptibility.[26]

These mystical states, which are brief, have much in common with those methodically cultivated by certain religions. James notes especially the prayer practices of Hindus, Buddhists, Muslims, and Christians. Yoga, the Hindu's *dhyana* (meditation), St. Teresa's orison of union, and the like all are characterized by detachment from outer sensations and verbal descriptions. James suggests the essentially hypnoid nature of these states but again notes their link to optimism.

Religious Feelings and Religion

James embraces the feelings elicited by the "eternal message of the arts" within the term *religion*. Formalized religion obviously grew from the impulses of religious feelings, and as already noted, these feelings must have been forerunners for the myths and religious rituals and their related institutions that later developed.

Until relatively recently, studies of religion have been predominantly sociological. Anthropologists have studied the myths, rituals, and totems of diverse societies; but while their approach has been essentially evolutionary, it was never especially biological. Social evolution was seen as some kind of progressive rise of civilization, from the primitive to the present, and along with that went the evolution of myth and religion. The classic text of such a view was *The Golden Bough*, by James Frazer (1854–1941), which examines rituals and magic practices in a wide variety of cultures and concludes there has been a natural evolutionary progression of thought, from the magic to the religious to the scientific.[27]

These Spencerian concepts were largely refuted by the sociologist Émile Durkheim (1858–1917). His main studies in this area concerned totemism, which he held to represent the earliest form of religion, and his work was largely about the beliefs and practices of the Australian aboriginals. *Pace* Frazer, Durkheim did not find an evolutionary progression of such human thought and activity, and he opined that study of a primitive culture, such as that of the aboriginals, would cast light on modern religions. He considered that religion was a fundamental and permanent part of humanity, but unlike James, he was concerned with its sociological significance: "A religion is a unified system of beliefs and practices relative to sacred things, that is to say, things set apart and forbidden—beliefs and practices which unite into one single moral community called a church, and all those who adhere to them."[28] Mana, the totemic principle, gives divine power to plants, animals, and the like, or to representations of them, and through ritual, human beings themselves become transformed.

Durkheim refers to "religious forces" and to a collective "effervescence" that religious ceremonies evoke. Religious force was conceived of as embodied in the totemic emblem, external to individuals and endowed with a kind of transcendence. Yet from another standpoint, and like the clan a totem symbolizes, it can be made real only within and by individual consciousness: "It is immanent in individual members."[29] The effects of the effervescence are extended by the totem, which has the power to reactivate the original feelings, like the effects of a drug or, in Pavlovian terms, acting as a conditioned stimulus.

Durkheim argued against one popular theory by opining that religion derives not from the fear and misgivings about the world that terrified primitive man but from a view of gods as friends and protectors, endowing a "joyful confidence" that lay at the heart of totemism. Jealous and terrible gods did not make an appearance until later in the history of religion.

Although Durkheim viewed religion primarily from a sociological perspective (that is, that societies need religion to bind them together), he also believed that by studying religion he could get to the origins of human thought. In his analysis, religious beliefs are not inexplicable hallucinations and delusions but are founded in the social forces that tie the faithful to their gods, a god therefore being a figurative representative of society itself. However, he discussed effervescence as a kind of ecstasy, which in religious ceremonies leads to unleashed passions and to "hyperexcitement of physical and mental life." He continues, "Men of extraordinary religious consciousness—prophets, founders of religions, great saints—often show symptoms of an excitability that is extreme and even pathological; these physiological defects predisposed them to great religious roles . . . It can be said that religion does not do without a certain delirium."[30]

With regard to the origins of religious thought, Durkheim suggested that while sacred things exist only in the mind, they also exist in the collective mind. Religious beliefs, in fact, are only a special case of a general law, namely, that the whole of our social world is populated with forces that exist only in our minds. The mental life of humankind is a system of representations in which the most commonplace objects can become sacred and the totem becomes real. Feelings expressed collectively in a religious ceremony are dispersed soon after the event but can be kept alive in the individual by being inscribed on things durable, such as totems and symbols, to which should be added poetry and music. Magic was born out of religion—not vice versa, as suggested by Frazer.

Mircea Eliade analyzed the religious experience, starting out by noting the earlier work of Rudolf Otto, *Das Helige*. In that book, Otto notes that religious feelings are a compound of terror before the sacred (the awe-inspiring mystery) and a fullness of being. The feelings are numinous, presenting as something *ganz andere* (wholly other). In other words, the sacred is a reality that is totally different from natural reality, and it is impossible to express the *ganz andere* in conventional language.[31]

Eliade contrasts the sacred and the profane and refers to the act of manifestation of the sacred as hierophany.[32] Essentially, the history of religions is constituted by many such hierophanies in which the sacred is manifest in ordinary objects or more "supreme" reflections of them, such as, for Christians, the incarnation of God in Jesus Christ. The object or person becomes something else; reality is transformed, as is the whole cosmos. Archaic societies lived as close as possible to the sacred because there resided power, and a special type of power at that, one with constancy and permanence: "Religious man attempts to remain as long as possible in a sacred universe." There are effectively two modes of being in the world, the sacred and the profane, and for the religious it is only in the sacred world that they have any true existence, the religious need expressing an "unquenchable ontological thirst."[33] Myth fixes the paradigmatic models for all human rites and activities; a responsible man therefore needs to imitate the gestures of the gods.

With the development of agriculture and the change in the nature of societies that came with it, Eliade notes, the value of the sacred changed, and religious experiences became more concrete. "Man let himself be increasingly carried away by his own discovery; he gave himself up to vital hierophanies and turned away from the sacrality that transcended his immediate and daily needs." However, a truly nonreligious man is difficult to find, even in modern societies, where so much is desacralized. Superstitions, taboos, "camouflaged myths," and "degenerated rituals" abound, and countless "little religions," sects, and schools, including political and other social utopianisms, are saturated with myth and religious fanaticism. Profane man is a descendant of *H. religiosus,* and he cannot wipe out his own history—that is, the behavior of his religious ancestors, which has made him what he is today. This is all the more true because a great part of his existence is fed by impulses that come to him from the depth of his being, from the zone that has been called the "unconscious."[34]

Freud and Beyond

Another psychobiological theory invoking the unconscious nature and the mythological origins of religious feelings comes from the neurologist-turned-psychologist Sigmund Freud (1856–1939). The Oedipus complex, a cornerstone of his psychoanalytic theory, is central to his ideas on the development of religions. Oedipus, a prince of Thebes, killed his father and married his mother, events that Freud holds are psychologically replayed during infantile development. The growing male child becomes aware of his parents' sexual relations, desires his mother, fears retaliation from his father, notes the lack of a penis in females, and fears castration. Healthy development demands resolution of these conflicts, with the eventual development of a superego. Freud argues that the Oedipus complex is central to the development of religious feelings both within the individual and within society. In *Totem and Taboo* he draws on much mythological material, including the works of Frazer, Durkheim, and Charles Darwin (1809–82). Primitive society consisted of bands of males driven away from a violent and jealous father who propitiated all the females. They retaliated, killed the father, ate him, and later felt guilt over these acts. The dead father became more powerful than the living one, the totem became a father substitute, and prohibitions and ceremonies were established around the totem to appease the ambivalence. The totem cannot be killed, except at specific ceremonies. Incest came to be forbidden; the totem had to be protected.

Freud argues that all later religions are attempts to resolve the same problem. In terms of the Oedipus complex, God is essentially an exalted father, and religion was founded on a longing for the father. He argues that totemism reflects a universal neurosis and that religious rituals protect against this by shielding individuals and societies from the latent forces of repressed Oedipal desire.

Two points stand out from Freud's thesis. First, the original traumatic incident is somehow biologically incorporated into the future psychological history of mankind, a kind of archaic heritage driving human behavior. Freud refers to a collective mind, which has somehow adopted the mental processes of the individual mind. This continuity he accepts, at least in part, as inherited, the result of biological and psychological necessities. Second, he unites his theory of the origins of religion with a theory of art and tragedy, especially ancient Greek tragedy. The hero suffers because he represents the primal father, and the tragic guilt of the chorus is relieved by his death and downfall. The hero becomes "the redeemer of the Chorus." For Freud, in the beginning was the deed, not the word.[35]

Interestingly, Freud tells us about his own conception of religious feelings. Responding to a friend who reproached him for not appreciating the true source of religious feelings, Freud replied, "This source is said to be a special feeling which (so my friend reassures me) never leaves him, the existence of which he finds confirmed by many others . . . It is a feeling which my friend is inclined to call 'a sensation of eternity,' a feeling as of something limitless and unbounded, as it were 'oceanic' . . . It is the source of the religious energy which is seized on by the various churches and religious systems." Freud himself, however, did not share this emotion.[36]

Although there were considerable differences between the theories of Freud and Carl Jung (1865–1961) on the origins of religion, Jung, too, in his elaboration of a theory of archetypes, refers to universal images of a collective nature that are "transmitted not only by tradition and emigration, but also by hereditary."[37] For Freud, the mechanism of transmission was biological evolution, although he professed not to understand the mechanism. However, he regarded religion as fundamentally pathological, a form of universal obsessional neurosis.

Edward Wilson has written widely on the biological underpinnings of culture, embracing a holistic sociobiology. He considers that the emergence of civilization related to hypertrophy of preexisting structures, basic social functions of our ancestors, metamorphosing from environmental adaptations to elaborate social behaviors. Religion is no exception, being an ineradicable part of human nature; religious practices can be "mapped onto the two dimensions of genetic advantage and evolutionary change." By "congealing identity," religious practices confer biological advantages, confirming group membership: for the individual, "his strength is the strength of the group, his guide the sacred covenant . . . This key process . . . is sacralization . . . The mind is predisposed—one can speculate that learning rules is physiologically programmed—to participate in a few processes of sacralization which in combinations generate the institutions of organised religion."[38] Belief in God is part of the human condition, which is ruled by myth.

Karen Armstrong, at one time herself a nun, has studied religions and their histories with meticulous curiosity. She writes this about her own experiences:

When I began to research this history of the idea and experience of God . . . I expected to find that God had simply been a projection of human needs and desires . . .
My predictions were not entirely unjustified, but I have been extremely surprised by
some of my findings, and I wish that I had learned all this thirty years ago, when I
was starting out in the religious life. It would have saved a great deal of anxiety to
hear . . . that instead of waiting for God to descend from on high, I should deliberately create a sense of him myself.[39]

Of the several psychological defense mechanisms that led to the development
of religions, Freud relies, in part, upon projection, hence the "illusion" in his title, *The Future of an Illusion*. Freud was not the first to consider such mechanisms
as operative. The nineteenth-century philosopher Ludwig Feuerbach (1804–72),
in his *Treatise on Christianity*, opines that the personality of God is nothing else
than the projected personality of man, an illusion. It is not so much that God created man in his own image but that man created God in his. Consciousness of
God is human self-consciousness, and religion therefore is a human rather than
a divine construction.[40]

Echoing Eliade, Armstrong notes that the images of God or the gods have
shifted with time: "When one religious idea ceases to work for [people], it is simply replaced." As humans who claimed direct contact with the gods faded into
mythological reality, at the boundary with the divine, God could still be revealed
and experienced through ritual and symbolism, though with an ever metamorphosing iconography.

By the time of the development of writing, religions were well developed, and
the shift from naturalism to animism had occurred, with a belief that things other
than man, including animals, possessed a spirit. It was a short step to endowing
such spirits with human capacities,[41] with the projection of the dichotomous
identities of the bicameral mind. Talking to spirits probably evolved into prayer:
the small tribe or clan elected a leader, who not only organized hunting but also
was quite likely elected the "religious" leader. Spirits needed to be appeased and
thanked, hence ceremonies evolved; and since ceremonies needed to be staged
somewhere, there came the endowment of sacred places. Space was divided,
some parts becoming qualitatively different—holy ground.

The development of agriculture almost certainly forged for *H. sapiens* the development of larger communities and a radical shift in the nature of what may by
then be referred to as worship. Cro-Magnon individuals lived in houses, in quite
large communities, and hunted and harvested. They practiced complex religious
rituals and had a conception of god.[42] The tribe had a priest, and the spirits be-

came worshipped as gods. Larger community groups brought with them problems of control of anarchic sections not found in smaller groups; hence laws,
which, once written, became enshrined. The priest was all powerful, in direct
communication with the gods or a servant thereof, a knower of the mysteries and
a controller not only of human bodies but also of human spirits—souls. Transgression of the written (laws) became sin, as the priests became high priests.
Rhadamanthine punishment followed transgression, the underworld became
Hell, and the gates of Elysium, Paradise, or Valhalla were seen as available only
to the few. The existence of the gods, whose own behavior portrayed all human
desires and follies, succumbed to the myth of the one creator God as monotheism erupted, in our time dominated by three major religions, Christianity, Judaism, and Islam.[43]

Religious experiences, however, are not solely the prerogative of believers in
one or several gods. For many, the divine is interpreted as a not-existing being or
even simply as a state of mind. Some hold that the human mind cannot grasp the
ineffable essence of God and that beyond the intellectual comprehension is only
that which is "speechless and unknowing."[44] Pantheists would hold that God is
represented in nature, echoed in the words of Albert Einstein, who refers to "cosmic religious feeling." This was a state in which an individual "feels the noth-
ingness of human desires and aims and the sublimity and marvellous order
which reveal themselves both in nature and in the world of thought."[45] In fact,
though he did not accept an interventionist God, Einstein revered some entity, revealed through the magnificent harmony of the physical laws of the universe. He
thought that traditional religions would have to abandon the idea of a personal
God, especially in the light of advancing scientific knowledge, but he puts scientific discovery itself in these terms: the scientist should have a "rapturous
amazement at the harmony of natural law, which reveals an intelligence of such
superiority that, compared with it, all the systematic thinking and acting of human beings is an utterly insignificant reflection." Such feelings are likened to the
feelings of past religious geniuses, and even his cosmology contains within it un-
explained factors, such as his concept of lambda, a cosmological constant, which
allowed him to create in mathematical terms a coherent (hence spiritual) model
of the universe.[46]

There are clear links here with the mystical tradition; in fact, some kind of mystical experience and a belief in the supernatural—in other words, a suspension
of belief in the laws of nature—underlie all faiths. God, as such, is not an essential component of such experiences, and belief in the paranormal is widespread.
Extending Eliade's list to a belief in UFOs, ghosts, the power of psychics, or the

fate within our astrological stars, it may be safely stated that the human mind is attuned to accept violations of physical reality. There is also a pervasive anthropomorphism, projections of our human selves onto objects and others in the world; but importantly, *ourselves* here also includes our minds.

Drawing on anthropological data, Pascal Boyer suggests that such attribution of agency is a common feature of the way the mind works generally and is not specific to religious experience. We hear a noise outside on a dark night and attribute it at first to a predator rather than a branch of a tree falling. Boyer points out that we constantly use such intuitions when interacting with others. Furthermore, attribution of minds to others is a stable feature of development and an essential component of human cognition, the so-called theory of mind. For Boyer, "Religious concepts are parasitic upon other mental capacities." However, "our capacities to play music, paint pictures or even make sense of printed ink-patterns on a page are also parasitic in this sense." In fact, Boyer points out that science, which offers an alternative to the religious explanation of why things are and why they happen in the world, represents an unnatural way of thinking, "a departure from our spontaneous intuitions . . . Scientific activity is both cognitively and socially very *unlikely,* which is why it has only been developed by a very small number of people, in a small number of places, for what is only a minis-cule part of our evolutionary history . . . Science is every bit as 'unnatural' to the human mind as religion is 'natural.'"[47]

Post-Kantian philosophy guarantees the limits of human reason, ensures that religious knowledge, as discussed by Eliade, is categorically different from empirical knowledge, and secures the religious experience as subjective, ad hominem but clearly compelling.[48]

As William James attempted to explore in his writings, in this book I examine religious experiences as universal phenomenological events that can be traced at least back to early hominid history. My work here is not concerned with any particular religion and has nothing to say on comparative values of any particular religious behaviors. The biological basis of religious experiences and practices are suggested by their universality through time and place, and the close relationship of these behaviors to both myth and music are evident. The ancients knew (through dreaming) of another world where ancestors dwelled, and, with the rise of self-consciousness, they became aware of death. Fear of death emerged, attempts were made to achieve the other world; gods were projected from and into the human psyche, and powerful feelings became attached to belief systems. For James, the origin of the Greek gods suggests a sense of reality in human consciousness, a sense of presence of something there, deeper than that given by our general senses. If this reality-feeling, as he calls it, touches on religious conceptions, they become believed. James relied on the existence of hallucinations as background evidence that such reality-feelings are a part of the human psyche, and he also discussed the feeling of a presence, localized but unseen, as part of this experience.

Objects of religious belief, then, become possessed by believers not as conceptions but as directly apprehended realities, Eliade's hierophanies. For Freud and the other authors quoted here, this was an illusion but a recognizable part of the normal human psyche. Although study of religious experience is best achieved by examining those with an ability to have feelings of unusual intensity, the underlying cerebral mechanisms involved are not seen as pathological but derive, in part or in total, from our evolutionary heritage.

Although James notes that fear is often held as a primary emotion underlying the development of religions, he doubly emphasizes joy, concluding that a person's religion involves both moods of contraction and moods of expansion of being. Joy, ecstasy, and melancholia are noted by several of the quoted writers as themes that underpin religious states and allow exploration of links between religion and mood disorders.

As should be clear from this introduction, religions have the potential, using the mechanisms of normal psychic activity, to hijack our primitive feelings and institutionalize them for the benefit not of the individual but of the high priests. Writing has been a potent instrument in this process. This brings us to at least one of the functions of art. Art and religious belief are close not only in terms of the huge amount of artistic expression that has an avowedly religious theme but also at the conceptual level. They both communicate through symbol and metaphor, they bring various special beliefs to a community, they use ritual, and they require an illusion, a suspension of reality. They represent a way of grappling with hidden connections in our lives and in our psyche. However, religion can usurp these processes, and "when religion becomes artificial, it is the prerogative of art to preserve its essence by means of mythical symbols, which religion would have us believe are literally true: however, it is through art that their symbolic value, and the profound truths they contain can be revealed . . . Myth is true for all time . . . and its content is inexhaustible for every age."[49]

CHAPTER TWO

The Neuroanatomy of Emotion

In 1994 the Nobel scientist and neurobiologist Sir Francis Crick wrote of his "astonishing hypothesis"—that "you, your joys and your sorrows, your memories and ambitions, your sense of personal identity and free will, are in fact no more than the behaviour of a vast assembly of nerve cells and their associated molecules."[1] Actually, the only thing astonishing about this astonishing hypothesis is why it should be, at the turn of the second millennium, astonishing. After all, Hippocrates (ca. 460–ca. 377 BC) had presented the same hypothesis twenty-five hundred years earlier. Writing about epilepsy, then referred to as the "sacred disease," Hippocrates opines, "Men ought to know that from the brain, and from the brain only, arise our pleasures, joys, laughter and jests, as well as our sorrows, pains, griefs and tears."[2] In his philosophy, the brain is also the seat of madness and of epilepsy.

Neuroscience has taken a veritable backseat in the public and scientific imagination for such a long time that even today the concept that the brain is the central organ of thought, feeling, and emotive energy, and that without the human brain there is no human endeavor, still astonishes. It is a fact, not a hypothesis, that consciousness and all that flows from it are dependent on the brain and its proper functioning.

To follow the progress of neuroscience over the generations since Hippocrates, a brief review of neurological history is in order before a more elaborate excursion into neuroanatomy as viewed from a twenty-first-century perspective. My review here probes the underlying neuroanatomy of emotional experiences and feelings.

The Seat of the Soul in the Brain

There is scarcely a mention of the brain in the Old Testament, and there is no neurological understanding to be gained from the readings of, for example, Egyptian theology or the texts of Judaism, Hinduism, or Buddhism.³ At some point in the development of thought in ancient Greece, a shift of emphasis occurred, from one that stressed the *pneuma animale*—the essential respiratory constituent of life, air being catalytic in transforming the *spiritus naturalis* into *spiritus vitalis* (the life spirit)—to one that posited a soul, which came to be seen as disembodied. This shift is discussed in detail in Bruno Snell's *The Discovery of the Mind*. Snell argues that the early Greeks, exemplified by the Homeric treatises, neither represented the body as a unit nor had words that characterized the mind or soul. *Psyche* was a force that kept humans alive and, at death, left the body through the mouth (the breath of life expiring).⁴

Homer also writes about *thymos* and *noos*, the former being a generator of motion, the latter providing ideas and images, but in his view action is the key to life and immortality, and the Homeric language aimed to express the essence of the individual act.⁵ The acts themselves, however, are attributed not to the individual but to external factors, particularly being given or driven by the gods. In Homeric times, humans were not thought to possess their own souls as the source of their actions. Furthermore, none of the three entities noted above, which Homer seems to have thought of as separate organs, is clearly anatomized to any particular location within the body. Snell makes the further point that Homeric man does not regard himself as the origin of his own decisions; that development was reserved for tragedy.

Gradually, in the post-Homeric texts, *psyche* took on a new meaning, with the development of concepts concerning the soul and its immortality. Snell credits Heraclitus with the early introduction of a concept of the soul, man consisting of body and soul, each of which has discrete properties; the soul has its own dimension, not being extended in space. This new *psyche* needed a home, provided by the developed concept of the *soma*, the living body. That the seat of the soul resides in the brain was firmly stated by several Greek philosophers, including Plato (427–347 BC) and Pythagoras (582–500 BC). The soul is variously divided; in one version the spirit (*spiritus naturalis*), which originates in the liver, is carried to the heart and the lungs and converted into the essential life spirit (*spiritus vitalis*), which is then distilled in the brain to become the animal spirit (*spiritus animalis*), the conveyer of thought, judgment, and memory.⁶ The embodied soul, or part of it, at last finds a seat in the brain, albeit, in those times, without clear reference as to where within the cranium the vital center might reside.

For Plato, at least a part of the divided soul, *psyche,* is immortal and vital, the rational element that comes from God and is located in the head, the part of the body nearest to heaven. Plato ascribes not only to a personal immortality but also to a transmigration of souls. The dualism that had invaded the integrity of the human being gave rise to acceptance of two kinds of reality, independent and contrasted: spirit and flesh, mind and body, the indivisible and the divisible.

In contrast, the school of Aristotle (384–322 BC) thought that the function of the brain is to cool the blood; it is the heart, they believed, that was the prime organ of the soul. This idea was echoed in the twentieth century and in the ideas of William James and found expression in Shakespeare's "Tell me where is fancy bred / Or in the heart or in the head."[7]

The Greeks knew that within the substance of the brain resided the ventricles, but, in part because of the concept of its ability to cool vapors, the brain itself was considered hollow.[8] However, gradually the solid parts of the brain attracted attention, and physicians such as Galen (129–ca. 199) attempted to unite the pneumatic and the solid doctrines, suggesting that the *pneuma* functions are ventricular, while the soul resides in the parenchyma.[9]

Aristotelian and Platonic philosophies continued to be influential in the development of European thought, but it was the establishment of Christianity as a major religious force, overwhelmingly supported by Platonism, that furthered the concept of the brain as the temporary residence of an immortal soul—an idea that in the Western world engulfed all others.[10] For many years, the ventricles were considered to be the essential location of the soul, but gradually, as the solid parts of the brain became distinguished, various thinkers applied their own theories of localization of function. The physician Thomas Willis (1621–75), the founder of the term *neurologie*, thought the human being a double-souled animal, possessing a sensitive soul, found in lower animals as well, and a rational soul. The latter, placed in the brain by God, was thought to be immaterial and hence immortal. It was located in the corpus callosum.[11] The philosopher René Descartes (1596–1650) opted for the pineal gland as the seat of the soul, while Albrecht von Haller (1708–77) placed it in the medulla oblongata.[12]

The earliest experiments, as opposed to speculation or anecdote, on cerebral localization were performed in the seventeenth-century by Emanuel Swedenborg (1688–1772). Working largely from earlier published texts, Swedenborg considered the cerebral cortex and basal ganglia vital for motor activity, stating, with remarkable prescience, that "the soul of the cerebrum issues its commands but the corporal striata execute them."[13] Although he later opined that the soul was distributed throughout the brain, rather than localized to any one part, by the time he died in 1772 the concept of cerebral localization of function was clearly becoming accepted, and neuroscientists were not averse to speculating on the cerebral representation of religious experiences.

Gall and the Localizationalists

The stage was set for an obvious battle, still in part unresolved today, as to whether any function could be localized, and if so, in which parts of the brain. On one side were those who espoused a strict localization of function, namely, that certain functions resided in specific brain loci and nowhere else; others preferred an interpretation of cerebral equipotentiality, negating the possibility of such specific incorporation. This debate was furthered by the schools of philosophy whose ideas enhanced these theories and the superb blending of eighteenth- and nineteenth-century literary theory with the developing discoveries of neuroscience.[14]

The hero and villain of the battle was Franz Joseph Gall (1758–1828). From clinical observations that certain people with various intellectual endowments had specific cranial prominences, he and his collaborator Johann Caspar Spurzheim (1776–1832) elaborated the system of phrenology and craniology.[15] Gall hypothesized that certain faculties of the mind were located in the gray matter of the cerebral cortex, and that, since the cerebral cortex was situated beneath the skull, examination of the contours of the cranium would reveal a person's potentialities and deficiencies. The brain was envisaged as made up of several independent organs (twenty-seven, later expanded to thirty-seven), each subserving a specific faculty but connected by white-matter commissures. The mind, and hence the soul, then, was not to be regarded as a unity, and religious sense and veneration were localized to the upper part of the ascending frontal convolution of the brain.[16]

The intellectual and philosophical outlook of the late-eighteenth and early-nineteenth centuries was dominated by two contrasting schools, one stemming from Descartes and his successors, the other from the empiricist Anglo-Saxon writers, most notably John Locke (1632–1704).[17] Descartes famously arrived at his *cogito, ergo sum*, while Locke posited the *tabula rasa*. Descartes supported the idea that the mind (*res cogitans*), which was indivisible and could be separated entirely from the divisible body (*res extensa*), possessed innate ideas from which the existence of God could be derived.[18] Locke and his followers considered that the mind was essentially blank at birth, a veritable clean slate upon which experience acted to produce ideas. For the empiricists, an intimate connection between the mind and the world allowed for speculation about the link between the two, including the role of the brain in such unity. Sensationalism, the theory that ideas are derived solely from sensation, was contrasted with rationalism, the view that reason is the basis of knowledge. A dominant philosophy at the time, supporting the sensationalists, was that of David Hartley (1705–57), which was referred to as associationism.

The Active Mind

Associationism posits that any idea tends to bring to mind other associated ideas through the principles of contiguity and similarity; the *tabula rasa* thus became structured through sensational experience and the association of ideas. In essence, these principles were passive conditions for the construction of the human mind, a problem being that, by themselves, they seemed unable to explain the vitality of human life and a vibrancy of the active imagination.

It was at this time, at the end of the eighteenth century, that the bubbling cauldron of experimental neuroscience met with not only the new developments in philosophy but also the onward rush of literary romanticism, all providing an escape from the rigidity of Enlightenment thinking and the struggle with Cartesian dualism. What was individual, and what motivated peoples' actions, became more relevant than establishing classifications and conformities. Springs of unconsciousness were discovered, for example, through dreaming and by the way the mind could be altered by the use of experimental substances. A central figure of the time was the poet and philosopher Samuel Taylor Coleridge (1772–1834).[19] What the Romantic poets sought was an explanation for the individual life force, the drive that underlies human action and achievement, and an understanding of inspiration—artistic and otherwise. Emotion rather than reason became a focus of attention.

The neuroanatomist-localizationalist school of Gall and his collaborators, and the continental philosophies of Immanuel Kant (1724–1804) and his followers, were of considerable interest to the Romantics since in all of these variant schools, the idea that the mind was an active processor, a synthesizer, and a creative force, not just a passive receptacle of sensory influences, was central. There was more to the mind than experience alone could provide; furthermore, they accepted the brain as the organ of the mind.[20]

It was Hartley's intention to break away from Cartesian dualism, and, with his associationism, to enable embodiment of the mind in the brain. His was an essentially materialist philosophy, which even ventured to posit unconscious mental functions. However, Coleridge, notably in his *Biographia Literaria*, disputed Hartley's ideas. He saw that without some organizing, synthesizing brain principle, there would be a chaos of association—no explanation for the formation of the associable and no room for rhyme or reason.[21] Alan Richardson, in his elegant reconstruction of the intellectual ferment of this era, observes that several scientists who were acquainted with Coleridge advocated an "organic" mind (the brain as an active organ); these included Erasmus Darwin (1731–1802) and Charles Bell (1774–1842) in England, Pierre-Jean-Georges Cabanis (1757–1808) in France, and, of course, Gall.[22] Hartley, as well as Cabanis and Gall, incorporated peripheral physiological events into their overall organic theories of the emotions. For these thinkers, "The mind, brain and body make up a single system, and mind-body reciprocity is the rule rather than the exception."[23] The mind was envisaged as an active principle, embodied, with innate structures, essentially creative; emotion came to dominate over human thought, and action over disembodied reason.

The Neuroanatomy of Emotion

Although great strides were made in neuroanatomy and neurophysiology in the nineteenth century, little progress was made in understanding how emotions were represented neurologically. At the end of the century, the James-Lange hypothesis became popular. William James and the Danish physician Carl Lange (1834–1900) independently developed the idea that the emotions were derived from sensory inputs to the brain that activate motor outputs; the resulting bodily sensations were perceived as emotion. We do not run away from something because we are frightened; rather, we experience fear because we are running away. However, there was no obvious cerebral location for the generation of emotion, although the sensory experiences were known to be received cortically, namely, in the parietal regions of the brain. About the same time that James was writing, the English neurologist John Hughlings Jackson (1835–1911) opined, *pace* the growing band of localizers of cerebral function, that localizing a lesion was not the same as localizing a function. Based on clinical observations of patients who had had strokes to the left side of the brain but could still express emotions, he stated that the right cerebral hemisphere was the dominant one for emotion.[24]

The Jamesian hypothesis was soon tested and shown to be wrong from two avenues. First, it was shown that in animals the removal of the cortex of the brain on both sides did not eliminate the expression of emotion. Furthermore, it was found that stimulation of various structures buried deep within the brain could lead to the release of emotion. These observations formed the basis for a neuroscience revolution, the impact of which is still poorly appreciated, not only by many in the scientific community but also by the public and media generally (hence Crick's astonishment).

The Emotional Brain

The unraveling of the cerebral mysteries of our emotional being has been one of the most fascinating neuroscience explorations of the past hundred years. We now appreciate that certain brain structures and pathways are crucial for the mediation and experience of emotion and that these are parts of our evolutionary inheritance, which developed eons before *Homo* developed into *sapiens*. The pioneers of this search were James Wenceslas Papez (1883–1958), Paul Yakovlev (1894–1983), and, in particular, Paul MacLean (1913–).[25] The developed concept related to what is referred to as the limbic system. However, before describing the limbic structures and their functions, a brief orientation of some key brain structures is warranted.

The Basic Components of the Brain

The brain is composed of neurons, which through a sophisticated machinery of ions, enzymes, and neurotransmitters carry signals that drive the system, and many other supporting structures. The latter include blood vessels and the glial cells.[26] The main constituents of neurons are cell bodies, axons, dendrites, and synapses. The axon, a long thin tube within which resides a host of biochemical machinery, extends from the cell body to a distant site, where it synapses with other neurons. In general, at the synapse, neurotransmitters are released that cross the synaptic cleft and exert a change in the postsynaptic membranes, which by and large are located on the dendrites of the postsynaptic neuron. These are small filamentous outgrowths of the neuron and the main points of information exchange in the neuronal system. Most neurons have a single axon but many dendrites. The number of neurons in the brain is estimated to be in the billions, and the number of synaptic contacts in the trillions; thus the number of potential brain states within the human central nervous system is extraordinary and virtually incalculable.[27]

The axis of the central nervous system is composed of several identifiable components: the cerebrum, the cerebellum (a smaller structure at the base of the cerebrum), the brainstem, and the spinal cord. Information flows up the spinal cord from peripheral sensory receptors, which send to the brain signals about the external and internal environments of the organism; many such afferent (inward-conducting) nerve tracts have been identified within the spinal cord. Information travels from the brain to the muscles down the spinal cord, again in identified pathways referred to as efferent (outward conducting). Many of the nerves that control autonomic functions, such as breathing, heart rate, and so on, and several of the cranial nerves begin or terminate in the brainstem.

The Brain and Its Divisions

The brain itself has been divided, purely on visual anatomical grounds, into four main lobes, the frontal, the parietal, the occipital, and the temporal. Some also refer to the insula as a lobe. The neocortex, so called because in phylogenetic terms it is more recent, is that which is generally seen on surface inspection of the brain.[28] The gyri and sulci form the irregular, undulating patterns of the cortical mantle, the former being composed of gray and white matter, the latter forming the spaces between the gyri. The gray matter is formed by the neurons, and the white matter is composed of the fiber bundles of myelinated axons, which stretch from one neuron population to another, interconnecting circuits of information.

Most sensory data initially terminate in a collection of nuclei situated subcortically in a structure called the thalamus. This is one of several identifiable subcortical collections of nuclei, which include the basal ganglia (striatal structures). From the thalamus, information is passed on to the neocortex, arriving in a primary sensory area, such as one selective for vision or for touch. These areas are mainly in the occipital and parietal areas of the brain. There then occurs a cascade of information flow from these primary receptive areas to the secondary, tertiary, and then association cortices of the brain, during which transfer the neural activity is fused, amalgamated, and combined such that while artificial stimulation of, say, the first visual receptive area will lead to the experience of flashes of light, stimulation in the temporal lobe association areas will lead to complex visual (and other) hallucinations. An exception to the above generalization is the olfactory system, which first enters parts of the limbic lobe without relay in the thalamus.

Information flow out of the brain descends from the motor areas of the neocortex down the pyramidal tracts to the spinal cord (the pyramidal system), where peripheral nerves emerge to influence movements by connecting with muscle cells. Other key structures that influence movement and permit the smooth pursuit of action are the cerebellum and the basal ganglia, the motor paths of the latter being referred to as the extrapyramidal motor system.

There is also much cross talk within the brain, with some white-matter bundles connecting areas within one hemisphere and others connecting points across the hemispheres. The largest of the latter is a commissure called the corpus callosum.

The four main domains of the cerebral hemisphere of mammals are the neocortex, the limbic lobe, the thalamus, and the basal ganglia. The neocortex, six layered and with extensive subcortical connections, provides the mantle for the structures of the other three divisions. Within the limbic lobe, the most relevant structures are the amygdala and the hippocampus and their afferent and efferent connections. The medial forebrain bundle is a continuum of interconnected neurons and pathways extending caudally from the hypothalamus into the midbrain (see figure 2.1A, 2.1B).

The basal ganglia are a collection of structures (the corpus striatum, the putamen, the globus pallidus, and the closely related substantia nigra and the subthalamic nucleus) whose efferents remain partly within the forebrain, forming so-called parallel distributed circuits, whereby the termination of a loop in the cortex is near to or at the site of the cortical origin of the loop. A scheme of these principal circuits is outlined in figure 2.2A and 2.2B.

The Limbic Lobe

The key structures of the limbic system, as originally outlined by MacLean and others, are the amygdala and the hippocampus, both neuronal aggregates of considerable complexity, and their immediate connecting structures, such as the orbital part of the frontal cortex and the so-called ventral striatum—that part of the brain's basal ganglia system that relates most closely to emotional-motor expression. The amygdala (from the Greek for almond, referring to its shape) is located at the anterior part of the temporal lobes and is central to the brain's regulation of emotion. It has two main components, a laterobasal part and a centromedial part. The former has extensive connections with other parts of the limbic lobe and with the ventral striatum and also with the neocortex, from which it receives polysensory information. The central-medial division forms part of the extended amygdala. The amygdala provides affective valence to sensory representations and is crucial for the emotional tone of memories. It also has reciprocal connections with the same cortical structures it receives information from, including

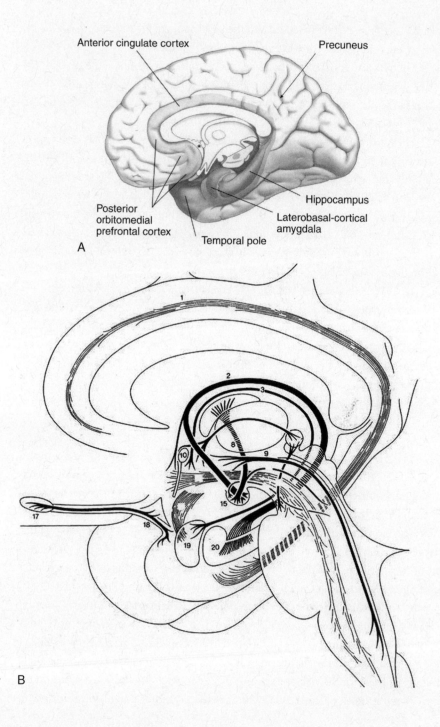

Anterior cingulate cortex

Precuneus

Posterior
orbitomedial
prefrontal cortex

Temporal pole

Hippocampus

Laterobasal-cortical
amygdala

A

B

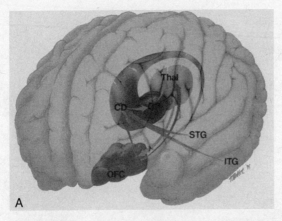

Frontal-Subcortical Circuits and Behavior-Cummings

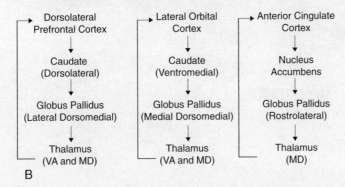

Figure 2.2. A, A circuit between orbital frontal cortex (OFC), caudate nucleus (CD), globus pallidus (GP), thalamus (Thal), and back to frontal cortex. STG = superior temporal gyrus. ITG = inferior temporal gyrus. *B,* A schematic representation of the frontal-basal ganglia-thalamic reentrant circuits, which have an influence on behavior. Reproduced with permission from (A) Salloway et al. (2001), fig. 4–11, p. 47, and (B) Cummings (1993).

Figure 2.1. A, The medial surface of the right hemisphere, showing some key structures of the limbic lobe, including the hippocampus and the cingulate cortex, and the positioning of the amygdala. Also shown is the area precuneus. *B,* The hippocampus and the amygdala connect with other limbic structures leading to connections with the pons and brain stem. 1, cingulum; 2, fornix; 3, stria terminalis; 8, mamillothalamic tract; 9, dorsal longitudinal fasciculus; 10, anterior commisure; 15, mammillary body; 17, olfactory bulb; 18, olfactory stria; 19, amygdala; 20, hippocampus. Reproduced with permission from (A) Heimer and Van Hoesen (2006) and (B) Nieuwenhuys et al. (1998), p. 307.

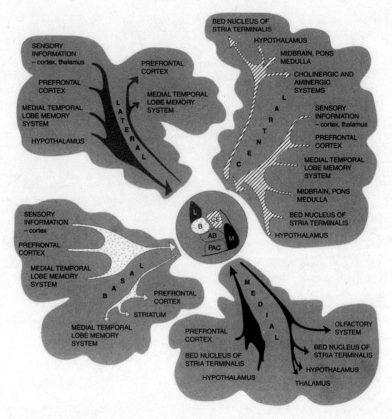

Figure 2.3. The extensive connections of the amygdala. Reproduced from Pitkänen (2000).

even the primary sensory cortical areas, allowing for an influence of emotional tone directly on cortical sensory impressions (figure 2.3).

The hippocampus (from the Greek for sea horse, so called because of its neat, curled appearance, resembling a sea horse) is also situated in the temporal lobe but is an elongated structure composed of several subdivisions, together referred to as the hippocampal formation (with the dentate gyrus). The main subcortical outflow path of the hippocampus is the fornix, which, like several other of the limbic components, curves around the thalamus and then descends to the mammillary bodies of the hypothalamus, forming a crucial link structure in the so-called Papez circuit (hippocampus, fornix, mammillary body, anterior thalamus, cingulate gyri, parahippocampal gyri, hippocampus) (figure 2.1b).

The parahippocampal gyrus lying over the hippocampus links posteriorly with the posterior cingulate gyrus. Anteriorly, it has a hook-shaped appearance, referred to as the uncus, which contains the cortical amygdala. The entorhinal cortex forms a substantial component of the anterior half of the parahippocampal gyrus. The entorhinal cortex sends much integrated polysensory information to the hippocampus beneath it through the perforant path.

The cingulate gyrus surrounds the corpus callosum, forming a C-shaped band, linking posteriorly with the parahippocampal gyrus and connecting extensively with neocortical structures. The cingulum has important connections with the parietal cortex, including an area referred to as the precuneus, located on the medial side of the hemisphere and involved in visuospatial processing and memory retrieval and somehow in an appreciation of one's sense of self. Widespread connections with the entorhinal area, the amygdala, the ventral striatum, the hypothalamus, and other subcortical structures allow the cingulate gyrus to have an important role in attention, motivation, and emotion.

The frontal lobes of the brain have many demarcated subregions, but the orbital, medial, and dorsolateral parts are the most frequently mentioned. The orbitofrontal cortex lies over the floor of the anterior cranial fossa and has intimate connections with the anterior insula, the amygdala, the ventral striatum, and sensory projection pathways.

The insula is a large limbic lobe structure that, in contrast to most limbic components, is not visible from the medial surface of the brain; it lies laterally, buried beneath folds of neocortex (figure 2.4). It, too, has many functions, including integration of limbic and cortical information, and it links anteriorly with the frontal cortex.

The Basal Ganglia

The discovery that the basal ganglia extend all the way to the ventral surface of the brain and that the inputs to the corpus striatum involve the whole of the cortical mantle allowed for a differentiation between the ventral and dorsal striata, which receive their main inputs from the limbic lobe and the neocortex, respectively (figure 2.5A, 2.5B). The accumbens, a main area of the ventral striatum, is heavily innervated by the basolateral amygdala and the hippocampus and the prefrontal and temporal association cortices. The main output from the ventral striatum is to the ventral pallidum and thence to the dorsomedial thalamus, which then projects back to the frontal cortex. This is but one of several cortico-

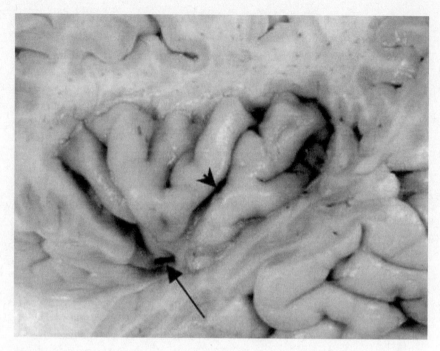

Figure 2.4. The position of the insula, buried underneath the cortex. The surrounding opercula have been removed. Picture taken from the lateral surface of the left hemisphere. Reproduced with permission from Mesulam and Muffson (1985).

striatopallidal-thalamic-cortical reentrant loops that have been defined, which have important regulatory properties governing behavior (figure 2.2B). The loop from the motor cortex through the dorsal parts of the basal ganglia (the motor loop) is involved with somatomotor activity, while the ventral limbic lobe–striatal circuits (limbic loop) modulate reward and motivation. The so-called extended amygdala is made up of those components of the amygdala (central and medial nuclei) that bridge the temporal lobe components of the amygdala with the bed nucleus of the stria terminalis and outputs to autonomic and endocrine areas in the hypothalamus and brainstem (figures 2.6A and 26B).

This brief sketch of some of the key components of the brain and how they interrelate sensory inputs and motor outputs has been developing for more than a century. In earlier times there was always the important question (a problem for William James) of how sensory information (the stimulus) actually drove the mo-

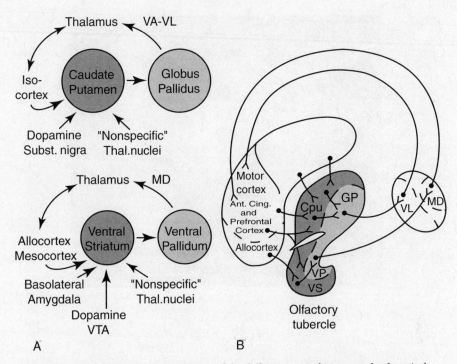

Figure 2.5. A, A schematic representation of the different cortical inputs and subcortical outputs for the dorsal striatum and the ventral striatum. The limbic inputs to the latter are clear. VA-VL and MD refer to different thalamic nuclei; VTA = ventral tegmental area. *B*, A schematic representation of the reentrant circuits; how the motor cortex outputs to basal ganglia (dorsal striatum) and how the output from the allocortex goes to the ventral striatum (VS) are shown.

tor system (the response). Was there not something else there—not a ghost in the machine but perhaps a poltergeist?[29]

The Development of the Limbic System Concept

As already noted, James had no idea how emotions could be represented in the brain other than by suggesting the sensory neocortex as a site of integration of bodily sensations that represent an emotional state. The concept that certain brain structures could form the foundation of an emotional brain system was a stunning departure for neurology, and the launch pad of the discipline of behav-

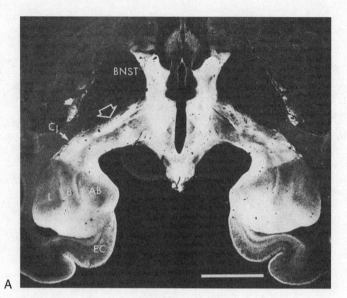

A

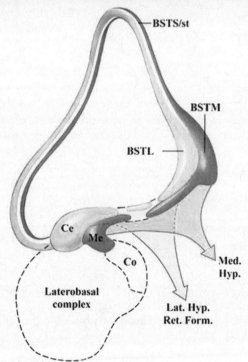

B

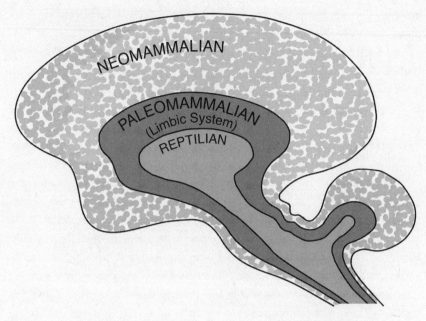

Figure 2.7. The triune brain. Reproduced with permission from MacLean (1990).

ioral neurology—the branch of neurology that tries to understand how the brain modulates and relates to behavior. *Behavioral neurology* is a term introduced by the American neurologist Norman Geschwind in the 1960s. It had a respectable predecessor in *neuropsychiatry.* Essentially, neuropsychiatry is a clinical discipline that studies the psychiatric associations of neurological disorders such as epilepsy and Parkinson's disease. Cognitive neurology, a third related area, is in reality a rejuvenation of nineteenth-century neuropsychiatry, reincarnated with the power and success of new brain-imaging techniques. The term *cognitive,* however, be-

---

Figure 2.6. A, The outline, with appropriate staining, of the extended amygdala in the monkey. *B,* The extensive outputs from the extended amygdala. The continuous nature of the extended amygdala, as it passes from the amygdala medially (central and medial nuclei, Ce and Me, respectively) to the bed nucleus of the stria terminalis (BSTL and BSTM, for lateral and medial components) and as it loops posteriorly and then courses around the basal ganglia to come anteriorly and then connect with the bed nucleus, is shown. The extensive outputs to the medial hypothalamus and the lateral hypothalamus and midbrain structures (reticular formation) are indicated. Reproduced with permission from (A) Amaral et al. (1989) and (B) Heimer et al. (1991).

lies the field's interests, since much work has been done in understanding emotional rather than cognitive neuronal circuits and systems.

In addition to the anatomists mentioned above, the key pioneers in unraveling this neuroanatomy, one of the most exciting neurological expeditions of all time, include neuroanatomists such as Lennart Heimer and his collaborators. Evolution, emotion, and epilepsy all played key roles in the development of the concept of the limbic system—the emotional brain, perhaps better referred to as the limbic lobe—and the unification of the anatomy of motion with that of emotion.

Papez delineated his proposed cerebral mechanism of emotion in 1937; the key components of his now famous circuit have already been noted. Papez thought the cingulate cortex was a receptive area for experiencing emotion, in the same way that the visual areas of the brain were receptive to visual information. While the hypothalamus was essential for the expression of emotion, the experience of emotion required the cortex, "the stream of feeling" depending on strong interconnections between the cortex and the hypothalamus. Papez sums this up thus: "The hypothalamus, the anterior thalamic nuclei, the gyrus cinguli, the hippocampus and their interconnections constitute a harmonious mechanism which may elaborate the functions of central emotion, as well as participate in emotional expression."[30]

MacLean took the story further, referring to the "visceral brain" and revealing how cortical information might reach the hippocampus by descending in stepwise connections from perisensory cortical areas to the parahippocampal gyrus and by noting the importance of the amygdala.[31] At the time he began his work, these limbic structures were referred to as the rhinencephalon. This moniker was based on a century-old assumption that the structures were primarily involved in the detection of smell, but MacLean wanted to convey a concept of strong inward feelings—hence the term *visceral*. The expression was soon misinterpreted as referring to a rather narrow physiological idea, and so in 1952 he adopted Paul Broca's term *limbic,* and the limbic system as a concept developed from that time.[32] The development of new techniques in neuroanatomy, such as the use of horseradish peroxidase, histofluorescence, autoradiography, and improved silver-staining methods, led to a renaissance of interest in and understanding of the structure, connectivity, and functions of the limbic lobe, especially its cortical-subcortical interactions, and the relevance of them for an understanding of the neuroanatomy of emotion and behavior.

The inputs to the limbic lobe have been shown to be both interoceptive (visceral) and exteroceptive (conveying information about the environment). The former derive from many structures that give information about the internal state of the organism and include modulating influences from substantial neuro-transmitter pathways, which originate in the midbrain and hindbrain, that help drive behavior and modulate mood, such as dopamine, serotonin, and noradren-aline. The exteroceptive afferents derive from all sensory systems and ultimately present complex integrated sensory information to the cortex of the hippocam-pus and the amygdala.

MacLean was a comparative anatomist, and he viewed brain development and animal behavior from an evolutionary standpoint. He developed several highly rel-evant concepts, which, although they have led to some misunderstanding of the limbic lobe and its role in behavior, were central to the developing field of neu-ropsychiatry. One central theme was the idea of the triune brain. This refers to a three-layered structure, the layers having different repertoires but all intercon-nected: the protoreptilian complex, in humans referred to as the striatal complex (basal ganglia); the paleomammalian formation (the limbic system); and the neo-mammalian formation (the neocortex and its connections to the thalamic appara-tus).[33] This triune brain represents the achievements of millions of years of evolu-tion of the neural axis but also of behavior. It is shown schematically in figure 2.7.

The striatal elements of the brain are involved in mastering daily behavioral routines and subroutines; these are repetitive and perseverative motor programs but also include rituals and communicative displays, best observed in reptiles but obviously applicable to much human behavior. The limbic system, in MacLean's

Limbic System Concept
(Yakovlev; Papez; MacLean)

Old version:
Non-isocortex (Limbic) $\longrightarrow$ Hypothalamus (Psychiatry)
Isocortex $\longrightarrow$ Basal Ganglia (Neurology)

New version:
(Nauta; Heimer)
Non-isocortex $\longrightarrow$ Basal Ganglia $\left.\right\}$ Neuropsychiatry
Isocortex $\longrightarrow$ Basal Ganglia

Figure 2.8. The conceptual change in the understanding of the limbic system concept. At one time it was considered that most limbic output was hypothalamic, whereas now its basal ganglia efferents are recognized. This provides an anatomical basis for the everyday observation that emotion and motion are closely entwined.

view, is involved in three key mammalian behaviors, namely, nursing and maternal care, audiovocal communications (vital for maintaining maternal offspring contact), and play. These neuronal structures developed extensively in mammals (much less so in reptiles), leading MacLean to state a most important dictum: "The history of the evolution of the limbic system is the history of the evolution of the mammals, while the history of the evolution of the mammals is the history of the evolution of the family."[34] The limbic lobe is thus a common denominator in the brains of all mammals and, in brief, represents two rings of cortex pivoting around the hilum of the hemispheres, an inner one of archicortex and an outer one of transitional mesocortex.

In other words, the development of the limbic system was an essential prerequisite for the development of characteristic mammalian behaviors. The key feature of being a mammal is, of course, the presence of and need for a mother, and everything that involves. A reptile hatching from an egg must not cry out for its mother, lest it be readily detected by predators and eaten. In contrast, a mammalian infant depends on the separation cry for security and succor. Furthermore, the development of family-, sibling-, and later peer-relevant behaviors, including interpersonal bonding, relates to the phylogenetic and ontological development of these limbic structures. Finally, in the triune brain the neomammalian formation is represented by the huge expansion in humans of the neocortex, leading to problem solving, complex learning, and language.

MacLean outlined three main subdivisions of the limbic lobe, which he referred to as an amygdalar division, a septal division, and a thalamocingulate division. These had to do with feeling and expressive states that relate to self-preservation, procreation, and maternal care and play, respectively.

One of the criticisms of MacLean's idea but also of Papez's scheme is that they somehow suggest that the limbic system is relatively isolated from isocortical structures, the latter being so important in the brain development of *H. sapiens*. It was as if the rider (cortical mantle) had few reins with which to control the horse (the emotional system), and neuronal interactions between these brain areas were limited. This is one reason to abandon the term *system*, which implies some self-contained arrangement, in favor of the designation *limbic lobe*, the term used by Broca and reinvigorated by Heimer and colleagues. To be fair to MacLean, this interpretation was not his intention, and indeed his scheme was much broader in regard to cortical-subcortical connectivity than that of Papez. In particular, MacLean was aware of important clinical data, not only from patients with temporal lobe epilepsy but also from some case reports of people with cortical lesions, especially frontal lobe lesions, that markedly altered personality and behavior. To quote MacLean, "Psychomotor epilepsy provides evidence that the limbic system is involved in self realisation . . . It is of great consequence apropos of a sense of being that the phenomenology of psychomotor epilepsy reveals that even the least obtrusive feelings generated by limbic activity are tinged with some degree of affect."[35]

Beyond the Limbic System

MacLean's contributions to unraveling the neural basis of emotional and social behavior were central to a revolution in the neurosciences that took neurology toward an understanding not only of mental illness but also of normal as opposed to abnormal social behaviors. However, in the past half century, the underlying concepts of the limbic system have altered considerably, not least owing to the anatomical explorations of neuroanatomists such as Walle Nauta and Lennart Heimer.[36]

As has already been noted, the neocortex is dependent on allocortical and subcortical structures not only for the relay of environmental information but also for memory and emotional valence. It has been further noted that these subcortical structures are phylogenetically much older than the neocortex, having evolved over millions of years, controlling movement and key species-specific behavioral repertoires. The circuitry of these structures is much more stabilized and perhaps less plastic than those of the neocortex, the represented behaviors being more ingrained (innate) within the neural apparatus. However, earlier conceptions of the limbic system had a further problem: the anatomical model of the time suggested that there were few direct projections from the neocortex to the hypothalamus (a structure that is important in regulating autonomic activity) and that the hypothalamus was to be regarded as the principal subcortical projection of the limbic system. This led to an interesting but rather damaging conclusion that had implications not only for understanding brain behavior relationships but also for the developing fields of behavioral neurology and neuropsychiatry: those neurologists who, a half century ago, might have reluctantly conceded that there was an underlying neurology of behavior could now say that the limbic system–hypothalamic axis was explanatory enough for them to understand how there might be a neurology of the emotions (and hence psychiatry), but this was very different from the existence of the neuroanatomy of neurological disorders. This involved essentially the neocortex and its main outputs, especially the basal ganglia and the pyramidal motor system.

Psychiatry and neurology, it was observed, could be separated by the Sylvian fissure[37] and were seen to have little in common from a brain-orientated perspective. This scheme, however, did not correspond to many clinical observations, including the obvious behavioral problems and psychiatric illnesses that accompanied movement disorders (such as Parkinson's disease and Huntington's chorea) and the obvious abnormal movements that were a part of the clinical picture of psychiatric disorders across the spectrum from anxiety (tremor) to schizophrenia (tics, dystonias, dyskinesias, and catatonias). Furthermore, the theory failed to connect with common English and everyday observations, namely, that emotion is six-sevenths motion (e*motion*) and that we express our states of distress and emotion with motion, including, of course, speech.[38] Turning to these puzzles, the next generation of neuroanatomists presented a totally different view of the limbic lobe and its connectivity and an integrated vision of the limbic forebrain. This conceptual change is illustrated in figure 2.8. Finally, it is now suggested from a comparative anatomy point of view that all three components of the triune brain are present in all vertebrates, different parts having developed more or less in parallel.[39] This allows for a much closer and more intimate integration of limbic, striatal, and cortical activity and hence a clearer neurobiological understanding of the observed links between emotion and motion and between thought and language.

The Limbic System beyond Emotion

Heimer and colleagues challenged the belief that cortical and subcortical systems are distinctly separated and noted that anatomical studies had revealed not only extensive efferent connections between nearly all of the neocortex and the basal ganglia but also serial linkage between the limbic structures, the basal ganglia, and the neocortex.[40] Furthermore, it became appreciated that the rostral parts of the basal ganglia, far from being exclusively motor in function, were actually innervated by the limbic system (figure 2.9). In fact, limbic structures exhibited a stronger connectivity with the basal ganglia than with the hypothalamus, overthrowing entirely the idea that the limbic system was a discrete system devoted to the hypothalamus and unable to influence the basal ganglia (motor systems) or the cortical mantle.

Nauta, in particular, extended the influence of the limbic system caudally through the medial forebrain bundle (a limbic traffic artery) and other structures to the midbrain (limbic midbrain) and hindbrain, including the cell structures we now know are the origin of the ascending monoamine systems. These innervate

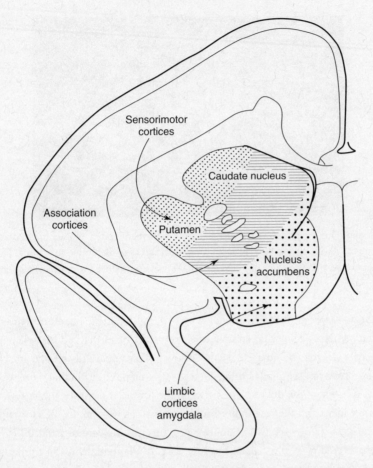

Figure 2.9. This image emphasizes the close association between the limbic cortex and the basal ganglia, particularly the outflows from the amygdale through the nucleus accumbens.

not only the ventral striatum itself but the frontal cortex and, for some neuro-transmitters like serotonin, probably the whole of the neocortex.[41]

Nauta also noted how limbic efferents influenced autonomic neurons and the cranial nerves that innervate the muscles of facial expression.[42] Furthermore, since the frontal lobes (especially the orbital and cingulate divisions) were also by this time revealed as being limbic related, Nauta was able to speculate that the frontolimbic connections enable the frontal cortex to monitor and modulate the activities of the limbic system.

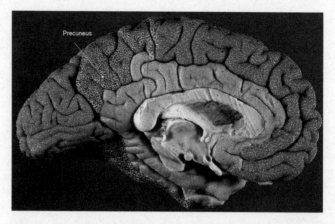

Figure 2.10. This image shows the medial cortex of the hemisphere of the human brain. This reveals the considerable size of the anatomical areas of the limbic structures. The area of the precuneus is also outlined (see figure 2.1). Reproduced with permission from Gary Van Hoesen.

The anterior ventral components of basal ganglia came to be referred to as the ventral striatum, a story taken up and elaborated by Heimer and his colleagues, especially George Alheid and Jose de Olmos.[43] This apparently striatal structure was now seen as essentially limbic. Heimer's group pointed out that there was an overemphasis on the distinctions between the limbic and basal ganglia systems, and they identified that the major limbic projections were to the olfactory tubercle and the accumbens, two of the key structures of the ventral striatum (sometimes referred to as the striatal fundus). This fundamental shift in thinking allowed a much better understanding not only of the neuroanatomy of normal behaviors but also of psychiatric illness.[44]

Following Heimer's scheme, the accumbens and related striatal structures (ventral striatum) receive cortical projections primarily from the limbic lobe and related areas of the temporal cortex. The information flow is to other subcortical sites (the ventral pallidum and mediodorsal thalamus) and then by reentrant fibers back to cingulate and other prefrontal areas (see figures 2.2 and 2.5).[45]

Another important idea was that of the extended amygdala. Many authors conceive of the amygdala as a nucleus, confined to a location in the medial temporal cortex. However, the amygdala seems anatomically to be coextensive with structures in the ventral forebrain, collectively referred to by Alheid, Heimer, and their colleagues as the extended amygdala (see figure 2.6A and 2.6B). This complex, like the ventral striatum, receives inputs from the limbic cortex and has extensive outputs not only to the ventral striatum but also to many other subcortical structures known to regulate emotion and motor function.[46] What this means, conceptually, is that the regions of the brain that modulate emotion and motivation have direct access to the brain's motor systems, down as far as the brainstem and beyond, to the neurons that control somatic and autonomic muscular activity.

The Limbic System as the Seat of the Soul

The cerebral structures that coordinate and modulate emotion have seen a considerable number of conceptual changes in the hundred years since James suggested a neurological approach to understanding the varieties of religious experience. There are well-defined structures in the brain that elaborate emotion, and, in contradistinction to our earlier attempts to understand rational man (*H. sapiens*), the growing evidence is that these are not represented by a confined system (the limbic system) but are all pervasive in influencing not only motion but also cognition. It has been convincingly shown that emotional valence contaminates all human interactions and beliefs, and it is obvious that disturbed emotions are reflected in all psychiatric disorders.[47] This argues for the dominance of allocortical and limbic lobe structures over the neocortex in regulating behavior, a continual triumph of the emotional over the rational. This idea seems logical if one places the brain of *H. sapiens* in the context of millions of years of evolutionary adaptation, during which time individual survival depended on rapid evaluation of the environment and any other organisms in it and rapid action—based on emotional appraisal of any given situation: fight or flight; no time to think.

Human studies using positron-emission tomography (PET) and other brain-imaging techniques have shown that we detect emotionally laden stimuli more quickly than neutral events and that the brain detects emotionally relevant stimuli even if the latter are not consciously appreciated. For example, Ray Dolan and colleagues at the Institute of Neurology, London, have demonstrated this with the technique of backward masking, in which a briefly given emotionally laden image is masked with the immediate longer presentation of a neutral one. The former image, then, is not appreciated consciously, but the emotional response of the amygdala can be shown. This preattentive emotional processing is heavily dependent on the amygdala and its outflow pathways. Furthermore, the amygdala, while receiving information about the visual world from the cascade of afferent projections from the neocortex, also projects back to the visual cortex, thus directly influencing, enhancing but also distorting, perception—the neural basis of paranoia.[48]

The amygdala is also involved in the laying down of everyday memories (episodic), in storing emotional memories, in fear conditioning, and in associative learning. In functional magnetic resonance imaging (fMRI) studies of conditioning for rewarding events, the amygdala, the ventral striatum, and parts of the prefrontal cortex are activated.[49] Indeed, it seems that the amygdala and the extended amygdala complex and other components of the nonisocortical brain already referred to are the crucial central representations of emotional states.

The biasing of judgment and thus personal knowledge by emotion can be observed on a day-to-day basis in human affairs. The neuroanatomical basis for such skewing seems to reside in the dominance of paleologically ancient neuronal structures in human behavioral regulation and cognition, circuits that developed eons before the six-layered neocortex to which so many of our human skills are attributed. Emotion is no longer seen as a counterpart to reason in human cognition but rather as a collaborator, and indeed constructor, of our reasons and thinking.

An interest in the neurology of emotion has now attracted the attention of many neuroscientists who are able, with new methods of investigation, especially brain imaging, to resolve some of these mysteries. More recent theories seem to be combining the hypotheses of MacLean and colleagues, celebrating a central regulator and generator of emotional experiences, with those of James and Lange, recognizing the role of peripheral sensations in emotional feelings and as markers for action. Most popular has been Antonio Damasio's somatic marker hypothesis. Consciousness begins as a feeling, which emerges from the processing of signals from the body and its internal milieu by brain structures, many of which are discussed above. A bodily response occurs (the somatic marker), essentially a feeling, which allows the organism to make a decision on what action to take in response to this feeling.[50] Emotions are essential to decision making, and the markers serve to speed the selection of biologically advantageous outcomes.

Before concluding this chapter on neuroanatomy, I would mention two topics of relevance for the overall theme of this book. The first relates to the anatomy and function of the parietal lobes; the second, to laterality, namely, differences between the left and the right sides of the brain.

The Parietal Lobes

Much attention in the behavioral neurosciences has been paid to the temporal and frontal lobes of the brain, and the close association of limbic structures to these lobes has been presented in this chapter. However, it had been known for

years that lesions of the parietal lobes in the human brain could lead to quite remarkable clinical syndromes, and one that has been well investigated is the phenomenon of neglect. This occurs particularly if the right parietal lobe is damaged,
for example, by a stroke, and the patient will fail to appreciate events and objects
that occupy the left side of his or her sensual world. Vision remains intact, but
the patient will not accept or describe objects in the left field of vision. Patients
may fail to acknowledge that the limbs of the left side of their body are theirs, and
if asked to draw, for example, a clock face, they will omit the details from the left
side of the dial.

This syndrome, which affects all sensory modalities, is seen much less following left-sided lesions, a fact that has lead to speculation about the differing
roles of the two parietal lobes in attentional mechanisms. In short, it is thought
that the left and right sides are specialized for motor and spatial attention, respectively, and that the left parietal lobe attends mainly to events in the right side
of body space, while the right parietal lobe attends bilaterally. Thus when the left
side is damaged, the events in space on the right side are still represented,
whereas a right-sided lesion will leave only the left hemisphere's view of the right
side and there will be an inattention to the left. It has long been held that the parietal lobes also play an important role in representing the body image in the brain
and its relation to external space and in integrating sensorimotor functions.[51]

Thus in epilepsy with seizures that arise from the parietal lobes, a number of
somatosensory symptoms have been reported, including alterations of the body
image, feelings of movement, and sensations of unreality. A variety of visual illusions and hallucinations are also recorded, with objects appearing smaller or
larger (micropsia and macropsia, respectively), objects diminishing in size seeming to be at a distance, perception of mirror images, and also complex hallucinations.[52]

In recent years, much attention has been directed to trying to understand the
role of the parietal cortex in such clinical syndromes. The parietal cortex is regarded as the brain's substrate for spatial behavior in primates, whereas in other
species the hippocampus seems the homologous structure. It is of considerable
interest, then, that there are extensive neuroanatomical connections between the
hippocampus and the parietal cortex in the human brain (especially through the
parahippocampal outputs), allowing for cooperation in the management of spatial tasks and the integration of systems for the spatial representation of personal
(within reaching distance) and extrapersonal space. Furthermore, the area most
involved in the neglect syndromes seems to be the inferior parietal lobule, an area
bounding the temporoparietal junction.

One area of the parietal lobe that is attracting much interest in the medial side of the hemisphere, is called the precuneus. Situated close to the tail end of the cingulate gyrus, the precuneus receives much input from that gyrus and also from the parahippocampal gyrus, and it has expanded in size considerably in the human brain. This area has been shown to be involved in visual imagery associated with memory for personal events and seems to belong to a medial prefrontal–midparietal neuronal network supporting the mental representation of the self.[53] Thus it seems that the right parietal cortex is part of a system that allows for the awareness of implicitly formed percepts of objects in space and has close and extensive connections with temporolimbic structures (figure 2.10).[54]

Laterality

The lateralization of functions within the cerebral cortex is now well accepted. Potentialities to lateralization that are suggested in some other species have actualized in the human brain over the course of its evolution. Many aspects of speech are linked, in right-handed people, to the left hemisphere, whereas emotional processing is more a function of the right hemisphere. The laterality of functions with regard to the parietal cortex has been noted above. This skewing of the brain's functional allocation must have had evolutionary advantages, placing representations that do not need to be bilateral—as, for example, those regulating vision or the motor functions of the two hands obviously do—in one or the other hemisphere. This would minimize brain size and energy consumption and allow for continued safety of the process of birth in mammals.[55] Neurons with the same type of computational activity are placed together, aiding the developing brain and minimizing the need for long-distance connecting axons.

Functional asymmetry in humans seems to begin early in life, blood flow showing a right hemisphere predominance until about the age of three, when a shift to the left occurs.[56] What is less clear is whether the primitive cortical, limbic, and subcortical structures of the brain also have lateralized functions and, if they do, how this may influence, or have influenced in the course of evolution, the overlying cortical development. The animal experimental literature suggests that this is indeed the case, as has recently been well reviewed by Giorgio Vallortigara and Lesley Rogers.[57]

Some suggestion of lateralization of function can be found in species all the way along the phylogeny from fish to nonhuman primates, which relates not only to basic behaviors but also to everyday social repertoires. For example, a variety of animals have been shown to react to predators in the left visual field more vigorously than in the right, while striking at prey is biased toward the right side. Aggressive responses of several species target preferentially the right side. Of course, there are exceptions to these generalizations, but the overall conclusion seems to be that lateralization of function in the brain is found across many vertebrate species. From an evolutionary point of view this must have conferred certain advantages, not only by increasing cerebral capacity but also in enhancing reaction times and, of course, in preventing the simultaneous action of a motor response from both sides of the brain in animals with two independent laterally positioned eyes.[58]

With regard to limbic structures, there is good evidence—from primates, from brain stimulation studies, and from patients with epilepsy—of lateralization. For example, in rhesus monkeys and marmosets a population bias for the right hemisphere to control emotional expressions has been found.[59] In humans, the right amygdala is associated with fear and panic.[60] Tachycardia recorded during seizures is associated with right temporal lobe epilepsy, and human micturition seems regulated by a group of cortical and subcortical structures that are predominantly right sided.[61] There is evidence for lateralization of function in the human insula, especially with regard to the control of autonomic activity.[62]

Several of the major neurotransmitter systems in the brain that drive and regulate behavior seem asymmetrically distributed in animal and human brains, including dopamine, acetylcholine, GABA, all with a left hemisphere predominance, and serotonin and noradrenaline, which have right-sided predominance. Separate processing abilities of the two hemispheres may relate to these observations, since such neurotransmitters, involved with the expression of motor behavior and attention, may link with the differing hemisphere capacities and the right hemisphere's capacity in *H. sapiens* for maintaining holistic, global representations, discussed in more detail in the next chapter, which are closely related to arousal and attentional mechanisms.[63]

The main theme of this book is the cerebral representations of emotional experiences that relate to music and religion and associated activities such as poetry. It is only recently that neuroscience has taken such topics as serious contenders for investigation and that the emotionally driven aspects of our behaviors are being viewed as dominant for so much of our ongoing behavior and intellectual activities. Until we can understand how we behave emotionally, how our brains modulate emotions, and how our thinking is driven by our emotions, we will never be able to influence human behavior in any meaningful way. Whatever the function of emotions, they enhance social communication and bonding and have survival value, but at the same time they bear the burden of destruction and death that has haunted mankind forever.[64]

The concept of the soul emerged through Greek philosophy and literature, but when Christianity became established around the fourth century, it integrated Gnostic and Greek myths into its traditions, including the concept of an immaterial, unembodied soul. Descartes reiterated the imperative of the immaterial, but his *res cogitans* was in actuality an individualistic ego and not some external cosmic order of Platonism. The problem of embodiment, incorporation, was clear, and Descartes, while completing the schism between the mind and the body, tinkered with an underlying neurological location for the soul, a quest that continues to this day.

Coleridge was one among the group of scientists, philosophers, and poets who embraced the excitement of the Romantic and idealistic theories of the eighteenth and early-nineteenth centuries. He appreciated the poverty of the current thoughts about the way the mind received and acted upon sensory impressions, the philosophy of associationism having failed to provide a matrix for creative thought and personal inspiration. Although himself a committed Christian, he was aware of the dangers of the fanatic mind. He wrote of the "magic rod of fanaticism preserved in the very *adyta* of nature [which] needs only the re-exciting warmth of a master hand to bud forth afresh and produce old fruits."[65] Like William James, he was aware of the geniuses of religion, but unlike James and several others from the Romantic scientific philosophical circle, Coleridge would not accept the complete embodiment of the human soul, in spite of his apparent recognition of the ancient nature of such feelings.

James was unable to take a neurology of religious experiences further, essentially because of a lack of neurological knowledge and experimental method. In the past half century, however, huge advances have been made in our understanding of the human brain, including an unraveling of the cerebral pathways that modulate emotions and our deepest feelings. The great conceptual leaps of Papez, MacLean, and Heimer and their collaborators have entirely altered our views of the relationships between the brain and behavior, a paradigm shift as relevant for an understanding of mankind as that of the Darwinian revolution.

MacLean derived some of his ideas from his study of patients with epilepsy, especially patients with seizures emanating from those very structures seen to be involved with emotional processing, the amygdala and the hippocampus. He concluded, "Something does not exist unless it is imbued with an *affective* feeling, no matter how slight . . . Without a co-functioning limbic system, the neocortex lacks not only the neural substrate for a sense of self, of reality, and the memory of on-going experience, but also for a feeling of conviction as to what is true or false."[66]

Nauta and Heimer's elaboration of the limbic lobe has integrated emotion, cognition, and movement. It is now understood that neocortex, allocortex, and basal ganglia seamlessly allow for the transmission and elaboration of all emotional and cognitive events within the brain—what an astonishing hypothesis.

CHAPTER THREE

Language and the Human Brain

The brain handles more than one form of language. Although in human discourse these various forms are usually embedded with one another, their identities are recognizable at once in the differences between poetry and prose. This realization becomes clearer when we examine what is known about the breakdown of language in various neurological and psychiatric disorders. The following discussion is intended not as an excursion through neurolinguistics but as an inquiry into modern theories of the relationship between the brain and language. However, any investigation of verbal creativity needs first to look at the evolution of human language, or at least what we know about it, since our brains and their functions can only be viewed as the outcome of those millions of years of evolutionary forces, driving our species forward to its present state of imperfection.

Language and Its Representation in the Brain

Although language is considerably more than just vocal expression and in everyday use includes gestures, pantomime, mimicry, and the like, for the purposes of the present inquiry it is spoken language that is most relevant. It seems axiomatic that competent linguistic abilities would have had immediate evolutionary advantage for our ancestors, and the latest estimates suggest that the capacity for some language abilities as we may know them arose perhaps some 2 million to 3 million years ago, probably with *Homo habilis*.[1] Although most animal species have some communication skills, the development of language, initially as an efficient method of transmitting danger signals and later as a social bonding system enhancing group activity, must be seen as of ultimate importance for the development of that particular culture we refer to as human.

Although the possibility has not yet been totally discounted, it seems unlikely that any animals other than humans have developed well-defined language abilities, and as far as we know no other species has developed a true grammar. Certainly, some proto *H. sapiens* may have developed early language skills similar to our own, only to be overturned in the tide of evolutionary choice by succeeding generations with more useful and therefore more successful language; but attempts to teach chimpanzees any language that involves the use of higher symbolic representational skills have failed, even after many hours of careful tuition. Recurrent apparent triumphs of some well-trained laboratory chimp-cum-pet emerge in the popular press, but, as Steven Pinker asserts, "deep down chimps don't 'get it.'"[2]

In fact, there is no reason to believe that the languages that developed in humans arose as an all-or-nothing phenomenon. Some kinds of protolanguages, with great simplicity but nevertheless substantial evolutionary advantages, presumably emerged in various places and at various times before the complex interactional grammatical systems that exist in the world today. Whether such protolanguages were composed of words with limited grammar or were essentially modes of delivering messages holistically, which then became segmented, is entirely unknown. Michael Corballis reflected on the development of language from gesture, the latter proceeding from primate grasping to pointing, and credited the neurologist MacDonald Critchley, among others, with the idea that gesture might have been a precursor of speech.[3] Corballis speculated that a gestural protolanguage may have developed some 2 million years ago. The making of simple tools emerged in a similar epoch. An increase in brain size occurred, along with the development of a hunter-gatherer way of life, and then, some evidence indicates, migration out of Africa some 150,000 to 200,000 years ago.[4] Cooperation became central to survival, coalitions came to be enforced, and with the development of our frontal lobes, certainly by the time of Cro-Magnon, the appreciation by one mind of the minds of others evolved.[5] Corballis dates the development of autonomous speech to perhaps some 50,000 years ago, at the same time as the flowering of technology, art, and music.

It is not my intention here to discuss in detail the various theories of language organization and such philosophical issues as the relationship of language to the external world in which an individual exists. However, it should be noted that there has been a considerable sea change about such matters in recent years, largely brought about by the development of the ideas of Noam Chomsky and the digressions of the linguistic philosophers.

Chomsky adopted an essentially rationalistic viewpoint, one that begins with an assumption that the world we live in, as we interpret it, is the product of our rationalizing minds. Although things obviously exist outside ourselves, our only access to them is indirect, that is, through our perceptual filtering organs, and embodiment through neurological distillation. These are necessities before apperception, and certainly any conscious representation, can occur. We simply do not have direct access to external (or for that matter internal) sensory gestalts; such crude and overwhelming information is by necessity pruned down for us into meaningful apperceptions by a process of which we are entirely unconscious. Although the alternative view, empiricism—that we have direct access to things outside of us and that such access is the sole source of our knowledge—is still adhered to by some philosophers and is the meat of folk psychology, a brief excursion into basic neuroscience reveals this approach must be wrong.

Chomsky suggested that the brain possesses in-built structures that are universal and allow for the development of language in any given individual.[6] These structures not only explain the unfolding of language but also are the underfelt of a common universal grammar, one that can be identified across all known languages. This is related to a genetically determined language faculty, allowing the expression of language universals through species-specific innate structures found in the brain. Human languages are known to be much more uniform than was at one time thought, which may be one reflection of their neurological basis. Chomsky refers to the faculty of language as a biological given, which, in its initial state, is an expression of certain genes. However, he departs somewhat from many others when he refers to language not so much as a means of communication as a system for expressing thought.[7] Indeed, language use is largely personal, solipsistic and self-reflective: planning the day, relating details of personal life, and so on.

The linguistic philosophers, like many thinkers before them, addressed the issue of the meaning of words and the relationship of thoughts to words and words to objects in the external world. In one account, the structure of language and logic are given by the structure of the world, and direct correlations are posited to exist between words and things. This view, sometimes attributed to the early Ludwig Wittgenstein (1889–1951), can be contrasted with the later postulates of the same philosopher, namely, that meaning rests not in the way words refer to objects but in the way language is used. In such a scheme, there are no direct external reference points; meaning is derived from context.

One corollary of this, according to the Sapir-Whorf principle of linguistic relativity, is that our cognates are given by our language; in other words, human beings' conceptions about themselves and the world in which they live are biased by the language they use. This view has been considerably challenged, and one good reason is that a distinction needs to be drawn between thought and language. This seemingly obvious proposition was unpopular with the schools of psychology that are referred to as behavioral and with the empirical philosophers.[8] As Charles Ogden and I. A. Richards note, "We shall find that the kind of simplification typified by this once universal theory of direct meaning relations between words and things is the source of almost all of the difficulties which thought encounters."[9] The primitive utterances of any protolanguage surely were urged by emotions and instincts, with limited cognates, the latter emerging later as thoughts. Words symbolize thoughts, not things.

The essential feature of human spoken and written languages is their symbolic nature. Symbols, which in some classifications are considered a class of signs, may also be viewed to differ from signs. The latter designate contiguous relationships and are metonymic in form, whereas the former are metaphoric.[10] Words act as more than signifiers for the thing signified; they have additional secondary (and then tertiary, and so on) links. Symbols are quite arbitrary; they need to be learned, and they are representative. Thus representations are arrangements of symbols, and it is such use of symbols in language that renders communication between humans "intelligent."[11] Symbols embody a power that allows us not only to think ahead but also to plan and to tell stories.

Because words are symbolic, they have no value in themselves and have no direct precise external referents; but they are also malleable and generally imprecise. The suggestion, conceived by George Orwell (1903–50), that a spoken language would develop, referred to as Newspeak, that would narrow the range of thought and in which every concept would be expressed exactly and only by one word can never be realized.[12] As Humpty Dumpty said in Wonderland, "When I use a word it means just what I chose it to mean—neither more or less." But it is this flexibility, and the variability of meaning based on context, that gives language its lively and dramatic nature. It also allows for two great attributes of language, ambiguity and metaphor.[13] Yet these are often the forgotten springs of linguistic achievement, in spite of their universal necessity.

Before verbal language comes thought. Coleridge sums this up with the following statement: "I believe that the process of thought might be carried on independent and apart from spoken or written language. I do not in the least doubt that if language had been denied or withheld from man, thought would have been a process more simple, more easy, and more perfect than at present." In the *Biographia Literaria* he notes that "an idea, in the highest sense of that word, cannot be conveyed but by a symbol; and except in Geometry, all symbols of necessity involve an apparent contradiction."[14]

Speech is only a part of the overall language system, as, for example, the whole world of gesture reveals, motor acts usually serving to highlight the emotional content and sometimes the meaning of spoken words. However, because speech is so obvious, both to ourselves and to others, it is often forgotten that the whole of our expressed output is preceded by thought, itself often only vaguely clarified in the mind and only finally represented to us in verbal terms, immediately preceding the verbal act itself. We know when we have said something that is not exactly what we wanted to say, and we strive for the lost word on the tip of the tongue. We derive satisfaction from the thought captured and succinctly phrased and communicated successfully to an appreciative listener. Mentalese is as symbolic as any representational language but is more richly textured, complex, and inchoate.[15] As Corballis reflects, spoken language is confined to a single spoken line, while thoughts are four-dimensional.[16]

Imagination and fantasy can proceed without the intervention of words, so not all thought requires the language of speech. This is further clarified from studies of people with acquired deficits of speech, referred to as aphasia, as may occur, for example, with a stroke or a brain tumor. While the retained experiences of the state of aphasia may vary dependent on the type of aphasia, thinking seems to continue. Jacques Lordat (1773–1870), a professor of physiology at the University of Montpellier, had a stroke in 1825 and later recorded the experience. He wrote that "the inner workings of the mind could dispense with words . . . While recognising the instrumentality of language in conserving ideas, in preserving them for future reference, and in transmitting them, I was unable to accept . . . [the] theory that verbal signs are necessary, even indispensable for thought."[17]

Another account that has been left to us relates to the stroke that Samuel Johnson (1709–84) suffered one night in June 1783, following which he was rendered partially aphasic.[18] Johnson set about demonstrating his retained intelligence by composing a prayer in Latin verse, although accounts of this feat vary. According to the novelist Fanny Burney, this prayer was composed "internally," and Johnson was unable to actually speak it aloud. He wrote several semicoherent letters describing his experience during this attack (from which he made a complete recovery), and the contents reveal the aphasic deficit.

There seems, then, to be an inner language, referred to by some as a linguistic *Vorgestalt,* from which the spoken language crystallizes, but with considerable texture that is beyond the capacity of the spoken word to express. This leads immediately into a consideration of the relationship between emotion, on the one hand, and thoughts and language, on the other, since there is also an affective texture that lies beneath all thought; as Nietzsche remarks, "Thoughts are the mere shadows of feelings."[19] The writer Ian McEwan describes this as follows: "This is the preverbal language that linguists call mentalese. Hardly a language, more a matrix of shifting patterns, consolidating and compressing meaning in fractions of a second, and blending it inseparably with its distinctive emotional hue which itself is rather like a colour. A sickly yellow. Even with a poet's gift of compression, it could take hundreds of words and many minutes to describe."[20]

We can conceptualize a development, then, from emotions to thoughts and thence to some preverbatim intermediary, all of which precede a final vocal declaration. As Pinker summarizes, "Any particular thought in our head embraces a vast amount of information. But when it comes to communicating a thought to someone else, attention spans are short and mouths are slow."[21] There is clearly considerable evolutionary advantage to our speech.

Speaking and Writing

Evidence from patients with neurological disease suggests that linguistic and writing skills develop separately, or at least have different cerebral representations. As we observe from our own experience, humans learn to speak before we manage to write. With writing comes the ability to express complex thoughts and emotions, beyond the capacity of oral presentation. The tradition of oral poetic verbal transmission preceded that of the written, and classic works such as those of Sappho and Homer were orally transmitted. It can be further speculated that these great stories of human strife, love, and war were recited in a poetic mode, not only for ease of learning but also because of the emotional intensity that the rhythmic musical patterns of the poetry imparted to the listener. People derived pleasure from the very act of listening, but they could also achieve emotional insights into questions, still baffling today, about the origin and meaning of life.

In contrast to the redundant and transient nature of speech, the written text demands a conciseness of expression and remains a permanent trace of the author's thoughts and emotions. There is time, in the act of writing, for the *Vorgestalt* to become modified, and the words available to the writer, as opposed to the speaker, are essentially more flexible, more varied, and greater in number.[22]

Neurological Disturbances of Language

The neurological underpinnings of language have been well discussed, and only a few of the basic details need be given here.[23] Essentially, the emphasis for well over a century has been on the left hemisphere of the brain, and the two main regions subserving language are referred to as Broca's and Wernicke's areas. In previous times, in the spirit of Gall, theories posited localization of functions, for example, speech and writing, to such specific brain areas. However, this rigid modular thinking of earlier generations about the way the brain functioned has been reviewed and renounced in recent times by two important developments in neuroscience. The first is the development of connectionist models of brain function, emphasizing circuits, parallel processing, and the cortical-subcortical representations of functions discussed in chapter 2. This stems, in part, from attempts to view brain activity using analogies with artificial intelligence and the language of computers. However, it also derives from observations that the same alterations of behavior can emerge from lesions at different sites in the brain and that lesions at apparently the same sites in different individuals may lead to different behavioral manifestations. The second is the information from studies using modern brain-imaging techniques to visualize cerebral activity of various functions, including language, in healthy volunteers.

The Localization Hypotheses

The idea that language, among other faculties, can be tightly located to certain brain regions has a long and respectable history. The modern era began way back in the eighteenth century, with the rise of the phrenology movement. Gall and his collaborator Spurzheim, it will be recalled, conceived of the brain as composed of many different organs, which they initially thought could be palpated through the scalp. These brain organs and their functions were faithfully plagiarized and delineated on the heads of busts, which, over time, became popular collectors' items. Various parts of the cortex were deemed to be the seats of different functions. Each of these functions was essentially localized to one part of the brain and one only—the seat of the passions, for example. Such contentions, and the popularization of the discipline (phrenology), opened the way to considerable misuse of the ideas and to exploitation of the vulnerable at the hands of charlatans. This led to the eventual downfall of the phrenology movement, but the ideas persisted, to permeate and influence thinking in neurology for the next two centuries.

Although there were intellectual and theological antagonists to such ideas, the theories proved powerful and seemed to be scientific in their conception, if not in their practice. They received considerable support from the early studies on aphasia, which began around the mid-nineteenth century.[24]

Who truly gave the first descriptions of an aphasic patient with left frontal lobe damage is still a matter of debate. Gall had actually suggested the orbital frontal areas of the brain as speech organs, but it was left to Broca, an anthropologist as well as a surgeon, to present cases and convince others that it was not just the frontal areas of the brain that were affected in cases of aphasia but more specifically the left frontal region. He presented eight cases of patients with acquired loss of language, all of whom had lesions in the third left frontal convolution.[25] This site was to be from then on referred to as Broca's area.

The original descriptions of aphasia were followed by many others that served to accentuate the idea of the modular nature of the brain and the way functions were localized to isolated brain regions. The sites of other skills, such as writing and reading, were identified, and the various parts of the cortex had their functions allocated to them, much as a jigsaw puzzle is filled out. The left hemisphere came to be referred to as "dominant" for language function, and for a century it reigned over its apparently silent counterpart, the right hemisphere. The latter was known to be involved in certain alternative functions, such as visuospatial abilities, but essentially these were considered nonverbal in nature and not really worth studying in much detail. One reason for this was the neuropsychiatric, as opposed to strictly neurological, flavor of the clinical presentations of right hemisphere lesions. It is rarely appreciated, even today, that acute insults to the left side of the brain are likely to be referred to a neurologist, whereas right-sided lesions often go to psychiatrists. The aphasia of the former directs to neurology, but the emotional disorder of the latter leads to psychiatry.

The second great pillar of aphasia terminology was given by Carl Wernicke (1848–1905).[26] In 1874 Wernicke described a different form of aphasia, essentially related to posterior rather than anterior left-brain lesions, with very different characteristics. His observations were soon followed by other observations of patients with brain lesions at one site or another and with differing forms of aphasia, as several speech areas were identified. The brain became a feast for diagram makers, who spotted their illustrations of the brain with so-called centers related to one function or another and demonstrated their interconnectedness by drawing lines.

Aphasic Syndromes

Present-day teaching still emphasizes the dominant role of the left hemisphere for speech and delineates several well-known speech disorders. These varieties of aphasia are given various names and imply rather specific underlying areas of cerebral damage. The main ones, and some of their distinguishing characteristics, are listed in table 3.1.

Speech disorders have generally been divided into fluent and nonfluent types.

TABLE 3.1
Varieties of Aphasia

Syndrome	Fluency	Comprehension	Repetition	Localization in Left Hemisphere
Wernicke's	Fluent	Impaired	Impaired	Post-sup-temporal
Transcortical sensory	Fluent	Impaired	Intact	Angular gyrus
Thalamic[a]	Fluent	Impaired	Intact	Thalamus
Conduction	Fluent	Intact	Impaired	Arcuate fasciculus
Anomic	Fluent	Intact	Intact	Anterior temporal: angular gyrus
Broca's	Nonfluent	Intact	Impaired	Inferior frontal
Transcortical motor	Nonfluent	Intact	Intact	Medial frontal or superior to Broca's area
Global	Nonfluent	Impaired	Impaired	Wernicke's and Broca's areas
Mixed transcortical	Nonfluent	Impaired	Intact	Lesions of transcortical sensory and motor aphasias

SOURCE: Based on Cummings and Trimble (2002), 90.
   [a]Thalamic aphasia is usually distinguished from transcortical sensory aphasia associated with cortical lesions by the onset with mutism, co-occurring dysarthria, and prominent hemipariesis.

The former characterize lesions of the posterior areas of the brain that subserve speech, and the latter relate to anterior abnormalities. The eponyms *Wernicke's aphasia* and *Broca's aphasia* are given to these two types, respectively. In reality, in most cases, an admixture of syndromes is found, and the clear stereotypes of the textbook descriptions are not so often seen in pure form. In fluent forms of aphasia, the speech output sounds fluid enough, but patients make mistakes with their word use, producing paraphasias. Patients have poor comprehension and often lack insight into their aphasic deficit. They might still be able to read, though this ability is variable, and their written output is also disturbed, containing paragraphias.[27]

The areas of the brain most often involved in this type of language disturbance are on the left side and cover the left superior temporal region and surrounding areas, especially the angular gyrus. From studies of patients with brain lesions and from brain stimulation studies, it has been suggested that these areas, especially the left superior temporal area, are important for language comprehension.[28]

In contrast, patients with Broca's aphasia experience an articulatory deficit, leading to reduced, nonfluent speech. Much effort is expended in the production of the halting, brief, mangled sentences; sometimes the resulting speech is referred to as telegrammatic. Nouns and verbs predominate, and prepositions and articles are virtually absent. In this second form of aphasia, comprehension is relatively intact for simpler grammatical constructs, but writing is limited, both by an agraphia and by the right-sided paralysis that inevitably accompanies this type of aphasia.

The lesions of Broca's aphasia are in the left frontal areas, specifically, in that region now referred to as Broca's area. Although there are continuing arguments about the exact site and nature of lesions that provoke this form of aphasia and its relationship to anarthria, the fundamental differences between language deficits following anterior as opposed to posterior hemisphere deficits are clear.[29]

Traditional views would have it that the language architecture of the brain is fixed at an early age and is rather invariant between individuals. However, studies of brain stimulation, in which patients remain awake and can respond to questions, reveal a rather different picture. The neurosurgeon George Ojeman has studied patients while they were being operated on to help their epilepsy, who were stimulated at various brain sites while simultaneously being shown pictures of objects they were asked to name or being given a reading task. Across several patients, the sites of language representation were actually very variable and extended far beyond the more traditional descriptions offered above. Ojeman's studies reveal the extensive involvement of the temporal lobes in language processing, sites of relevance that pass anteriorly as far as the temporal pole in some patients.[30] Unfortunately, as these and most other stimulation studies have been done on patients with known brain lesions, it is unclear how reliably such information can be extrapolated to the normal population.[31] This work also fails to clearly demonstrate the two major subdivisions of language specialization, the receptive and expressive being only poorly defined—another example of the dictum in neurological practice that it may be possible to localize a lesion but not a function.[32] Thus in spite of strongly held scientific opinions about the fixed and confined nature of the cerebral representations of language, it should not be surprising that several outstanding voices were raised against the likelihood of such close links between structure and function, especially with regard to speech.

A Centenary of Dissenters

Until recently, the left hemisphere attracted the lion's share of attention when it came to language mechanisms. It was also considered relevant for many other cognitive tasks, including calculation and the execution of planned motor actions, and to generations of neuroscientists it seemed truly dominant in the overall scheme of brain function.[33] However, there have been a considerable number of opponents to the view that language could be so discretely localized in the brain, and good evidence has now accumulated revealing that the right hemisphere has an important role in the organization of our cognitive abilities, especially for language.

Even Broca and the early localizers faced opposition to their views that language could be organized in such a discrete way, in the left hemisphere of the human brain. Some of the first arguments were of a religious nature: symmetry is God's way, and to suggest that the human brain, the finest organ of creation, is lopsided was considered heresy.

An early English neurological dissenter was John Hughlings Jackson. Although initially persuaded by Broca's arguments, Hughlings Jackson gradually drew away from the localizationist views of his contemporaries and firmly posited a role for the right hemisphere in language. He emphasized the dual nature of the brain and two fundamental modes of expression, the emotional and the intellectual.[34] He opined that damage to the left hemisphere interfered with intellectual expression but emotional expression remained intact. He developed his ideas after careful evaluation of patients with aphasia, observing the language that remained with aphasics rather than trying to work out what had been lost. In particular, he was impressed by the involuntary and emotional nature of their expressions.

For Hughlings Jackson, the basic aphasic deficit was the failure to propositionize, both in the speech act and internally. He recognized that aphasic patients could have thought and hypothesized that the right hemisphere was receptive for speech and was also expressive for the automatic reproduction of words. However, Hughlings Jackson saw no clear boundaries between the automatic and the voluntary, such that in health, in the act of propositionizing, mentation was dual.[35] He was particularly impressed with the ability of the aphasic patient to utter emotional expressions: "His emotional language is apparently unaffected. He smiles, laughs, frowns and varies his voice properly. His recurring utterance comes out now in one tone and now in another, according as he is vexed, glad, etc.; strictly we should say he sings his recurring utterance: variations of voice being rudimentary song; he may be able to sing in the ordinary meaning of that term."[36]

These early observations seem to have been ignored by several generations of neurologists and neuropsychologists, who persistently, and seemingly almost deliberately, played down the role of the right hemisphere in cognitive manipulations. Even today, supporters of a strict localizationalist view of brain function still exist, and the approach does find use in a clinical neurological setting. However, a considerable shift in emphasis has occurred over time. This has historical and medicopolitical dimensions.

In the last quarter of the nineteenth century and the first half of the twentieth, as the value of the clinical localization of the site of brain lesions by examination of the patient was realized, neurology expanded and developed as an intellectual discipline. Along with the mystique of the patella hammer and red carnation (to test smell and color vision), the neurologists' equivalents of a stethoscope, went the considerable skills of interpreting a patient's signs and symptoms as a consequence of one or several lesions in the central nervous system and pronouncing on the site of the cerebral disturbance. More and more specific brain functions were described or hypothesized as localized to specific brain areas, continuing the intellectual trend of the phrenological ideas of Gall and Spurzheim. However, one important consequence of this was that behaviors that could not be so localized fell from mainstream neurology and floated helplessly in a sea of assorted flotsam and jetsam, only partially rescued by the good ship psychiatry.

The latter discipline had, up to the midpoint of the nineteenth century, been the neurology of the times. It was at that time better referred to as neuropsychiatry, and those physicians interested in the brain and its functions were likely to be excellent psychopathologists as well as pioneering neuropathologists.[37] But as more and more discrete neurological syndromes were identified, psychiatry was left to contend with the more complex (and fascinating) but apparently nonlocalizable disorders of motion, sensation, and emotion. These inevitably were disorders of higher mental function and social behaviors, including schizophrenia, epilepsy, and a vast array of emotional syndromes, which became the psychiatric illnesses of today's classification schemes.[38]

Initially, because most of these disorders seemed culturally bound and involved problems of thinking and communication rather than seeing and walking, they were embraced by psychology and the pioneers of psychoanalysis.[39] The decline and fall of psychiatry over the next half century was inevitable, as its practitioners shifted away from its medical base and any interest in the role of the central nervous system in patients' symptoms waned. It became the era of the mindless brain and the brainless mind.[40] A new treatment was offered for the untreatable—psychoanalysis—and was enthusiastically taken up, particularly in the United States.

The Americans had always been unimpressed by the hereditary models of neuropsychiatric illness espoused by the Europeans. These models emphasized such concepts as moral degeneration, which implied an inevitable decline of abilities over time within the diseased individual but also a handing on of such illnesses to their future progeny, based on shaky principals of inheritance.[41] In contrast, in the New World view, a person achieved or failed on account of his or her own individual enthusiasm and enterprise and not because of genetic heritage. This split between endowment and achievement amplified the Cartesian echo, that lingering but powerful philosophical constraint that so deceptively but neatly split mind from body and neurology from psychiatry.

The past forty years have seen considerable advances. Psychiatry has been rescued from the wilderness, and in many countries neuropsychiatry is an accepted clinical and academic discipline, with its own corpus of literature and its dedicated practitioners. It is a psychiatry with the brain in mind. An allied specialty, behavioral neurology, has also flourished, attributable, in part, to the convincing contributions of the American neurologist Norman Geschwind (1926–84).[42] From these developments, the right hemisphere, Hughlings Jackson's emotional hemisphere, has gradually emerged to become an equal player in the overall game of human communication.

The Right Hemisphere

Gradually, from about the midpoint of the twentieth century, case reports appeared of patients with right hemisphere damage and various intriguing neuropsychological symptoms, but initially little attention was paid to language. Often strikingly abnormal behavior was noted, with, for example, visuospatial disorders with total neglect of the sensory fields on the opposite (left) side of the body. Celebrated cases described by Oliver Sacks, such as the man who mistook his wife for a hat, represent other examples.[43] Sacks makes particular play of patients with parietal lobe lesions, who lose their ability to recognize things or people despite intact visual pathways (visual agnosia).

Gradually we have built up a picture of the main functions of the right hemisphere, aside from those of language, and these have been discussed in some detail by the neuropsychiatrist and philosopher John Cutting, in one of the only comprehensive texts on the subject to be written.[44] What is also now clear is that the right hemisphere is very much involved with language in a different way from the left hemisphere; and central to its involvement is the concept of prosody.

Prosody

Our ability to understand the meaning of spoken language goes far beyond the capacity to understand the words uttered or even the rules of the grammar in which they are embedded. The tone of what is said often betrays far more, hence the expression that it is not what someone says that is relevant but the way it is said. Prosody here refers to poetic rhythm and intonation rather than to an alternative meaning, which might relate it to speech rhythm in general.

It was clinically observed that patients with right hemisphere brain lesions, while superficially seeming to have intact language skills, responded literally to questions and often missed the entire point of a conversation, focusing on the superficial and making inappropriate interpretations. It was further noticed that patients with right-sided brain strokes spoke with a flattened tone of voice and a lack of emotional expression: they lacked prosody.

There are several elements to prosody, including tone, pitch, melody, stress, and rhythm. These aspects of spoken language were probably first brought to the attention of neurologists by the Norwegian physician Lars Monrad-Krohn, who emphasized stress, rhythm, and pitch as elements of what he called the prosodic quality of speech. In particular, he noted their importance for the conveyance of meaning.[45]

Critchley discussed the creative writing skills observed in aphasiacs and made some special references to poetry. He reported on several aphasic patients whom he personally studied. One was able to write "advanced" poetry with his left hand, and one of his poems was published. It seems that this patient, and another who also composed adequate lines, had not written poetry before the aphasia but afterward found poetry easier to write than prose. Two other patients Critchley wrote of were able to resume a former skill of writing poetry after their acute illnesses, and another, who had enjoyed reading poetry before his stroke, was successfully encouraged to take up writing it after the stroke. While the quality of much of the poetry quoted seemed limited, the emotional tone, rhyming, and often the rhythm were maintained.[46]

A physician who left his own testimony to his aphasia was August Forel (1848–1931), a neuropsychiatrist from Zurich. Forel suffered a stroke in May 1912 and later reflected on its effect on his intellectual functions. Interestingly, like Samuel Johnson, he wrote a poem while aphasic, to test his abilities; he later wrote a second version and compared the two. His main observation was that the first version had "l'incapacité a maintenir la cesure et le rythme approprie, ansi que 'd'autres fautes' mais avec une bonne ordonnance des rimes."[47]

The behavioral neurologist Eliot Ross expanded on these observations, and he described in some detail what are now referred to as the aprosodias. He proposed that affective prosody is a dominant function of the right hemisphere and that the areas of the right hemisphere that subserve this function are analogues to those involved with propositional language on the left side of the brain. He tested patients with right-sided strokes on special language tasks designed to detect prosody and defined several forms of aprosody, mirroring the several different forms of aphasia.[48]

Patients with right hemisphere lesions were shown to have problems with the expression of, recognition of, or even the ability to feel emotions. On the basis of a series of investigations into the underlying neurology of prosody and the way the right hemisphere modulates emotions, Ross elaborated a theory of the neurology of the emotions that takes into account his observations and, at the same time, embraces some evolutionary aspects of the development of human language.[49]

Ross noted Charles Darwin's suggestion that certain emotions are wired innately into the nervous system and are found across all cultures. These include anger, fear, panic, surprise, interest, happiness, and disgust, and they are referred to as primary emotions. Anatomically, these can be linked to structures in the limbic system of the brain. In contrast, there are also social emotions, which are thought to derive from the need to bond with others and include pride, embarrassment, guilt, shame, and the like. Both primary and social emotions have positive and negative valences. Based mainly on work with stroke patients, some researchers had earlier suggested that positive emotions were linked almost exclusively to the left hemisphere and negative ones to the right. This fitted in with the reported observations, discussed later, of depressions emerging after left hemisphere strokes and emotional indifference after right-sided lesions. However, Ross pointed out some of the inconsistencies in the results of the quoted studies and arrived at a different interpretation. He noted that primary emotions have a predominantly negative bias, and social emotions are more evenly distributed with regard to positive or negative valence. Furthermore, in social situations, there is always a tendency to express positive emotion at the expense of the negative. We prefer to say that things are all well, even when they are not. Ross therefore suggested that the right hemisphere modulates the primary emotions, while the left enhances positive emotions but also suppresses negative ones. This interpretation is but one reflection of the controlling influences of the left hemisphere over the right.

Following further experiments, using the sodium amytal technique (see chapter 4), Ross published results that suggest that the left hemisphere memorizes the social emotional experiences of life while the right stores primary emotional experiences. During inactivation of the right hemisphere with the barbiturate, patients were asked to recall primary emotional life experiences, which they had identified to the investigator before being given the injections. However, they related social, not emotional experiences, some patients actually denying the emotional content of their experiences.

On account of these observations, Ross was able to put forward the view that social emotions and related behaviors, including voluntary control of emotional displays, are modulated by the left hemisphere but that primary emotions are mediated by the right. These hemisphere differences are part of a body of work that reveals the right hemisphere to be of utmost importance in regulating not only the emotional tone of speech but also the complexity of our emotional lives. The right hemisphere is involved in the interpretation of language in a more global, less focused way than the left and is central not only in the analysis of the multiple meanings of language narrative but also to the understanding and expression of rather specific emotional contexts.

Spoken language seems to be an exclusively human attribute, and we could not speak to ourselves and communicate with one another without the appropriate neurological apparatus, facilitating the learning and use of our generative grammars. The brain circuitry underlying this fabulous evolutionary achievement has been developing for eons, but it is only in the past 50,000 to 150,000 years that the full potential for language use burst onto the planet with *H. sapiens,* and for an even shorter period of time has language served as the rich symbolic, metaphoric, and prosodic pitch, prattle, and patter of our daily discourse.

The modular, phrenological constructions of an earlier neurology have given way to an understanding of brain function based on circuits and parallel processing, with an emphasis on cortical-subcortical and right and left hemisphere cooperation and coordination in normal brain functioning. Until quite recently, the left hemisphere has been viewed as the dominant hemisphere, exclusively modulating language, but recent research has challenged this view, and in the past few years the functions of the right hemisphere have become clearer. In this chapter, its role in language and emotion has been suggested, themes taken up in the next chapter.

CHAPTER FOUR

The Other Way of Using Language

One of the central aims of this book is to relate certain human cultural achievements, especially religion, poetry, and music, to their underlying neurological basis. These cultural activities, I suggest, are deeply embedded in our nature and could not be so ingrained without corresponding brain structures, which have developed over millenniums of evolution. Language forms the central bridge for both religion and poetry, and music, or musical expression, can also be discussed as a form of language. The left hemisphere can no longer be considered as dominant for language skills in the way envisaged by our neurological forefathers; the right hemisphere is now known to play a significant role in our language and emotional life. Before exploring this role, it is useful to examine the differences between two forms of language: prose and poetry.

What Is Poetry?

Poetry, as one aspect of language, can be considered to be different from prose, and there are biological, evolutionary, and neurological underpinnings to this sentiment. One way to begin to explore these ideas would be to start with a definition of poetry itself, and at first sight this would seem to be a relatively simple task. After all, everyone would recognize the following as a poem:

Drink to me only with thine eyes,
And I will pledge with mine;
Or leave a kiss but in the cup
And I'll not look for wine
The thirst that from the soul doth rise
Doth ask a drink divine;
But might I of Jove's nectar sup,
I would not change for thine.[1]

Over the years, few literary critics have come up with a good definition of po-etry, or, for that matter, a definition of good poetry. In fact, arguments rage as to the limits and boundaries of poetry and where, indeed, the border between po-etry and prose, if there is one, lies. This is a controversial subject, especially since the twentieth century, and it is accepted at the outset that there are critical bor-ders between prose and poetry—free verse, which departs from meter but still has underlying ordering and pattern, being an obvious example. These discus-sions are not pursued further here, in part because they are predictable. Neither will the issue of *when* poetry becomes prose, and when prose becomes poetry, be pursued. What is more relevant for the theme of the book relates to the basic in-gredients of poetry: Can we define what seems to be essential for a poem to be a poem and not something else? Here, there may be some agreement.

Unfortunately, no definitive work on the question exists for easy reference. Many distinguished poets shy away from attempting an answer. This is perhaps because they worry that the exception will always disprove their rules, and they do not want to be caught out; or perhaps they are fearful of the boomerang criti-cism that some or all of their own work will fail to match up to the standards they would wish to lay down.

Many classical theorists imply that whatever poetry is, it comes close to an early form of the human language. Jean-Jacques Rousseau (1712–78), in his text on the origin of languages, writes, "It seems then that need dictated the first gestures, while the passions stimulated the first words . . . The language of the first men is represented to us as the tongues of geometers, but we see that they were the tongues of poets." In some way he seems to be hinting that poetry came before prose, which was "bound to be, since feelings speak before reason."[2] Although he obviously does not mean that primitive man came out of his cave spouting an ur-form of Homer, Rousseau argues that, as languages developed, they became more monotonous and less passionate, a change linked to the developing em-phasis on reason over passion. Interestingly, Rousseau further notes that the ori-gins of music must have been closely allied to these early prosodic speech forms.

It is not surprising that one of the first discourses on the nature of poetry came from the Greeks, since the early Greek era was a fertile age of poetic invention, and the origins of tragedy, a further theme of this book discussed later, stem from that culture. The word *tragedy* derives from two Greek words, *tragos* (goat) and *aei-dein* (to sing); thus the goat song, or *tragodia*. The feasts of Dionysus were the set-tings for tragedy, Dionysus being the god of vine and vegetation whose sacred an-imal was the goat. The poetic-musical performances of the tragedies were, then, religious ceremonies, but they also placed the nature and meaning of human suffering in art.

Greek philosophy includes extensive discussion about poetry, much of which would seem irrelevant for our modern understanding of the value of the art. Nevertheless, some points are worth noting. Plato objected to poetry mainly on the grounds that, like all art, it is imitative and involves the representation of falsehoods rather than truth. It diverts man's attention away from the true nature of things and stimulates irrational tendencies. Poets and poetry were therefore banished from his Republic, or ideal state. He issued a call for someone to defend poetry, and Aristotle, Plato's student, took up the challenge.

Aristotle, who considered Homer to be the perfect poet, wrote his *Poetics* around 360 BC, essentially in response to Plato.[3] Aristotle, in contrast to his teacher, recognized that poetry, and imitation of life in play form, can reveal human experience and that the emotions it arouses can be positive in their effect, provoking what he refers to as a "catharsis." While much of the *Poetics* has to do with tragedy and how a good tragedy should be written, Aristotle also outlines the principles of poetry, as he saw them. Since much of the tragedy written at the time (at least that which survives for us today) was based on the Homeric legends, it is not surprising that Aristotle admired Homer's work, and he suggests that Homer was the first writer of poems in iambic meter, the form "most speech-like of verses."[4]

As a discipline, poetry, unlike history, was thought to be philosophical in nature, speaking more of universals than of particulars. In part, the skill of writing poetry rests with the use of "alien" words:

> So then, poetic expression should have some mixture of this kind in it; the one ingredient, that of foreign words, metaphor, ornamental words, and all other varieties, will ensure that it is not commonplace or low . . . It is important to make fitting use of all the devices we have mentioned, including compounds and foreign words, but by far the most important thing is to be good at metaphor. This is the only part of the job that cannot be learned from others; on the contrary it is a token of higher native gifts, for making good metaphors depends on perceiving the likeness in things.[5]

The Elizabethan age produced a considerable amount of literary criticism about poetry, evoked, in part, as a defense of poetry against a developing Puritan opposition. The Puritans associated poetry with degeneracy and all the sins of foreigners (especially Italians), harking back to the aphorisms of Plato and his banishment of poets from the ideal Republic. These attacks on poetry also stemmed from a distaste for the low ballad form and the bawdy rhymes of popular writing and for the playhouse. Several authors attacked rhyme, blaming its intrusions into a poem for disturbing the meter, and attacked its foreign origins, especially as a heritage of the Goths and Huns.[6]

The rebuttal was led by an appeal to classical models and hence attention to style and decorum and an insistence on appropriate syllable count and meter. Continental poets such as Dante, Petrarch, and Boccaccio were praised as models, and poetry was claimed as a superior, albeit artificial, form of composition compared with prose. One of the earliest critical reviews was that of George Puttenham (1520–90), who notes that "speech by meeter is a kind of utterance more cleanly couched and more delicate to the eare than prose is, because it is more current and slipper upon the tongue, and withal tunable and melodious, as a kind of musicke, and therfore may be tearmed a musicall speech or utterance, which cannot but please the hearer very well."[7] Poetry, in Puttenham's view, is the skill of speaking and writing harmoniously. It requires knowledge of Pythagorian proportionality, and it is musical.

The succeeding two hundred years, including the Enlightenment, produced some of the most elegant works of and on English poetry, for example, the poems of Alexander Pope (1688–1744) and John Dryden (1631–1700) and the criticisms of Samuel Johnson (1709–84).[8] However, it was a later generation of poets, the Romantics, who advanced the discussion of the form and meaning of poetry in new ways. Two texts of relevance are William Wordsworth's introduction to *The Lyrical Ballads* and Coleridge's *Biographia Literaria*.[9]

The Lyrical Ballads first appeared anonymously in 1798, but the second edition included the preface, which seems to have been written by Wordsworth at the suggestion of Coleridge. Both poets were attempting to alter the style of poetry and to write on themes of ordinary life in straightforward, everyday language. Wordsworth contended that the important thing about a poem is the emotion it arouses, and although it was his view that there is really little difference between the language of prose and that of poetry, he did state that rhythm has an effect of "tempering and restraining" the passions and that meter "greatly contribute[s] to impart passion to the words."[10]

In the *Biographia Literaria,* Coleridge asserts that he learned from his tutors that poetry, even that of the loftiest and, seemingly, that of the wildest odes, had a logic of its own, as severe as science. He considered that "poetry is distinguished from prose by meter or rhyme or both." However, he also suggested that there are fundamental differences in the purposes of the writing and in the contents of poetry and prose, which led him to the proposition that "a poem is that species of composition which is opposed to works of science by proposing for its *immediate* object pleasure, not truth; and from all other species (having this object in common with it) it is discriminated by proposing to itself such delight from the whole as is compatible with a distinct gratification from each component part."[11]

For Coleridge, then, mere rhyming or metering are insufficient for a "legitimate" poem; the individual parts must support and "explain" one another, harmonizing with the influence of the metrical arrangement. Reading the poem is like being carried forward toward the ultimate solution, and the mind is pleasurably excited along the way.

One of Coleridge's objects in writing the *Biographia Literaria* was to develop his philosophical ideas, but he also wished to analyze the poetry of earlier ages and the contemporary contributions of Wordsworth. Coleridge had read a considerable amount of continental philosophy and was especially influenced by the writings of Kant and Friedrich Schelling (1775–1854). The mind for Coleridge is an active, synthetic organ and not the passive *tabula rasa* of the empiricists; and fancy and imagination are two distinct psychological faculties.[12] The former has shaping or modifying power, the latter aggregative or associative power, and both are free from the laws of association. These faculties allow for the development of the poetic imagination and genius, which Coleridge saw as exemplified in the works of Shakespeare and in the poems of Wordsworth. In short, for Coleridge, poetry unites passion with order.[13]

Percy Bysshe Shelley wrote his *Defense of Poetry* in 1821, inspired by *The Four Ages of Poetry*, written by his close friend, Thomas Love Peacock (1785–1866). In this work, Peacock argued that progress in civilization coincided with a decline in the power and social relevance of poetry. Shelley's essay, in contrast, highlights in some detail the social role of poetry and ends with the words, "Poets are the unacknowledged legislators of the world." Shelley offers some general rules for the definition of poetry: The language of poetry is "vitally metaphorical; that is, it marks the before unapprehended relations of things." Language itself is produced by the imagination, he suggests, and poetry expresses arrangements of language originating, therefore, in the imagination. He emphasizes the importance of "a certain uniform and harmonious recurrence of sound . . . with its relation to music, [which] produce metre, or a certain system of traditional forms of harmony and language."[14]

Twentieth-Century Contributions

A. E. Housman, in his *Name and Nature of Poetry*, referred to an underlying set of facts and natural laws by which versification can be conditioned, but, like most before and after him, he would not be drawn out on what they might be. However, he makes the following revealing statement, much quoted, about the recognition of poetry:

> I could no more define poetry than a terrier can define a rat, but . . . we recognise the object by the symptoms which it provokes in us. One of these symptoms was described in connection with another object by Eliphaz the Temanite: "A spirit passed before my face: the hair of my flesh stood up." Experience has taught me, when I am shaving of a morning, to keep watch over my thoughts, because, if a line of poetry strays into my memory, my skin bristles so that the razor ceases to act. This particular symptom is accompanied by a shiver down the spine; there is another which consists in a constriction of the throat and a precipitation of water to the eyes; and there is a third which I can only describe by borrowing a phrase from one of Keats's last letters, where he says, speaking of Fanny Brawne, "everything that reminds me of her goes through me like a spear." The seat of this sensation is in the pit of the stomach.[15]

The critic Northrop Frye, in his *Anatomy of Criticism,* had a lot to say about the functions of poetry but, again, rather less on the actual definitions. The class of things called a poem, as representative of a part of a larger class referred to as art, presents "a flow of sounds approximating music on one side, and an integrated pattern of imagery approximating the pictorial on the other. Literally, then, a poet's narrative is its rhythm or movement of words." It is the "regular pulsating metre that traditionally distinguishes verse from prose."[16]

T. S. Eliot also wrote about poetry and its uses. Like most other commentators, he shied away from giving definitions, questioning the value of any even if they could be given. We only learn what poetry is by hearing it or reading it, but he seemed to acknowledge that we have some innate idea of what it is. Eliot suggested that one of the great accomplishments of Elizabethan poetry is the development of lyric, and he emphasized the relationship of poetry to music. He also discusses the "auditory imagination," "the feeling for syllable and rhythm, penetrating far below the conscious levels of thought and feeling, invigorating every word; sinking to the most primitive and forgotten, returning to the origin and then bringing something back, seeking the beginning and the end."[17]

He echoes these sentiments in his "Burnt Norton":

Words move, music moves
Only in time; but that which is only living
Can only die. Words, after speech, reach

Into silence. Only by the form, the pattern,

Can words or music reach

The stillness, as a Chinese jar still

Moves perpetually in its stillness.[18]

Poetry began, according to Eliot, "with a savage beating a drum in a jungle, and it retains that essential of percussion and rhythm; hyperbolically one might say that the poet is *older* than other human beings . . . I have insisted . . . on the variety of poetry, variety so great that all kinds seem to have nothing in common except the rhythm of verse instead of the rhythm of prose."[19]

Frederick Pottle, in an essay titled "What Is Poetry?" notes that it is a matter of historical fact that people generally distinguish the "poetic" quality of writing from prose by the use of meter in the former; on similar grounds, alliteration, assonance, rhyme, and parallelism are also recognized. All these serve to "concentrate the poetic effect." However, like others, Pottle wished to decrease the emphasis on the more formal structure of poetry and to concentrate on the experience, or the illumination, of the poem itself: "Truth attained by rational inquiry seems generally a tame thing as compared with the immediate illumination of great poetry . . . because we proceeded by conscious steps to the result and know how we got there. In poetry we know of no intermediate steps, because there were none."[20] This sentiment is echoed by the French poet Charles Baudelaire (1821–67): "Death or deposition would be the penalty if poetry were to become assimilated to science or morality; the object of poetry is not Truth, the object of poetry is Poetry itself."[21]

In a discussion of descriptive poetry, Pottle goes on as follows:

> Successful descriptive poetry does not attempt to catalogue objects precisely, in the scientific manner. It becomes successful when it realises that its real subject matter is not lakes or mountains, rivulets or precipices, birds or flowers, but man's inner life, the motions and changes of which, in some mysterious fashion, may be symbolised by the elements of landscape. And perhaps it does not become successful even then. It must realise the precise quality of this mental life which is its subject matter and not only select its symbols but direct them."[22]

This brief introduction serves to remind us that for well over two millennia something called poetry has been recognized and discussed by scholars, most of whom have been poets, but few have been willing to define poetry. In fact, many will just dismiss much of the above as the prating of out-of-date theorists; so be it. This account certainly ignores much of modern literary or narrative theory, which may give definitions of poetry in terms such as it being a structure of signifiers that absorbs and reconstitutes the signified. The point is, however, that throughout history a body of writings can be identified that most people would agree is poetry, and this designation implies certain characteristics about the use of words and the structure of the piece. The authors who have been considered here seem to posit a view that poetry somehow differs from prose and consistently refer to several features that for them distinguish the poetic.

The Form of Poetry

This is not the place to give cookbook descriptions of the various forms of poetry in an attempt to identify common patterns that will give a description of poetry true for all time. Nonetheless, in a popular sense, there are certain structural elements that are usually identified as essential to poetry, including meter, rhythm, and stanzaic form. Of these three, meter and rhythm have been traditionally the most important.

Meter is related to the stressed and unstressed syllables in a line of poetry, and the feet by which these patterns are described include the well-known iamb, spondee, trochee, anapest, and dactyl. Some kind of stressed verse has been a part of English literature since old English times, although other metered patterns have dominated some continental poetry, notably, that based on syllable count.[23] The iambic pentameter is the most common form, as in Thomas Gray's "The *curfew tolls* the *knell* of *passing day*."[24] The effect of meter is magnified by the additional sound effects of alliteration, assonance, and rhyme. Alliteration, a primary structural principle of old Germanic and Middle English poetry, refers to the repetition of initial consonant sounds, as in, Shakespeare's "Full fathom five thy father lies." Assonance is the repetition of vowel sounds, as in the line that follows, "Of his bones are coral made."[25] Both alliteration and assonance contribute to the emotional tone of poetry.

Rhyme became popular in England in the twelfth century with the growing influence of the French culture on the English language. Although much poetry, especially modern verse, is unrhymed, rhyme, when present, is ideally a part of the playful, musical character of the piece. As courtly love and stories of King Arthur and his gallant knights spread through Europe, new French words were gathered into the rapidly developing English language; poetry was one medium of language, and rhyme flourished. Rhyme, an ancient device, makes lines easier to remember and may well have been a vital ingredient for the oral communication of early poetry. Rhyme, of course, can be internal, within a single line, or stanzaic, within the pattern scheme (couplets, for example) of the poem. The subtleties of rhyming add considerably to the intellectual complexity of a poem, but banal rhyme can destroy an otherwise creative piece.

Poetry, then, has rhythm as a consistent element, and dramatic metrical forms and irregular meter can add to the complex excitement of some modern poetry. The "sprung rhythm" of Gerald Manley Hopkins and the effects of various forms of repetition, as revealed by Walt Whitman in some of his so-called free verse (in which the importance of meter is diminished but which still has rhythm), are two good examples.

The Language of Poetry and Metaphor

The language of poetry uses words in a rather special way—"Poetry is the other way of using language."[26] Some literary devices seem central to this discussion. First and foremost is metaphor.

The significance of metaphor in poetry has been noted by many writers since the time of Aristotle. Simply stated, metaphor is the use of the name of one thing to suggest something else.[27] It is fundamentally symbolic; and with the symbol, that which would stream out of us, and be lost in a void, is caught.[28] Metaphor is but one of a number of linguistic tropes in which words are used figuratively rather than literally. Other common figures of speech include simile, metonymy, and synecdoche. In simile, the nature of the trope is signaled by terms such as "like" or "as if." In metonymy, there is substitution of a name of an attribute for the thing that is meant (such as *turf* for "horse racing"). Synecdoche refers to the use of a part for the whole or the whole for the part—for example, "a sail upon the sea"—or the use of the name of a material for the thing itself—for example, *willow* for "cricket bat."

A common use of metaphor in poetry is personification, in which an inanimate object or an abstraction is given personal, human qualities ("There is a garden in her face / where roses and white lilies grow").[29] Personifications of love and death are common:

Because I could not stop for death—
He kindly stopped for me—
The carriage held but just Ourselves—
And Immortality.[30]

The power of metaphor as a linguistic device has been long recognized. It was sufficient to have Plato banish poets from his Republic, and Dr. Johnson referred to it as representing "the most heterogeneous ideas . . . yoked by violence together."[31]

Obviously, metaphor is not the prerogative only of poetry, since the use of metaphor is central to all language. Some suggest that language is almost entirely composed of metaphor, literal language being metaphorical in origin. However, for a metaphor to work in poetry it has to have a liveliness, and it must fit—it must feel right to the reader. "The re-animation of 'dead' or 'background' metaphors is part and parcel of the poet's art."[32] Furthermore, the metaphor is embedded with the other poetic elements—rhyme, rhythm, and meter—thus furnishing the whole with poetic power.

The symbolic nature of metaphor was particularly exploited by the symbolist poets. When Baudelaire states that it is through poetry that the soul perceives the splendors lying beyond the grave,[33] he is referring to the power of poets, through language, to see beyond reality, a neo-Platonic vision. The symbolists strongly equated poetry with music (rather than painting or sculpture) and considered written text that was not musical to be prose literature. Another poetry movement, imagism, used stark metaphors intended to shock—as, for example, in the images given by Eliot: "Let us go then you and I / When the evening is spread out against the sky" and the succeeding simile "Like a patient etherised upon a table."[34]

The discussion of metaphor leads to a consideration of ambiguity. Words that have multiple meanings hardly lend themselves to precision of communication, explaining why, to some writers, metaphor represents all that is wrong with poetry. However, ambiguity is central to poetry, as it is to music (discussed in chapter 6). The most quoted text in this regard is William Empson's *Seven Types of Ambiguity*. Empson opines that the "machinations of ambiguity are among the very roots of poetry."[35] He uses *ambiguity* to mean any verbal nuance that leaves room for alternative reactions to the same piece of language. Ambiguity therefore is at once a device for compression of language and for exploitation of its richness. This tendency of poetry to continually alter, however slightly, the meaning of words through syntax is quite opposite to the use of language in science, in which terms are always being refined and stabilized and where ambiguity is poorly tolerated. For Empson, all good poetry contains ambiguities, and in these ambiguities opposites converge.

This brief introduction to poetic devices is not intended to be an academic linguistic treatise, but it is necessary for consideration of one of the main themes of this book, namely, the different modes of language that are subserved by the brain. Although the differences between poetry and prose are, and perhaps will forever be, open to discussion, the resonance of the above is, I hope, clear. For more than two thousand years many writers have addressed the differences between the two forms of linguistic expression. Since most modern commentators seem to avoid this question directly, it may seem foolhardy to attempt to more precisely delineate such differences. However, there is some agreement about certain elements that seem relevant to poetry. These are rhythm, meter, rhyme, music, repetition, alliteration, assonance, metaphor, and ambiguity.[36]

The essence of poetry is contained by both form and content. With regard to form, rhythm and meter are quintessential (Shelley, Coleridge, Eliot); musicality is created by these and such poetic devices as assonance and alliteration and a use of language that appeals to a primitive, unconscious prototype (Eliot), which has an almost religious intensity (again, Eliot). Metaphor is a vital poetic trope, and tolerance of ambiguity a sine qua non. In our own times, with its creeping legalism, political correctness (read political corrosion), and the ossifying influence of ever more administrative mandates, precision of expression is seen to be essential for even the slightest day-to-day discourses. There is a curse on ambiguity.[37] However, when Auden noted that "it is a poet's role to maintain the sacredness of language," he must have had in mind the genealogy of poetry and the tragedy of the loss of linguistic richness that identified the twentieth century.[38]

Linguistic Expression and the Right Hemisphere

Much of what is known about the brain's relationship to language was gathered by examining patients with strokes or brain tumors, and, as noted, for many years the left hemisphere was revered as the dominant partner of the bicameral brain, especially for language. Only recently has the role of the right hemisphere been recognized, not only for language but also in relation to human behavior more generally. Distinctions having been drawn between at least two forms of human language, one related to prose and the other to poetry, the differences in brain responses to these different forms of communication can now be explored further.

Lesion Studies

Some observations of patients with lesions, especially to the left side of the brain, have already been presented. These have mainly to do with speech, but in the course of clinical research, several investigators have also reported changes of patients' mood and behavior.

The first lesion investigation was done in the nineteenth century by the French neuropsychiatrist J. L. Luys (1828–97). Luys was impressed with the differences in personalities between patients who had suffered brain damage to the right and left hemispheres. He noted the euphoric tendencies of the former and postulated an emotional center in the right hemisphere.[39] Beginning in the 1950s, this theme of emotional release in patients with certain brain lesions, either strokes or tumors, was taken up by several investigators, who commented on the so-called indifference reaction noted in patients with right hemisphere disease, this disposition being accompanied by "jokes, mockeries, and disinhibition."[40]

More recent studies of patients with strokes have essentially confirmed these earlier findings. Robert Robinson and colleagues, who have carried out extensive studies of patients who developed psychiatric disorders after strokes, note a close association between lesions affecting the left hemisphere and the development subsequently of a depressive illness. In patients who developed bipolar, manic-depressive illness, they find that the right hemisphere is usually involved. Among the latter series of patients, all the reported lesions have been in the subcortical structures.[41]

Exploring the Intact Brain

The problem with studying people with such pathologies as strokes and tumors is that it does not yield information on how the intact brain actually works. Luckily, there are several other ways of probing the brain to yield up its secrets. Four main lines of investigation have been pursued; the findings have considerably increased our awareness of the functions of the right hemisphere and have stoutly challenged the view of the overriding dominance of the left brain when it comes to language.

One study used the novel approach of temporarily inactivating a hemisphere by injections of a sedative, sodium amytal, into the arteries that supply that part of the brain. A second related to the invention of a new operation for epilepsy: transection of the large white-matter bundles that connect and straddle both hemispheres, the corpus callosum. A third is referred to as dichotic listening. The most exciting, and potentially the most revealing method of all, is the use of modern brain-imaging techniques.

Some of these methods are linked to the exploration of epilepsy. It had long been known that in one form of epilepsy, referred to as temporal lobe epilepsy, a structural lesion is often found in one or another of the temporal lobes, and in the 1950s neurosurgeons began to remove this part of the brain, if abnormal, in patients with intractable seizure disorders. The operation, known as temporal lobectomy, is often successful in relieving seizures.[42] However, because the temporal lobes are involved in laying down memory traces, and the left hemisphere is involved in certain language functions, to avoid any postoperative aphasia and to assess the potential for memory loss after the operation surgeons need to know, before brain resection, which hemisphere is dominant for language and whether the other temporal lobe alone is capable of sustaining memory.

The chosen method to investigate these issues is to inject the arteries of each hemisphere separately with sodium amytal, thus sedating one hemisphere, and then observe the subsequent effects on memory and language. During the course of such studies, several investigators have reported additional behavioral effects of injecting the hemispheres, including changes of mood and emotion.

Early on, following injections into the left hemisphere, "appearances of a characteristic emotional reaction of a depressive-catastrophic type" were observed and, of course, patients became aphasic. However, when the injection was made in the contralateral (right) side, the emotional reaction was of "the opposite type, euphoric and maniacal," and language disturbance was absent. With right hemisphere inactivation, "the patient appears without apprehension, smiles and laughs and both with mimicry and words expresses considerable liveliness and sense of well-being." The responses were variable between patients but could reach the intensity of a "maniacal reaction."[43]

The patient's euphoric reaction has been identified as "a relaxed attitude and then the extremely optimistic view he takes of everything, by his smiling and making jokes, and by his breaking into actual laughter."[44] The reported depressive reaction was usually less intense than the euphoria; both lasted several minutes. Of importance was the time relationship between the paralysis of the limbs on the contralateral side of the body (the right frontal cortex controls the limbs on the left side of the body, and the left frontal cortex the right-side limbs) and the emotional responses. The paralysis of the limbs on the contralateral side of the body was briefer, and the emotional response outlasted the motor impairment by several minutes, usually coming on after the paralysis had resolved. It was also possible in these studies to provoke these emotions with small doses of the amylobarbitone, which did not appear to lead to even mild impairment of motor functions or speech. The electroencephalogram (EEG) associated with the phase of emotional change was described as "activated." Thus the psychological changes, which were not seen in every case, were noted to have occurred some short time after the injections, at a time when the EEG traces, which were carried out continuously, revealed an activated, rather than a sedated, cortex. Taken together, these results suggest that the euphoria may reflect, if anything, a release (activation) of right hemisphere function.[45]

The split-brain procedures were devised as a treatment for severe epilepsy; in the operation, the corpus callosum, that large fiber bundle of more than 200 million white fibers, is divided. The intervention stops the spread of seizure activity from one side of the brain to the other and lessens the severity of the attacks. Although there are other commissures that link the two hemispheres, the corpus callosum is by far the most important, and if the transection is complete, much of the interhemispheric transfer of information is blocked. For example, a right-handed patient becomes unable to name an object if a picture of it is flashed only into the right side of the brain from the left visual field. This is because, while the sensory information can get across to the right visual cortex by its subcortical pathways, the information about what the object is cannot be transferred to the language-eloquent left hemisphere for verbal description because the main highway for that transfer, the corpus callosum, has been cut off. That the information has been received and decoded, however, is revealed by the patient's ability, with the left hand, to correctly indicate the object from a group of objects shown simultaneously.

The split-brain investigations confirmed much that was already known about the left hemisphere, especially with respect to language, but they also revealed a lot of new data about the right hemisphere. The latter was shown not only to possess a rich lexicon but also to have some control over syntax. The right hemisphere was shown to be sensitive to emotional expression: it can recognize the emotional tone of pictures—for example, faces—selectively shown to it, and patients respond with appropriate emotions. In one study, patients were noted to blush when salacious pictures were directed to the right hemisphere, even though the left hemisphere was unable to verbalize the reason for the shame.

The outcome of these studies was to help define in considerable detail the possible functions of the right hemisphere. However, they were all conducted on patients with essentially abnormal brains, affected by many years of epilepsy. There are several ways to examine brain function in nondamaged brains, which have also been applied to the investigation of the role of the right hemisphere in language. One technique is dichotic listening.

In this method, auditory information is given to one ear or the other, or to both simultaneously, with the underlying knowledge that each hemisphere subserves the auditory input from the contralateral ear. In these investigations, the type of auditory information given to each hemisphere can thus vary in form and content, and hemisphere preferences for various types of information can be explored. The number of such studies is legion, and no attempt is made here to review them. However, it has been possible, using such methods, to show that the left ear has the advantage over the right when it comes to recognizing the emotional intonation of speech and nonverbal emotional sounds, supporting the view that the right hemisphere has an advantage for emotional recognition.[46]

Functional Brain Imaging

Using modern brain-imaging methods, many investigations have been carried out on healthy volunteers. Subjects are asked to carry out various time-locked tasks, during which some image of the brain is captured. Most investigations about language to date have used the technology of either PET or fMRI. As time goes by, the latter is likely to supersede the former for such neuropsychological enquiries.[47]

In PET, a radioactive substance that is metabolized by the brain (such as oxygen or glucose) is given to the patient or volunteer. It is rapidly taken up by the brain's neurons; the more active the neurons are, the greater the uptake. Thus the pattern of radioactivity given back from the brain at a given moment in time will reflect those parts of the brain particularly active in any given task the person is performing. By comparing the metabolic rate patterns of the brains of people in different conditions, for example, at rest and moving the fingers of the right hand, it is possible to determine those areas of the brain associated with such movements. Furthermore, the patterns can reveal the distributed network associated with particular tasks and functions, not merely isolated brain regions related to a function. Developments in the actual processing of imaging, and in the sophistication of the techniques for statistical handling of the results, have led to considerable scientific power for this research methodology.

These imaging techniques have once again confirmed the significant role of the left hemisphere in mediating language, and they substantiate much of what is already known.[48] At the same time, they have allowed for the analysis of what is going on in other brain areas during language tasks. The results reveal that the areas of the left brain involved in language are far more extensive than the traditional models imply, extending well beyond Broca's and Wernicke's areas, and crucially involve the insula and the prefrontal areas of the brain. Furthermore, it has been confirmed that parts of the right hemisphere, notably, the superior temporal cortex, are activated when listening to words and when repeating heard words.

Speech output has been shown to activate bilaterally the Sylvian sensorimotor cortices and the anterior superior temporal lobes. The involvement of larger areas of the brain for language skills has considerable bearing on the use and understanding of aspects of language that may be called creative, based on symbolic representations of the highest order.

Higher Language Function

A growing body of evidence in the past thirty years suggests that the right hemisphere has much more to do with language than previously thought; additionally, several researchers have highlighted its importance in emotional behavior. John Cutting summarized this in 1997 as follows: "The overwhelming role of the right hemisphere in emotion, will, and action, has only been uncovered in the last 10 years or so, and the implications of the main findings for the traditional ideas about mind and brain are startling."[49] Before discussing in detail the relevance of these data for understanding linguistic expression, it is germane to consider those investigations that have examined the role of the right hemisphere in the linguistic tropes that are the language of poetry, as outlined above.

There have been several studies of the role of the right hemisphere in the interpretation of humor and metaphor. Howard Gardner and colleagues examined the ability of brain-injured patients to understand jokes by investigating patients who had damage to either the right or left hemisphere.[50] Subjects were shown cartoons with varied captions and were asked to indicate which was the "funny" version. Additional cartoons without captions were also shown. Patients with left hemisphere lesions behaved normally in many ways, smiling or laughing appropriately when they understood the cartoon. In contrast, those with right hemisphere damage seemed to exhibit one of two reactions, either laughing at nearly everything or, more commonly, showing little reaction, even when they seemed to understand the joke. The cognitive and affective aspects of the responses seemed dissociated. Another study has found the ability of patients with right hemisphere lesions to choose an appropriate punch line for a joke to be impaired compared with those with no brain lesions.[51]

Gardner also examined the use of metaphor in brain-damaged patients.[52] Patients with damage to one or the other hemisphere were asked to match sentences containing metaphors with their pictorial equivalents. Patients with left-sided damage were better able to choose the metaphorically relevant pictures than were those with right-sided lesions. The latter tended to select pictures with literal interpretations and, unlike patients with lesions of the left hemisphere, did not find these literal pictures amusing or absurd.

In yet another investigation, patients were asked to choose word sets based on either antonymical (warm-cold) or metaphorical (warm-loving) relationships. Aphasic patients with left hemisphere damage mainly selected metaphor, while right hemisphere patients relied mostly on the antonyms and showed a decreased sensitivity to an understanding of metaphor.[53]

In more recent studies using PET, Richard Frackowiak and colleagues at the Institute of Neurology, London, have been examining brain function and some higher language abilities in normal people.[54] They gave volunteers three language tasks, two involving sentence interpretation. One sentence was literal, the other was metaphorical, and the third task used random word strings, with or without a single nonword. The subjects were asked whether each of the metaphorical and literal sentences was plausible, and, in the control task, whether a nonword was present. Using this design, the researchers were able to show that the cerebral processing of literal sentences activated regions of the left side of the brain and that metaphors activated several right hemisphere areas. The latter included parts of the frontal lobe, the cingulate gyrus, the middle temporal areas, and the precuneus.[55]

These studies examining function in the normal brain confirm the findings of the lesion studies that the right cerebral cortex is important for the processing of complex linguistic information, such as metaphor. One explanation, especially with regard to the right-sided precuneus and frontal activation, is that somehow mental imagery is involved in metaphor interpretation, these areas being associated with such imagery, especially for personal events. The interpretation of metaphor requires an evaluation of a sentence's violation of the denotative rules of language, which itself is related to personal experience.

Using the PET technique, Tim Shallice and his colleagues have shown that while memory encoding activates the left prefrontal cortex, retrieval of past personal events involves the right prefrontal areas;[56] other studies, especially from epilepsy, have revealed a role for the right lateral temporal areas, the hippocampus, and the precuneus in such memory processing.[57] It may be that such idiosyncratic personal memories are retrieved through a process involving the right hemisphere yet are revealed to us in consciousness through the verbal interpretations of the left hemisphere.[58]

Taken together, these imaging investigations reveal a substantial role for the right hemisphere in modulating some important aspects of language and also memory. The memory system involved is personal, and the linguistic skills are related to metaphor and idiom interpretation, especially the ability to recognize alternative meanings of phrases and those statements that defy the literal rules of the language. It might also be concluded that the right hemisphere has a dominant role in the processing of emotional language. Norman Cook summarizes this view as follows: "At every level of linguistic processing that has been investigated experimentally, the right hemisphere has been found to make characteristic contributions, from the processing of affective aspects of intonation, through the appreciation of word connotations, the decoding of the meaning of metaphors and figures of speech, to the understanding of the overall coherency of verbal humour, paragraphs and short stories."[59]

The Lopsided Brain

There was clearly a time in the evolutionary development of the human brain when the distributed laterality of functions with regard to language, which we now recognize, was not present. Just why pressures grew for the eventual evolution of the "lopsided ape" is unknown, but there is much speculation.[60] The theories are well laid out by Corballis, whose own view is that verbal language grew from gesture. As the climate of the African continent changed, becoming drier and cooler, forests turned to grassland, and food sources were dispersed. This meant that the Pleistocene hominids came under selection pressures for the development of bipedalism, which freed up the hands.

The brain capacity of *Australopithicus* (about 400 cc) was insufficient for these changes, while *Homo habilis* (handy man), with longer limbs and a larger brain (600–750 cc), was the more successful and is thought to have made the 1.8-million-year-old stone tools found at Olduvai Gorge in Tanzania. It is in casts of the brains of *H. habilis* that the first suggestion of Broca's area is seen, although the anatomical developments of the chest, throat, and mouth were probably not yet sufficient for a full vocal language.[61] These physical developments emerged between 400,000 and 1.6 million years ago, with *H. erectus*, whose leaner and taller body was directed by a larger brain (800–1,000 cc) and who may have developed a vocal social language, albeit far short of the languages of today.[62] *H. erectus* was probably the first hominid to use fire, to cook food, and to have migrated out of Africa, remains found in China and Java reflecting their presence there some million years ago. These migrations required sophisticated planning and conditional thinking (what if?), perhaps suggesting that our grammar may have evolved about 1 million years ago. However, the complex, self-referencing syntax of human languages was thought not to be complete until perhaps 150,000 years ago or even later, with a further increase in brain size (to 1,355 cc).

One interesting fact relates to the brain size of *H. neanderthalensis*, who flourished in Europe and West Asia some 200,000 to 300,000 years ago and existed alongside other *Homo* species, including *H. sapiens*, until about 30,000 years ago. The brains of the Neanderthal were actually larger than those of *H. sapiens*, yet the fossil evidence seems to suggest that *H. neanderthalensis* disappeared fairly rapidly off the face of the earth with the sudden spread of *H. sapiens* across the globe. This achievement of *H. sapiens*, modern man, our direct ancestors, can only have been achieved by the flourishing of a culture based on human cognition and an intolerance of any competition from alternative species. The effective use of language must have been central to this transition.[63]

The rise of syntax required the development of appropriate cerebral structures and circuitry to accommodate its complexity. These became the province of the left hemisphere, as dramatic reorganization of the human cerebral cortex occurred. Whether this was the result of a random genetic mutation or genetic variations acting on preexisting biases for dextrality is simply unknown, but laterality evolved, and with it the skewing of cerebral development.[64] Clearly, this development did not relate only to brain size but must have been related to a reorganization of cerebral connectivity and greater neuronal selectivity.[65]

The grasping primate had a highly developed visual system, with binocular vision. Attention was directed to both visual fields and presumably controlled equally by both hemispheres, as were motor and sensory systems. Such symmetry must have been advantageous for the immediate generation of actions in response to external events and in manipulating, controlling, and commanding the environment. Representations were a unity of object images, and the actions to be performed needed to be appropriate to a given situation. Knowledge was kinesthetic and emotive. However, the advantages of symmetry do not apply to internally generated actions, such as language, and the loss of cerebral symmetry was the price paid for increased brain efficiency.

In humans, the parietal cortex is enlarged relative to other primates. Wernicke's language-efficient association area, on the left, and complex visuospatial processing areas, on the right, are part of this development, as is the expansion of the area precuneus. However, there is evidence that the right hemisphere has maintained some of the earlier functions relinquished by the left, and the clinical phenomenon of neglect is one piece of evidence. This fascinating clinical phenomenon is noted after right parietal lesions and does not occur (at least not so obviously) with lesions of the left parietal lobe. One explanation of this is that the right cerebral hemisphere controls attention for both visual fields, whereas the left side controls only the contralateral hemispace.[66] As Corballis noted, the invasive presence of language deprived the left side of the brain of its former role in spatial awareness, but such awareness is retained by the right.[67]

Henry Hécaen and colleagues suggest that sensory data may be differently organized in the two halves of the human brain, undergoing a complex conceptual reorganization in the left, dominant hemisphere on account of language. Such information may be processed in a more primitive way by the right hemisphere, which retains a more immediate and affective valence.[68] Tatyana Glezerman and Victoria Balkoski refer to the symbolic-situational thought and symbolic-object thought of right hemisphere activity. They suggest that "the left hemisphere extracts typical features of objects and phenomena, abstracting from the 'whole,' the right hemisphere, on the contrary, 'deepens' into the single, having the individual symbol as the highest cognitive step."[69]

In fact, over recent years there has been a growing awareness of the different cognitive styles of the two hemispheres, and Cutting has summarized the historical progress on the views of the function of the right hemisphere (table 4.1). After careful consideration of the data, Cutting was led to conclude that "an apparatus in tune with the ups and downs of real life, as is the right hemisphere's, is more likely to reflect the emotional side of things than an apparatus designed to categorise and condense, to desiccate and strip things of their individuality, as is the left hemisphere's."[70]

TABLE 4.1
The Historical Developments of Ideas about the Functioning of the Left and Right Hemispheres

Era	Left Hemisphere	Right Hemisphere
1860–1940	Language	Little (excluding Hughlings Jackson)
1950s	Language	Spatial function
1960s	Verbal	Nonverbal
	Analysis of parts	Synthesis of wholes
	Piecemeal processing	Holistic processing
1970s	Local aspects of things	Global quality of things
	Detailed approach	Gestalt approach
	Serial processing	Parallel processing
	Propositional mind	Appositional mind
	Logical, abstract	Creative, imagistic
	Judging for difference	Judging for sameness
	Focal organization	Diffuse organization

SOURCE: Based on Cutting (1990), 23.
NOTE: Emphasizing the increasing acknowledgment that the right hemisphere had different, often complementary, roles to the left hemisphere in organizing activities.

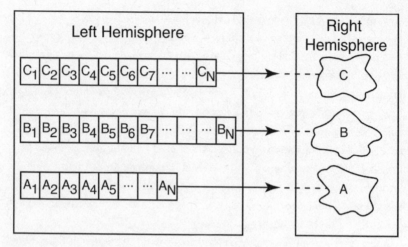

Figure 4.1. A schematic representation of interhemispheric specialization, illustrating analytic versus holistic information processing. Glezerman and Balkoski (1999), 22.

In addition to the differences in handling language, patients with right hemisphere lesions seem unable to grasp overall textual themes, and they often confabulate, talking past the point at hand. Representations exist in the left hemisphere as discrete units and combinations of units, combined together as continual logical series; in contrast, the right hemisphere interprets information holistically (see figure 4.1). These suggested differences in hemisphere specialization are relevant to the discussion of the potential differences between poetry and prose but also to an understanding of different cognitive styles of creativity.

The neuroscientific community has generally shown little interest in exploring the finer aspects of human behavior and thought, especially aesthetic experience and creativity. With regard to the themes developed in this book, this sentiment clearly extends to language other than the categorical and propositional. This neglect may stem from the fact that scientists, in the main, have traditionally had little interest in such matters as aesthetics and art, and that those who have a responsibility to fund research are similarly stuck in administrative potholes, unable to give merit to anything that is not seen as directly applied; curiosity, for them, is simply not enough. Thomas Love Peacock's observation of an inverse relation between the power of poetry and civilization seems to have continued to hold.

However, the neglect of creativity also derives from the relative neglect of neuroscience of the role of the right hemisphere in behavior, and the undue prominence given to left hemisphere abilities in our culture, so dominated by written and spoken prose. Things are now changing. It is abundantly clear that the right hemisphere has a significant role in mediating activities that are exclusively human (such as language, and also music, as discussed in chapter 6). It is involved in important speech functions, including giving emotional tone to language, essential to conveying some aspects of meaning. Of course, in the normal intact brain, the right hemisphere does not carry out such functions in isolation but only in cooperation with the left side of the brain. Nevertheless, the right hemisphere's contributions to language, communication, and the emotions seem reliably demonstrable.

The work cited in this chapter emphasizes at least two ways of using language: the propositional and the prosaic, the detailed and the gestalt, the parts and the whole. The suggestion is also made that prose is a different form of language from poetry. The musical character of the latter is recognized, its physicality has been introduced (Housman not even daring to shave while composing), as has its phylogenetic and ontological relevance (including Eliot's note of its appeal to the "most primitive and forgotten"). The central elements of meter and rhythm for both music and poetry seem obvious, and metaphor is perhaps the common ingredient.

Commentators often distinguish between the language of description (history, order, reason) and that of emotion (passion, imagination), and there are hints even of two kinds of truth, subserved by the two modes of language: a rational, reductive logic (the language of history, science, and the law) and an alternative, personal truth—that which we know. Such implications arise in some languages from the very words used for knowing, when more than one is used—for example, the distinction in German between *wissen*, to know that (a fact), and *kennen*, to know personally.

The distinctions between poetry and prose that have been discussed in this chapter can be seen as one consequence of the divisions of function within the human brain. These have developed over the past few hundreds of thousands of years of evolution, but they allow for a potential understanding of how the functions of the right hemisphere mantle follow closely the cloth of poetry.

The main conclusions drawn from this chapter are that an intact right hemisphere is crucial for certain aspects of language, that these aspects are especially relevant for poetic expression, and that disturbance of that hemisphere disturbs affect and prosody. There are several ways to study the linguistic representations of the right hemisphere, and some have been noted in this chapter. They may also be explored phylogenetically or ontogenetically, from the study of older languages or the prespeech of developing infants. Here, the method adopted is to note the breakdown in language in certain neuropsychiatric disorders and the effect on the language of poetry.

CHAPTER FIVE

The Breakdown of Language

After years of neglect, the contribution of the right hemisphere to language processing is beginning to be recognized by the neuroscience community. There is also a growing understanding of the neurological underpinnings of speech, language, and thought. Poetry, one of the subjects of this book, is itself highly dependent upon an efficient function of the right hemisphere. In this chapter I discuss some other neuropsychiatric conditions in which alteration of speech, language, and thought occurs. Although for traditional neurology, acquired disorders of speech imply aphasia, or a variant of it, it is by now clear, I hope, that such a narrow view of speech and language is untenable.

Examining the form and content of expressive language is central to the detection of most severe psychiatric disorders. Psychopathology usually reveals itself through disturbed language, which implies abnormal underlying thought processes. The important disorders now to be considered are schizophrenia, epilepsy, and disturbances of affect, especially bipolar affective disorder.

Theories of Psychiatric Illness

Early theories of madness attributed mental illness to the unwanted intrusion of spirits and evil forces, often as a sign of punishment for wrong doing. These understandings have gradually given way, in Western cultures at least, to the view that the disturbances of language and behavior that indicate psychiatric illness are reflective of changes in the brain. These changes may be the outcome of a number of processes, and, if they all could be known, then the road to even more enlightened treatments would be apparent. The second half of the twentieth century saw unparalleled developments in the neurosciences, and we now have a much fuller understanding of the underlying neuroanatomy and neurochemistry of many neuropsychiatric disorders. Part of this progress has been driven by close observation of patients and detailed recording of their behavior and speech.

Over the years, the physicians who have been observers of human behavior and its vagaries have developed different classifications to distinguish one syndrome from another; they then use their nosologies to help clarify underlying causes of the behavior aberrations. Like all previous systems, the ones in current use are likely to mature or disappear and be replaced by others.[1] It is interesting to note, however, that over many centuries some concordance has appeared, at least with respect to the descriptions and classifications of some of the more severe forms of behavior disturbance.

Plato distinguished three kinds of madness: melancholia, mania, and dementia. Aretaeus was probably the first physician to recognize that mania and melancholia were somehow related.[2] However, the first comprehensive classification of nervous diseases was that of William Cullen (1710–90).[3] Cullen defined a separate category, *vesania*, to distinguish disorders of intellectual function that occurred without pyrexia (fever) or coma.[4] Both melancholia and mania were included under this heading. The French alienist Phillipe Pinel (1745–1826), who translated Cullen's work into French, also recognized these two states in his system, while another Frenchman, Jean Paul Falret (1794–1870) more clearly described the alternating moods of mania and melancholia (*folie circulaire*). In Germany, Wilhelm Griesinger (1817–68) identified states of mental depression, mental exultation, and mental weakness.[5] The condition we now refer to as bipolar disorder, formerly and perhaps better described as manic-depressive illness, has, then, a long and respectable history; the propensity of the human nervous system to cultivate manic and melancholic moods seems to be primitive.

Another disorder recognized since antiquity is epilepsy. It was at one time referred to as the falling sickness, and it was often given sacred embellishments. In certain places, the sayings of patients with epilepsy had oracular appeal, and close links between religiosity and epilepsy have been observed since ancient times.[6]

The concept of schizophrenia has had a somewhat different history from these first two and is more controversial. Classic signs and symptoms of the disorder are not readily found in the literature before the nineteenth century, although Cullen's *vesaniae* must have included that disorder we now call schizophrenia.[7] The best descriptions derive from the late-nineteenth- and early-twentieth-century writings of Emil Kraepelin (1856–1926) and Eugen Bleuler (1857–1939).[8] The name migrated from the French *démence précoce* to Kraepelin's *dementia praecox* and thence to Bleuler's *schizophrenia*. It was Kraepelin, however, who established the importance of the two stable pillars of psychiatric classification in use today, namely, schizophrenia and manic-depressive illness.

Psychiatric disorders, unlike many in medicine, are almost entirely based on symptoms and signs; their classification is syndrome orientated and pragmatic. They are essentially diagnosed clinically, but embedded within their descriptions are concepts that seem to stretch back to the origins of clinical medicine itself. Within the various diagnostic handbooks and classification manuals, the tricky concept of personality disorders is also found.[9] It is by his or her personality that we get to know a person. In Karl Jasper's words, a man is known by the way "he expresses himself, in the way he moves, how he experiences and reacts to situations, how he loves, grows jealous, how he conducts his life in general, what needs he has, what are his longings and aims, what are his ideals and how he shapes them, what values guide him and what he does, what he creates and how he acts."[10]

The link between a personality type and the susceptibility to develop any particular psychiatric illness remains unclear but there are strong associations between so-called cyclothymic personalities and manic-depressive disorder. Cyclothymes are those people who have a lifelong tendency to fluctuating depressive and elated moods; many believe that cyclothymia is, in fact, a part of the manic-depressive spectrum of disorders.[11] Cyclothymes easily tumble into affective highs or lows.

Varieties of Psychiatric Illness
Bipolar Disorder–Manic-Depressive Illness

The essential feature of a mood disorder, such as bipolar disorder or manic-depressive illness, is the change of mood, which comes before everything else.[12] That is, the change of mood is primary, not secondary to some physical ailment or, for example, to another psychiatric disorder such as schizophrenia. The mood disorders are usually classified today, as in the past, into depressive, manic, and mixed varieties.[13] If cyclothymia is not classified under the personality disorders, it is placed within the spectrum of affective disorders, but its manifestations must not be of sufficient severity or duration to meet the full criteria for one of the affective disorders.

In the depressive state, a patient loses vitality, ceases to enjoy life, and admits to a general loss of emotional well-being. Concentration problems, poor memory, increased apathy, loss of appetite for food, loss of libido, and changes in sleep patterns are all central symptoms. Loss of energy is reported, and as the disorder progresses abnormal thoughts, even delusions, may arise.[14] The latter are typically somber, of guilt, worthlessness, and impending doom.

In contrast, the moods of hypomania and mania are of an increased sense of well-being, with euphoria.[15] Alterations of sleep, appetite, and sexual interest occur but in a direction opposite to those in depression. These can be accompanied, in mania, with delusions, notably of splendor, success, and grandeur.

In both depression and mania, disturbances of thought, speech, and language are typical. In depression, patients' thoughts become slowed, ideas dwindle or become fixated on themes, often seemingly trivial or irrelevant, and speech becomes monotonous and sparse. In contrast, at the hypomanic-manic end of the spectrum, ideas flow freely (up to a point), speech is speeded up, and the use of words alters. The former two are referred to by clinicians as a flight of ideas and pressure of speech, respectively.

In a flight of ideas, thoughts follow one another rapidly, sometimes triggered by outward distractions and often seeming to have only random connections with one another. The psychopathologist Frank Fish has commented that "the progress of thought can be compared to a game of dominoes in which one half of the first piece played determines one half of the next piece to be played. The absence of a determining tendency to thinking allows the association of the train of thought to be determined by chance relationships, verbal associations of all kinds, such as assonance, alliteration, and so on, clang associations, proverbs, old saws, and cliché." Flight of ideas, Fish continues,

> is typical of mania. In hypomania so-called "ordered flight of ideas" occurs in which, despite many irrelevancies, the patient is able to return to the task in hand. In this condition, clang and verbal associations are not so marked, and the speed of emergence of thoughts is not as fast as in flight of ideas, so that this marginal variety of flight of ideas has been called "prolixity." Although these patients cannot keep accessory thoughts out of the main stream, they only lose the thread for a few moments and finally reach their goal. Unlike the tedious elaboration of details in circumstantiality, these patients have a lively embellishment of their thinking.[16]

The Schizophrenias

Several different forms of schizophrenia are recognized, and it is likely that there are several different etiologies. In schizophrenia, thought, logic, and hence speech are primarily disturbed, and any change of mood, such as depression, is seen as secondary, in contrast to the affective disorders, in which change of mood is central. Indeed, the affect in schizophrenia is most often blunted, and emotions are flattened and inappropriate.

Competent psychiatrists readily recognize the symptoms of schizophrenia, which, interestingly, are the same all over the world. The cardinal symptoms will not be listed here and can be found in any textbook on the subject. However, what is important for the overall theme of this text are the distortions of speech and language in schizophrenia, which have been well described.[17]

The speech of some schizophrenics may fragment to such an extent that it resembles that of a frank neurological disorder, some writers likening the condition to one of the aphasias. The term *schizaphasia* is, in fact, used in clinical practice to describe just such a deterioration. Bleuler recognized "every imaginable abnormality" in schizophrenic speech, and Kraepelin referred to the abnormal expression of thought in such speech as *akataphasia*.

A summary of the results of several studies that used computer-assisted analysis of speech to discriminate schizophrenic speech from normal language notes that "schizophrenic subjects, as a group [compared with normals], uttered speech of reduced syntactic complexity, made more syntactic and semantic errors, and were more dysfluent."[18] Schizophrenic speech is less predictable, it contains less redundancy and less information, it uses fewer words, and it is more concrete than normal speech.

Cutting based his careful analysis of schizophrenic language on his own extensive research and personal contact with many patients.[19] He observes in schizophrenia "a combination of reduced concern with pragmatics and incompetent selection of individual words within a category, coupled with a hyperefficiency of the syntactical and categorical semantic systems." He views the left hemisphere in this disorder as "working overtime" and notes that "meaning is arrived at by trawling the linguistic structure itself . . . The conveyance of meaning to others is not the object of the exercise. Meaning is simply presented in the form of all the connections of the word itself; if this can be unraveled by the listener so be it, but it is not a matter about which the schizophrenic cares."[20]

Some authors have commented on the clang associations of schizophrenics, but as the psychiatrist Andrew Sims has pointed out, these are not the same as those of hypomanic utterances or of "poetry and humour." In the examples he gives, the clang occurs with the initial syllable of a previous word, rather than with the terminal ones.[21]

The term *formal thought disorder* is used by clinicians to specify disorders of conceptual and abstract thinking in schizophrenia, and the category includes such interesting forms as condensation, interpenetration of themes, overinclusion, derailment, tangentiality, driveling, and fusion.[22] In schizophrenic speech, conceptual boundaries are lost, and a private speech form, with its own idioms, develops. Thoughts are blocked, broken, and withdrawn from the mind, and language disintegrates. Another type of thought disorder, also seen in patients with organic, especially focal, neurological lesions, is perseveration, in which "mental operations persist beyond the point at which they are relevant and thus prevent the progress of thinking."[23]

Cutting distinguishes between the pragmatic aspects of language—the value of language as a form of meaningful communication—and the other components of language such as syntax and semantics. In schizophrenia, there is a defect in pragmatics, almost the converse, therefore, of aphasia, in which the syntax and structure fail, the pragmatic aspects may be seemingly intact, and any failure of the latter is secondary and is a reflection of the impoverished speech output.[24]

With respect to the themes developing in this book, one writer has said, "In poetry, there is usually a tension between private and public meaning. In schizophrenic writing, there is a drastic skewing towards the private. Further, what appears as metaphor in schizophrenic writing is often private language."[25]

The Epilepsies

Much less has been written about the changes of language in patients with epilepsy than about the other disorders so far described. As with the schizophrenias, there are many different epilepsy syndromes, and, as with the other classification schemes outlined, the classification of seizures and the classification of the epilepsies is subject to the flux of history.[26]

The epilepsies are divided into two main groups. In one, patients have a focus or lesion in the brain that can be assumed from the clinical description of the seizure or detected either with an EEG or some form of brain imaging. Patients from this group are referred to as having lesion-related or focal epilepsy. Patients in the other main group have a different presentation, primary variants having no obvious brain lesions and sometimes an obvious genetic basis. This form is known as generalized epilepsy. Similarly, the seizures patients suffer from are divided into two main groups, those that are focal in origin (partial seizures) and those that from the outset are generalized.

Many partial seizures are secondary to a change in the structure or the function of the temporal lobes of the brain, hence the term *temporal lobe epilepsy*. In the current classifications, this is a form of lesion-related epilepsy. Temporal lobe epilepsy has some defining characteristics, which include a typical seizure pattern with specific signs and symptoms, often an identifiable change of structure and function in one or both of the temporal lobes, and a tendency to be difficult to treat.[27]

Patients with temporal lobe epilepsy seem more likely to suffer from secondary disabilities, including psychiatric problems, than those with generalized epilepsy. They have an increased liability to develop depression and schizophrenia-like disorders, and a special form of personality change—known as Gastaut-Geschwind syndrome—has been described in a subgroup. This condition is named after two neurologists who more clearly formulated the features, Henri Gastaut from France and Norman Geschwind from the United States, although clear descriptions of this personality anlage can be found in the English and continental medical literature of the nineteenth century.[28] These clinical pictures represent forms of an organic brain syndrome, a behavior disorder that evolves from the continuing presence of chronic brain dysfunction.[29]

The affective disorders seen in patients with epilepsy are similar to such problems in people without epilepsy, with some exceptions, such as the associated emotional lability, the increased presentation of irritability and anxiety, and the tendency for the episode to be short lived. Of considerable interest is the frequently cited clinical observation that in epilepsy, classical bipolar disorder is rarely reported.[30]

Gastaut-Geschwind Syndrome

The symptoms of Gastaut-Geschwind syndrome include alterations in sexual behaviors, irritability, and viscosity, the latter being a tendency to slow, labored thinking, as if thoughts are emerging from treacle. This sometimes is revealed as circumstantiality: "Here thinking proceeds slowly with many unnecessary trivial details but the point is finally reached. The goal of thought is never completely lost and thinking proceeds towards it by an intricate and devious path. This disorder has been explained as the result of a weakness of judgement and egocentricity. It is an outstanding feature of the epileptic personality."[31] Two other fascinating features of Gastaut-Geschwind syndrome are hypergraphia and hyperreligiosity.

HYPERGRAPHIA

Geschwind and Stephen Waxman were the first to clearly describe hypergraphia, in a report on seven patients with temporal lobe epilepsy.[32] The writing of these patients, all of whom were hypergraphic, was extensive and characteristically meticulous; in four patients the written themes had moral and religious overtones. In a later paper, the authors discussed three additional cases, in one of which the patient was reported to have undergone multiple religious conversions. This patient's writing revealed a preoccupation with detail, and there was a compulsive quality to much of it. Repetition of words, and often of sentences, was seen. Waxman and Geschwind note that in some patients the desire to record was especially strong: one patient hired a stenographer to take everything down for him; others engaged in extensive drawing and painting that, the authors suggest, may be seen as variants of hypergraphia.

Since publication of these papers, several other studies of hypergraphia have been conducted.[33] Some have been clinical, others have used some form of rating scale to assess the extent of the writing, and the feeling of a need to write, in patients with epilepsy. The results tend to confirm the assertions of the original investigators, namely, that hypergraphia is associated with temporal lobe epilepsy, especially from a site of seizure focus from the medial (that is, limbic) structures.[34] The relationship of cerebral laterality to hypergraphia is at present unclear, although at least one report noted an overrepresentation of right-sided foci.[35] While the relationship between the hypergraphia noted in epilepsy and the ability to produce creative written text must for the moment remain speculative, the phenomenon is obviously the opposite of the effects noted with left hemisphere lesions, with the subsequent development of aphasia and agraphia.

Hypergraphia has been linked to several other disorders of the central nervous system, including schizophrenia and mania. It is also seen rarely following certain strokes that affect cortical and subcortical (thalamic) structures and are lateralized to the right hemisphere, and it may be noted as a reflection of the utilization behavior seen in some people with frontal lobe lesions.[36] However, these are entirely different in quality from the hypergraphia of Gastaut-Geschwind syndrome. The writing associated with epilepsy is more conscious and attentive than the automatic compulsive writing seen in stroke patients;[37] patients with frontal lesions perseverate on tasks, simply continuing to use (hence utilization) the pen.

Kraepelin writes of the hypergraphia of schizophrenia, "Beside negligent want of connection in the train of thought, repeated change of construction in long spunout periods, mixed metaphors, abrupt interspersing of sudden ideas, rhymed effusions, we find a slovenly external form, irregular hand writing, flourishes on single letters, underlining, deficiency or superfluity in marks of punctuation, and monotonous contents with verbal repetitions."[38] The content of the writing is, of course, often incomprehensible, and the incoherent thought processes of the schizophrenic can be easily recognized. Critchley has drawn attention to the veritable *cacoethes scribendi* of the schizophrenic, the writings being embellished with "ornate flushes" and often the page being "barely large enough to contain all that he wishes to impart."[39]

As noted, the hypergraphia of epilepsy may manifest instead as a prodigious output of painting or drawing. The same is typical of schizophrenia. Hans Prinzhorn, who studied both the history of art and medicine, began collecting artwork from some 450 schizophrenic patients in the 1920s, mainly in asylums in Heidelberg. He brought together examples of paintings and drawings, ostensibly for their visual appeal. However, many of the examples are strewn with written marginalia, of precisely the type Critchley describes (see figure 5.1).[40]

Elevation of mood is associated with the hypergraphia in epilepsy, often showing a close temporal relationship to the hypergraphic activity. The tendency to

Figure 5.1. An example of schizophrenic art taken from the *The Cevelar Mary* by Adolf Wölfli (1864–1930), who was a long-stay mental hospital patient at the Waldau Mental Asylum near Bern, Switzerland. Note the extensive marginalia that completely adorn the page.

write is present when the patient is euphoric and disappears as the mood settles. Hypergraphic patients with epilepsy also often seem to report déjà vu experiences. The latter, in which patients feel they have seen or lived through (*déjà vécu*) the period of time they are now experiencing, represents an interesting disturbance of biographical memory and is typically evoked by abnormal stimulations of the right side of the brain.[41]

The content of the writing from hypergraphic patients with epilepsy often reflects religious or mystical themes. Of fifteen cases in one published study, nine expressed hyperreligiosity or comparable metaphysical beliefs, but those who see these patients regularly in the clinic, and who ask about such phenomena, recognize its more frequent occurrence.[42]

RELIGIOSITY

The association between epilepsy and religion stretches back to antiquity. Oswei Temkin, in his brilliant account of the history of epilepsy, noted several ancient religious explanations for the illness: either a god sent it, or a devil entered the patient, or the patient had sinned against Selene, the goddess of the moon. Superstition has always veiled epilepsy, the old name for the disorder, "the sacred disease," lingering on even today in some parts of the world. While at some times and in some places, patients with epilepsy were considered to be unclean, touched by evil forces, and contagious, at others they were considered divine, magic, and their utterances were thought to be prophetic.[43] Much more about the association is discussed in chapters 7 and 8. For the present, it is sufficient to note that certain forms of epilepsy seem to be linked with a recognizable pattern of behavior, referred to as Gastaut-Geschwind syndrome, the central features being religiosity, hypergraphia, and often elevation of mood, and that a focal epilepsy of the right hemisphere may be overrepresented in this group.

Neuropsychiatric Illness and the Language of Poetry

Since certain forms of language are associated more with poetry than with prose, and since in both neurological and neuropsychiatric illness a breakdown of language is often present, it is of interest to examine the form and content of language in such illnesses to see if they provide further insights into the cerebral representation of language skills, especially those relevant to poetry and religion. This assumes that the underlying neurobiology of these disorders is understood. Although in reality we do not yet have a complete picture, these illnesses are slowly yielding up their secrets to neuroscientists, and sufficient clues are available, especially with regard to laterality of brain function, to provide further evidence for the differences between poetry and prose and their respective underlying neurological circuits.

Poetry in Hypomania and Mania

Kay Redfield Jamison has described in some detail the mental experiences of hypomania, reliant to a good degree upon her own personal testimony. In *Touched with Fire*, she gives excellent examples of poets who were likely to have been cyclothymic or manic-depressive.

During hypomanic episodes, Jamison notes, thought is "fluid and productive," and there is a "loosening of normal patterns of association and racing thoughts and flight of ideas"—fertile ground for the writing of poetry.[44] One idea calls up another with ease, the person is inspired, feelings intensify, sensations are keener. The psychiatrist Eliot Slater describes it thus:

> The majority of mankind are moderately equable in temperament, and their moods of joy or sadness, elation or depression, occur within a narrow span and are a natural consequence of the circumstances of the time. There are some however, whose mood is constantly varying, and not from any external cause but from an internal biological rhythm . . . In the upswing there is abundant unflagging energy, spontaneous joy in life, swift flow of ideas, bodily well-being . . . It is a well-known fact that a high proportion of creative workers find that there are periods of life when they have more than usual productivity, others in which they are more or less sterile. The lay observer, and indeed the man himself, will be inclined to say that he was happy because he was working well, that he was unhappy because he could not work. This may sometimes be true, but sometimes it is quite certain that cause and effect should be placed the other way round.[45]

With respect to creative work in particular, Slater continues:

> Whereas the cyclothymic is rendered incapable of imaginative work in a well-marked depression, he has the compensation of finding such work exceptionally easy, of having his ideas flowing richly and abundantly, in the opposite phase. Furthermore, the cyclothymic man is generally an extrovert, impressionable, with warm and strong emotions generally; and I think everyone would agree that there is not such a thing as a major work of composition without a rich emotional content.[46]

Asylum physicians observed long ago that in manic phases some patients would spontaneously write poetry, and in hypomania the tendency to hypergraphia was often seen. This was accompanied by a compulsive feeling, also noted in the hypergraphia of epilepsy; but unless the illness episode progressed to a manic collapse, the output was likely to be contained and, Slater suggests, materialized as productivity, at least in certain people: not all patients with bipolar disorder become poets, of course, nor are all poets manic-depressive.

Poetry in Schizophrenia

Clearly, there are good grounds for believing that the development of schizophrenia acts against the creative process, especially in the ability to create poetry and music. In contrast to the large numbers of quotable poets with manic-depressive illness, poets with schizophrenia are few, and for those few, once the illness becomes established, their creative ability withers.

Poets with schizophrenia in the canon are difficult to identify, and those biographies that are available inevitably reveal a descent from skill in the use of language to schizaphasia.[47] One exemplar is Christopher Smart (1722–71), who skedaddled from being a major prizewinning poet while at Cambridge to living as an inmate in a private asylum, scribbling so-called religious poetry such as his "Song to David" or the now more famous "Jubilate Agno."[48] Others include Friedrich Hölderlin (1770–1843) and John Clare (1793–1864), both of whom spent many of their last years in asylum, and the lesser-known William Collins (1721–59) and Georg Trakl (1887–1914). Considering the relative frequency of schizophrenia (with a community prevalence rate of about 1 percent), this scarcity of poets with the disorder is remarkable.[49] The psychiatrist Felix Post, in an extensive trawl through the biographies of 291 talented creative people, including artists and scientists, notes a low lifetime prevalence for schizophrenia (1.7 percent) and opines that "schizophrenic genes only rarely favoured artistic creativity."[50]

Other authors have specifically speculated on associations between poetry and schizophrenia, but most have suggested an inverse relationship, supported by the comments above. The suspicion that there may be some positive influence of schizophrenia on poetic creativity derives from speculations about links between psychological processes such as condensation, in which many different elements of thought are fused together, and, for example, metaphor.

There are clear differences, however, between the language of poetry and the language of schizophrenia. In the latter, the metaphors are sterile, concretized, and so literal that they cease to be metaphorical. Words become objects themselves and are purposeless, without an "intellectual goal," as Bleuler puts it.[51] The language hides rather than reveals: "In poetry there is displacement from symbol to reality and the two are concordant; in schizophrenia the reality is replaced by the symbol, and the two become increasingly discordant."[52] The language of the schizophrenic is private, not public, and the utterance is for the patient alone, not for general consumption. Schizophrenic rhyming is senseless, the words do not reflect or emanate from the writer's emotions (that is, there is an incongruous affect); in short, there is no artistic intention.

Critchley draws the following distinctions between schizophrenic utterances and poetry: "The one is clinical and compulsive: the other is compulsive too, but it may also at times prove lucrative. One is uninhibited and sincere, while the other may be redeemed by its much contrived euphony. Psychotic writing may or may not have been intended to be read, the other was written not only to be read, but also to be declaimed."[53]

Bleuler suggests that there may be some potential for creativity early on in the course of schizophrenia: "It cannot be ruled out that very mild forms of schizophrenia may be rather favourable to artistic production. The subordination of all thought associations to one complex, the inclination to novel, unusual range of ideas, the indifference to tradition, the lack of restraint, must all be favourable influences if these characteristics are not over-compensated by the association disturbances proper."[54] However, the conclusion can only be that the language disturbances of schizophrenia, in contrast to manic-depressive illness, destroy rather than nurture poetic expression.

Poetry in Epilepsy

The number of people with epilepsy who have become well-known poets is also remarkably small, especially considering the relative frequency of the condition.[55] The clinical sign of hypergraphia might be expected to lead to productive poetic output, but sadly the hypergraphic outpourings of patients with epilepsy are rarely creative; they are often loosely mystical and both perseverative and vague in content. An example is given in figure 5.2.

Poetry and the Affective Disorders

Before discussing what is known about the underlying neurobiology of schizophrenia, manic-depressive illness, and epilepsy of relevance for the theme of this book, it is germane to consider further the link between poetics and bipolar disorder and the incompatibility between schizophrenia and a measured creative po-

Figure 5.2. An example hypergraphia. Patients bring such books with them to the hospital. The open book has poetry within it, but with much repetition and limitation of style. On the right-hand page, "Islands are lovely and rugged, islands are lovely and bare" is written repeatedly.

etic output. The main interest of epilepsy for this text relates to the theme of religiosity, which is discussed in some detail in chapters 7 and 8.

In contrast to the relative paucity of poets with either schizophrenia or epilepsy, the number of poets suggested to have had some form of affective disorder is legion. Melancholy, in particular, has been a common subject for English writers since the publication of Robert Burton's *Anatomy of Melancholy* in 1621.[56] It is a predominant theme in texts of Elizabethan and Jacobean times, and in the eighteenth century *The English Malady*, by George Cheyne (1671–1743), who suffered from depression, was a bestseller.[57] The theme was revived by the Romantics, especially in Germany, with *The Sorrows of Young Werther,* by Johann Wolfgang von Goethe (1749–1832), and in England, through poets such as Coleridge.

There are a great number of poets who seem to have been either cyclothymic or manic-depressive. In an appendix to *Touched with Fire,* Jamison lists many writers and artists with probable cyclothymia, depression, or manic-depressive illness, although some of the poets cited there, including Clare, Trakl, and Hölderlin, might be more accurately classified as schizophrenic.[58] Neither is it clear which poets had typical bipolar disorders, as opposed to depression, or a lifelong angst intertwined with a personality disorder, mistakenly identified as depression. Nonetheless, the list is long, and manic-depressives are amply represented, in numbers far greater than those with schizophrenia or epilepsy.

Jamison especially concentrates on the life and works of Lord Byron, although she quotes the poetry of many others, noting the melancholic lilt to their verse and commenting on the phases of productivity and inactivity that probably reflected the cyclothymic or bipolar nature of their mood swings. A list of the most famous poets with bipolar disorder would include William Cowper (1731–1800), Robert Lowell (1917–77), and Anne Sexton (1928–74), brief biographies of whom are given in appendix 1 for the interested reader.

In spite of this apparent association between poetry and bipolar disorder, only one attempt has been made to correlate mood swings with literary productivity.[59] According to one study, John Keats (1795–1821) went through periods of high productivity, and his low moods were described in his letters. However, the study includes only those poems that could be dated, omitting about a third of Keats's body of work. Although his correspondence reveals the lows, it is assumed that the periods of revealed productivity represent episodes of hypomanic overactivity. Certainly, in a fashion often noted in bipolar patients, the intervals between the episodes of activity seemed to decline as Keats became older; who knows what might have emerged had he lived beyond his meager twenty-five years?

Studies of Associations between Creativity and Mental Illness

Associations between creativity and mental illness have a long history. Over time, creativity has been viewed as a sign of mental illness or a palliative for insanity; at other times, no particular relationship is thought to exist. The legacy of the mad or divinely inspired poet, which goes back to the Greeks, saw some reappraisal in the writers of the nineteenth century, from both neuropsychiatric and psychoanalytic points of view. In fact, the debate shifted from studies of associations between insanity and genius through the concept of moral degeneration to the nature of the creative process itself. In psychoanalytic terms, creativity was viewed by some as a substitute for neurosis, but such theorizing was hardly examined with experimental vigor.

One early-twentieth-century investigation failed to find any link between creativity and mental illness. Havelock Ellis, in his *Study of British Genius*, examined reports of insanity in 1,030 British men of genius taken from the *Dictionary of National Biography* and found an incidence of insanity of only 4.2 percent but an 8 percent incidence of melancholia, which was, however, higher among poets.[60]

Adele Juda undertook a considerable study, which took nearly twenty-six years to complete, of some 19,000 people from German-speaking countries. Five thousand people were personally interviewed, and from these, 294 gifted personalities were selected, a group that included 113 artists and 181 scientists; among the artists were 37 poets. Psychopathy was noted in 27 percent of the artists and was highest among poets (48 percent) and musicians (34.6 percent). Psychosis occurred in both artists and scientists more frequently than expected. This included manic-depressive psychosis, which was higher in scientists (3.9 percent) than artists (0 percent). Manic-depressive illness was more prevalent overall than schizophrenia. The character deviations were referred to as schizoid or emotionally unstable. Juda also identified an intermediate group of people, not so highly gifted but nonetheless of high intellect and able to interpret the works of genius, who possessed a good capacity for reading and writing. Among these, psychoneurosis was observed in 19.1 percent, with an overrepresentation of cyclothymes.[61]

Juda concluded that there was little support for the general proposition of a relationship between creative capacity and psychic health or illness but that schizophrenia was detrimental to such ability. Sadly, a major problem with this study, reflective of the era in which it was carried out, was the poor definition of the psychiatric terminology.

Post reviewed the biographies of 291 "world famous men" from six professional categories: forty-eight visual artists, fifty scholars and thinkers, forty-five scientists, forty-six statesmen and national leaders, fifty-two composers, and fifty novelists and dramatists. Only males were studied because of the lack of availability of sufficient female biographies. Unfortunately, he excluded from his work people whose fame rested solely on poetry. Diagnoses were made according to the *DSM IIIR*. The results are summarized in table 5.1. Affective disorder was noted in 72 percent of writers, 42 percent of artists, and only 33 percent of scientists. Post noted that among writers, 90 percent had some personality disorder, and in 20 percent this was "seriously disruptive." Bipolar disorder was not specifically discussed, but schizophrenia was noticeably absent from all groups.[62]

Post's study emphasized several important points. First, many of the men studied, especially the novelists and dramatists, had had unhappy childhoods and family histories of psychiatric illness. Second, the personality features most overrepresented in writers consisted of avoidant, obsessive-compulsive, dependent, and affective traits. Third, alcohol dependence was above average in artists, politicians, and writers. Fourth, there was a remarkable absence of schizophrenia in

TABLE 5.1
Incidence of Psychopathology in Talented People

Category	Marked or Severe Disorder	Personality Disorder	Schizophrenia	Affective Disorder
Scientist	44.5	42.2	0	33.3
Composer	50.0	61.5	0	34.6
Politician	58.7	63.0	0	41.3
Artist	56.3	75.0	0	41.7
Thinker	62.0	74.0	0	36.0
Writer	86.0	90.0	0	72.0

SOURCE: Data from Post (1994).

this sample. Finally, he found no bipolar type-1 patients, that is, patients with classic manic swings.

Arnold Ludwig carried out a ten-year study of the link between mental illness and creativity by gathering together biographies of 1,004 "extraordinary men and women." One-quarter of the sample was female, and all were selected from biographies that had been reviewed in the *New York Times Book Review* from 1960 to 1990. Eighteen different professions were represented, including 53 poets (5.3 percent of the sample). Ludwig analyzed the family backgrounds, looked for broken homes, and noted family size and birth order, physical health, education, social behavior, encounters with the law, and several other factors he considered relevant to the nurturing of creativity. He also developed a Creative Achievement Scale to measure relative eminence, the scores on this scale correlating highly with the number of lines allotted to the individual in the *Encyclopaedia Britannica* and the *Encyclopedia Americana*.

Among those inclined toward alcohol abuse, depression, mania, psychosis, and suicide, poets were well represented compared with other creative artists. Ludwig concludes that although people in the creative arts suffer from more psychopathology than other creative people,

> no single pattern of mental illness characterises all of the creative arts professions. Although alcoholism and depression are widespread within the creative arts, each profession in its own way shows a distinctive pattern of psychopathology. Illicit drug use is more common among musical performers and actors. Musical composers, artists, and nonfiction writers suffer mostly from alcoholism and depression throughout their lives. Musical entertainers, architects and actors are relatively free from depression. Poets show a high prevalence of both mania and psychosis. Poets, actors, fiction writers, and musical entertainers are more likely to attempt suicide.

Among all those in the creative arts, only architects and designers, and to some extent non-fiction writers, show few signs of mental instability.[63]

About 15 percent of those suffering from depression also had manias. Ludwig was unable to give good statistics for schizophrenia because of a historical diagnostic confusion, especially in the United States, among the psychiatrists of an earlier era, who poorly differentiated between affective and schizophrenic psychoses, which effectively meant that there was an overdiagnosis of the latter at the expense of bipolar disorders. So in place of *psychotic* Ludwig simply uses the term *schizophrenia-like,* recognizing that this embraces schizoaffective disorders, psychotic depressions, and florid mania. Poets seem to be well represented in this group.

Bipolar Disorder and Creativity

One early modern observation on the relationship between genius and bipolar illness was given by W. R. Brain in 1960: "The form of insanity which is most closely related to genius is cyclothymia, the manic-depressive state." His list of cyclothymic men of genius includes the poets Smart, Cowper, and Clare.[64]

One of the authors who have examined the relationship between creativity and psychopathology in a systematic way is Nancy Andreasen, a distinguished psychiatrist and English scholar. In her study comparing thirty writers, most of whom were men, with a control group, writers had significantly more lifetime prevalence of affective disorders (80 versus 30 percent), especially bipolar disorders (43 versus 10 percent) and alcoholism (30 versus 7 percent). Andreasen noted the absence of schizophrenia in her sample.[65]

A similar result was obtained by Ludwig in his comparison of fifty-nine female writers and the same number of nonwriters. Both studies confirm a high rate of psychiatric illness, especially affective disorders, in the families of the writers, and Ludwig also noted other potentially relevant factors overrepresented in this group, such as a history of physical and sexual abuse and other comorbid psychiatric disorders but not schizophrenia.[66]

Jamison studied forty-seven writers of talent, most of them males, including eighteen poets. A high proportion (38 percent) of the total sample had received treatment for an affective disorder; a summary of her results is shown in table 5.2. The greatest degree of overlap was between creativity and hypomanic episodes, characterized by enthusiasm, energy, self-confidence, an increased speed of mental associations, and fluency of thoughts.[67]

TABLE 5.2
History of Treatments for Affective Disorder
in Creative Writers
(Percentage)

Category	Treated for Bipolar Disorder	Treated with Antidepressant	Total Treated for Affective Disorder
Poet	16.7	33.0	55.2
Playwright	0.0	25.0	62.5
Novelist	0.0	25.0	25.0
Biographer	0.0	20.0	20.0
Artist	0.0	12.5	12.5

SOURCE: Data from Jamison 1989.

TABLE 5.3
Psychopathology in Writers and Poets
(Percentage)

Study	Affective Disorder	Bipolar Disorder	Schizophrenia
Post-1994 (writers)	72	?	0
Post-1996 (poets)	25 (cyclothmic) 42 (major affective disorder)	"High prevalence"	0
Ludwig 1995 (poets)	77	13	?
Andreasen 1987 (writers)	80	43	0
Ludwig 1994 (writers)	56	19	0
Jamison 1989 (poets)	55	17	0

Several studies have specifically explored psychiatric illness in poets (see table 5.3). Brain noted that of fifty poets included in the *Oxford Book of English Verse*, only 15 percent were insane or grossly psychopathic, while Harold Nicholson found that of the thirty-two most famous British poets from the fourteenth to the nineteenth centuries, four had major psychopathology (Swift, Cowper, Dr. Johnson, and Shelley). Nicholson opined that all creative writers were hypochondriacs, mainly worrying about the state of their minds, and that it was customary for gifted writers to hear voices and see spectres.[68]

Jamison reported that, compared with playwrights, novelists, biographers, and artists, poets suffered from significantly more bipolar disorder than schizophrenia (17 versus 0 percent) and had received significantly more treatment with lithium, the primary treatment for bipolar disorder at the time of her study. In another study, Jamison reported on the lives of all major British and Irish poets born between 1705 and 1805. The biographies are briefly summarized in her book, *Touched with Fire*. Many are listed as manic-depressive (one-third) or as suffering from recurrent depressions; the catalogue is impressive. She calculates that manic-depressive illness in her sample was thirty times greater, and cyclothymia ten to twenty times greater, than expected.[69]

Ludwig gives the lifetime incidence for mania in poets as 13 percent, almost certainly an underestimate. His sample of depressives included bipolar patients, and his psychotic sample contained both manics and schizoaffectives.[70]

Post gave special consideration to poets in an extension of his study already quoted. Again, only males were sampled, and *DSM IIIR* diagnostic categories were used. Among the hundred artists in the sample, including poets, playwrights, and writers, thirty-five were poets. Of the seven writers whom he considered to have affective psychoses, five were poets (Clare, Randall Jarrell, Vachel Lindsay, Lowell, and Theodore Roethke), and all had a bipolar illness. Of the writers, 48 percent had had a major depressive episode without psychoses, and cyclothymic personalities were noted in 25 percent of poets, as opposed to 7 percent of the rest of the sample. There were eight suicides, six of whom were primarily or secondarily poets. Alcoholism was lowest in poets (31 percent) and highest in playwrights (54 percent), three poets having alcoholic psychoses (Berryman, Hart Crane, and Edgar Allan Poe).[71]

Neurobiological Associations of Schizophrenia and Bipolar Disorders

The past three decades have seen an explosion of work on the brain abnormalities found in schizophrenia. Neuropsychology, EEG, and brain imaging have all been used to examine generalized and focal abnormalities in patients, and several series of brains from schizophrenics have been subjected to postmortem studies. The medial temporal lobes, especially the left hippocampus and the frontal cortex and related structures, have been the main target of interest, and various reports have associated irregular cell patterns, diminished size, and abnormal organization of the hippocampus associated with schizophrenia.[72]

Such studies suggest that in schizophrenia the left side of the brain is abnormal, initially from a structural perspective and then also from the point of view of function. Most neuroscientists now accept that schizophrenia is a developmental disorder, associated with subtle genetic-structural brain abnormalities that may be detectible early in life. However, the main functional changes and the clinical psychotic manifestations evolve and do not usually become manifest before the later teenage years. It has now also been shown that, while left limbic disturbances are a common feature in schizophrenia, other brain areas are also dysfunctional, including the subcortical structures and the frontal lobes.[73] Although much of the literature implicates abnormalities in the left hemisphere, it is clear that the right hemisphere is also involved.[74] The accumulating evidence suggests that left medial temporal abnormalities are present early in the brains of many patients who develop schizophrenia and that they display evidence of language problems long before the development of their psychosis.

Furthermore, recent brain-imaging studies have found that the disorganization of speech in schizophrenia increases in proportion to the decrease of activity in, among other areas, the left superior temporal cortex, part of the circuitry for processing speech.[75] Some characteristic hallucinations and delusions of schizophrenia, so-called first rank symptoms of Schneider, have been linked with bilateral brain changes, such as decreased cerebral blood flow in the cingulate and lingual gyri on the left and increased flow in the superior parietal cortex on the right.[76] The hallucinations, which carry with them a sense of reality and also usually a spatial location, have been associated with right-sided activation of superior and middle temporal gyri and the right inferior and superior parietal lobule. In some studies, the activation associated with hallucinations is actually greater on the right side.[77]

At the present time, schizophrenia is conceived of as a developmental disorder with a genetic basis. Tim Crow suggests that the gene (or genes) responsible for the development of laterality differences, handedness, and cerebral dominance in the normal human brain is likely to be involved in schizophrenia, somehow leading to an abnormal pattern of development affecting the brain's maturation, especially in the left medial temporal areas.[78] The assumption is that disorganization of left hemisphere function is fundamental to the pathogenesis of schizophrenic mental states.[79] However, as the disorder becomes more apparent, the anterior lobes of the brain are more and more implicated, as are areas of the right hemisphere. Cutting's carefully considered view is that in schizophrenia the right hemisphere is underactive relative to the normal state, an obvious contrast to the overactive right hemisphere cortex associated with disturbances of affect as revealed through the studies reviewed in chapter 4.[80]

In contrast to the wealth of information on the brain in schizophrenia, there is much less information about the underlying biology of manic-depressive disorder. There are no postmortem studies and few imaging studies. There are, however, many reports of patients with manic-depressive profile who have developed a secondary mania—that is, a manic swing—following some brain insult, such as stroke, head injury, and the presence of tumor.[81] The reports implicate brain structures, which are a part of well-identified cerebral circuits running from the frontal lobe to the basal ganglia to the thalamus and back to the cortex, also involving the temporal cortex. The reported lesions are nearly all right-sided and involve the frontotemporal cortex or subcortical structures or both. Postictal mania, when seen in epilepsy, is also usually associated with a right temporal lobe seizure onset.

The imaging studies in bipolar disorder are complicated by the issue of state versus trait effects—that is, whether the brain is imaged while the patient is in the hypomanic or depressed phase of the illness or while he or she is in remission. Imaging a manic patient is a difficult and potentially expensive procedure. Most patients investigated are on medication, and while this is also a problem in many of the schizophrenia studies, the conclusions from imaging in schizophrenia are supported by other data, such as pathological studies, not readily available for manic-depressive illness.

The few brain-imaging studies that have been done suggest that in contrast to depression, in hypomania brain activity is increased, and the temporal and frontal areas are particularly involved.[82] But the picture is complicated and far from complete. Using a PET technique, Mark George and colleagues serially imaged a bipolar patient during different phases of the illness. In summarizing their data they state that in mania, "there may be persistent hyperactivity in the right temporal lobe when euthymic, which becomes hypoactive during states of acute mania."[83]

One of the few studies to image patients while they were actively manic (rather than hypomanic) scanned five females and compared their results with matched controls. The investigators noted that the manics had lower blood flow in the right medial temporal cortex. In another investigation of secondary mania using PET, three patients were also shown to have decreased metabolic changes in the right medial temporal cortex.[84]

From their extensive review of the literature, George concludes that "bipolar affective disorder—specifically the state of mania—likely involves distributed networks that involve both cortical and subcortical structures in both hemispheres, with an emphasis on the right."[85]

This chapter has reviewed the relationship of three neuropsychiatric disorders to alteration of language. Schizophrenia, epilepsy, and affective disorder, especially states of hypomania and mania, lead to a reorganization of linguistic ability, albeit in different ways. An analysis of these differences has relevance not only for an understanding of the structure of language systems in the brain but also for the quest to understand the cerebral origins of verbal creativity and the relationship of brain organization to poetic expression and related activities. The brief biographies and studies cited in this chapter serve to emphasize that schizophrenic thought disorder, certainly as the disorder progresses, is not conducive to poetic linguistic creativity. In contrast, there is an observed link between manic-depressive illness and cyclothymia, on the one hand, and verbal fluidity, especially poetic inspiration, on the other. The biographies in appendix 1 are given to reinforce the association and to contrast it with the dearth of poets with schizophrenia or epilepsy. There are no specific studies of epilepsy and creativity, but the number of writers and poets with reported epilepsy is small, and Post, in his large study of creative people, does not mention epilepsy, with the possible exception of William Faulkner's alcohol-related seizures. It is, therefore, of considerable interest in this context to be reminded that published reports of bipolar disorder occurring in people with epilepsy are rare. The inverse association is, then, not only between epilepsy and verbal, especially poetic, creativity but also between epilepsy and bipolar disorders.

Obviously, the flight of ideas and increased output of hypomania, associated with a sense of well-being, is conducive to creativity and may be helpful for poetic inspiration and expression. However, not all poets are manic-depressive, and not all manic-depressives are poets. One interpretation of such clinical observations is that bipolar disorder and cyclothymia are markers for right hemisphere activity, and so is poetic expression. In other words, poetry and mood instability are linked through common associations to the functions of the right hemisphere of the brain.

In terms of neuroanatomy, it is important to note the biological associations between schizophrenia and alteration of function of both the left and right hemispheres, but with a bias toward earlier and greater dysfunction of the left. With hypomanic activity there is alteration of function predominantly (but, of course, not exclusively) of the right hemisphere. The data sometimes may seem difficult to reconcile, and indeed perhaps contradictory, which reflects on patient selection, the state of the illness at the time the investigations are carried out, and methodology. However, a tentative conclusion drawn here is that it is overactivity of the cortex, associated with alteration of activity of subcortical structures in the right hemisphere, that predisposes to hypomanic release, consistent with the findings of the EEG recordings carried out during the emotional states released by amytal injections as reviewed in chapter 4.

This should be seen in the context of the right hemisphere dominance for certain aspects of language, including prosody and linguistic tropes such as metaphor, and for the recall of biographical memories. In other words, the "other way of using language" seems to rely heavily on the "other" so often called nondominant hemisphere.

CHAPTER SIX

Music and the Brain

Many writers have discussed the affinities between poetry and music, and considerations of rhythm and meter are fundamental to the analogy. "Everything in life is rhythm," so says Novalis.[1] I. A. Richards refers to the expectancy that rhythm in poetry evokes in a listener and the absence of such a "getting ready" process in prose. The rhythm brings a "texture of expectations, satisfactions, disappointments, surprisals . . . and the sound of a word comes to its full power only through rhythm."[2] This expectancy is increased by the presence of meter. Both poetry and music are sound patterns playing on a background of time.

The close association between poetry and music is ancient and is reflected in mythology by the Greek god Orpheus. The son of a muse, Orpheus was a poet famous for his skill with the lyre. Early musical forms were perhaps derived from the sounds of nature: for example, the musical scale of Indian music is likened to the sounds of animals (*sa*, the cry of a peacock; *ri*, the lowing of a bull; *ni*, the trumpeting of an elephant; and so on). Lyric poetry was so termed because it was originally composed to be sung and accompanied by the lyre: Scottish Gaelic poetry contained much song poetry. The word *ode* derives from the Greek for "song," and many early ballads were written to be sung.[3] The sonnet is one of the oldest verse forms in the English language, and the very term implies a song. Poetry and music sublimely combine in the tradition of the *Lied*, the art song, standing at the center of German musical life, in which a poem is set to music, generally for a solo voice accompanied by the keyboard.

Much common versifying is found in songs, those of religious inspiration being hymns, and many early carols stemmed from the works of the Franciscan poets. Madrigal composers used verse themes, and early English poets, notably Geoffrey Chaucer (1342–1400), William Langland (1330–1400), Edmund Waller (1606–87), and Sir Philip Sidney (1554–86), wrote a lot of their poetry to be accompanied by music. Indeed, much pre-Elizabethan poetry was embedded in a musical tradition: "It is not an accident that the English lyric poets of the golden age of English literature were steeped in music, any more than it was an accident that Robert Burns should have written his lyrics always with a tune in his head. The poet who writes to a melody instinctively writes verses that come trippingly from the tongue, whereas the poet of the printed page is heavy with sibilants and successive consonants."[4]

The musical nature of poetry is one of the means by which it becomes memorable, and one of the difficulties with much modern poetry is that it is difficult to remember, often lacking both musicality and rhyme. As Ezra Pound has said, "Poetry withers and dries out when it leaves music, or at least imagined music, too far behind it. Poets who are not interested in music are, or become, bad poets."[5]

Echoing similar sentiments, the poet Basil Bunting repeatedly emphasized the links between musical sound and poetry, noting that "it was very late in literary history before poets began to forget the origin of their art and tried to do without music . . . The poets gradually lost touch with music. They lost sight of the vast variety of possible rhythms. The noise they made became monotonous . . . The monotony was infectious—the wit, the syntax, the diction, all became stereotyped. They aimed at neatness. They achieved the sterile emptiness of a hospital corridor."[6]

The Language of Music

There has been considerable debate as to whether music can or should be considered a language. It has been argued that, unlike the spoken language, musical abilities are uneven, some people being tone deaf, and in any case most adults simply do not play an instrument.[7] What kind of survival value could music have conferred to early hominids? Foot-tapping hedonic "cheesecake" sums up one such view of music, which considers it nonadaptive from an evolutionary point of view and at best a vestigial appendix from some one-time more useful hominid activity.[8] The neurologist Jason Warren has replied in response that after the destruction of the human race, music may be the only thing of our civilization to survive, should the Voyager probes be intercepted by some other intelligence.[9]

An alternative view has been strongly argued. This notes the value of music for communication and cooperation, between infant and mother, between groups of individuals, and within groups by way of sexual selection and bonding. Others have stressed the benefits of a positive hedonic tone for the health of the individual. Supportive of innate neuronal biases for responding to music are the rare cases of a condition referred to as congenital amusia, a specific failure of the development of any musical aptitude, in spite of normal other cognitions and exposure to music, and its mirror image, the rare musical idiots savants whose outstanding musical talents stand alone among their otherwise limited abilities. The philosopher Peter Kivy has put forward the view that perhaps we are hardwired by evolution to respond to sounds as animate, as emotional expressions, which has given us the advantage of knowing how another will respond to our presence (for example, positively or with anger), suggesting that our response to music remains with us as a vestigial relic from our evolutionary past.[10]

Musical instruments have been discovered that are thought to be more than fifty thousand years old, and it is safe to assume that singing and dancing predated that time. Some earlier commentators, such as Rousseau, suggested that language somehow developed from musical intonation, and Charles Darwin, who considered music to have evolved from primate sexual selection calls, argued for a common origin of music and language.[11] More recently, Steven Mithen has argued that both spoken language and music evolved from a protolanguage. He notes that both have a hierarchical structure, being composed of acoustic elements that combine into phrases that provide numerous expressions. He suggests in his book *The Singing Neanderthals* that a precursor for both music and spoken language, which he refers to as a musilanguage, evolved from primitive primate calls. The singing Neanderthals used a language that lacked words but was intensely emotional. Living in small intimate communities, they communicated by gesture and vocalizations, which, Mithen suggests, had intonation, rhythm, pitch, and melody.[12]

Clearly, music and spoken language are both communication devices used to express emotional meaning through high-register socially accepted patterned sound, and a musical grammar akin to language grammar may perhaps be discerned. Anthony Storr quotes with approval the psychoanalyst Anto Ehrenzweig:

> It is not unreasonable to speculate that speech and music have descended from a common origin in a primitive language which was neither speaking nor singing, but was something of both. Later this primeval language would have split into different branches; music would have retained the articulation mainly by pitch (scale) and duration (rhythm), while language chose the articulation mainly by tone colour (vowels and consonants). Language moreover happened to become the vehicle of rational thought and so underwent further influences. Music became a symbolic language of the unconscious mind whose symbolism we shall never be able to fathom.[13]

Storr concludes that "language and music were originally closely joined, and that it makes sense to think of music as deriving from a subjective emotional need for communication with other human beings."[14]

Musicality, then, is a crucial aspect of the poetic. The word *melody* is derived from the Greek *melos*, which refers to both lyrical poetry and the music to which it was set. Music has some similarities with the spoken language, in the sense of being a means of communication, in having its own kind of grammar, and in being universal in all cultures. Like the spoken language, it must have evolutionary origins but is perhaps older, and it may be more intimately linked with emotional displays, gesture, dance, and ultimately singing. As Corballis comments, "Given the rather diffuse yet pervasive quality of music in human society, it may well have been a precursor to language, perhaps even providing the raw stuff out of which generative grammar was forged." Bunting suggests that poetry arose from the grunts and cries of primitive dancers, both poetry and dancing being tied to the body and its movements.[15]

Deryck Cooke, in his book *The Language of Music*, makes a strong case for music as a language of the emotions. He suggests that one can only wonder how certain patterns of tone setting ever came to correspond with certain emotional reactions on the listener's part in the first place, unless the correspondence is inherent. He shows that there were close natural associations between the emotive effects of certain notes of the scale and their positions in the acoustic hierarchy and quotes the writings and sayings of several composers in terms of what music actually conveyed to them. His view is that the medium of words and the medium of music both evoke emotional responses, and the overall emotional organization of a piece of music is similar to that of a poem or drama. He concludes that, with regard to Western music, at least, "music is a language of the emotions akin to speech."[16]

The link between music and emotion seems to have been accepted for all time. Plato considers that music played in different modes arouses different emotions, and as a generality most of us would agree on the emotional significance of any particular piece of music, whether it be happy or sad, for example. Major chords are cheerful, minor ones sad; the ups and downs of life and of cyclothymia. The tempo or movement in time is another component of this, slower music seeming less joyful than faster rhythms. This reminds us again that *motion* is a significant part of *emotion* and that in dance we are *moving*—as we are moved emotionally.

The theme of music as a language was taken up by the composer and conductor Leonard Bernstein in his Harvard lectures. He structured these around the

TABLE 6.1
The Grammars of Music and Language

Music	Language
Note	Phoneme
Motive	Morpheme
Phrase	Word
Section	Clause
Movement	Sentence
Piece	Piece

SOURCE: Based on Bernstein (1976), 58.

linguistic concepts of phonology, syntax, and semantics and supported the contentions not only of the common evolutionary origins for music and language but also of a universal grammar for music, in the manner of Chomsky.

The triad of the tonic, third, and dominant (the major triad) is the foundation of Western music. Bernstein reflects that there is "an analogy between Chomsky's innate grammatical competence and the innate musical-grammatical competence which we may all possess universally."[17] His musical language elements include notes, motives, phrases, sections, movements, and pieces, with possible spoken language counterparts (see table 6.1). He refers to musical noun phrases (morphemes) as motives, to chords as adjectival modifiers of musical nouns, and to the verb function of rhythm.

Bernstein discusses Chomsky's ideas of transformational grammar, noting the processes by which deep structures are transformed to superficial structures, and then he describes their analogies in music. Through processes such as deletion (of words in language, notes in music) and embedding (of one clause in another, in music or language), music and language become supersurface grammars, and aesthetics are created. "And once we have established this aesthetic surface structure, above and beyond the prose Chomskian surface, then we can have a true parallel with music-poetry."[18]

Analogies between the languages of speech, especially poetry, and music have been made by several other writers, although some would caution against taking the comparison too far. They are disliked by many of those who are either linguists or neuroscientists, but they find echoes in philosophy. Kivy refers to music as a sort of language, but one which is untranslatable (as is poetry to a significant extent). The composer and philosopher Roger Scruton has pointed out that only rational beings make and listen to both language and music. He refers to human beings as having "tacit knowledge" of music, in the same way we have, according to Chomsky, tacit knowledge of language.[19] In this context, a robust finding is that previous exposure to a musical piece shapes musical preference and leads to a positive bias when the music is heard again. This is like implicit learning, and it occurs without subjective awareness on the part of the listener.

Others refer to universals in music, like language universals, that are essentially innate and have evolutionary significance. The structure of music is understood to be related to unconscious processes in the same way that we unconsciously comprehend the deep structure of language.

Bernstein sees many common linguistic elements shared by poetry and music, including metaphor (of such transformations are metaphors made, and of such metaphors is beauty born), ambiguity (germane to all artistic creation), repetition (it is repetition, modified in one way or another, that gives poetry its musical qualities, because repetition is so essential to music itself), and devices such as alliteration, anaphora, and chiasmus.[20] In short, all the identified components of poetry listed in chapter 4 are common to music, drawn from Bernstein's scheme.

Leonard Meyer explores in detail the meaning of music, especially from an emotional point of view. He notes that musical theorists, in the main, have concerned themselves with the grammar and syntax of music rather than with the affective experiences that arise in response to music.[21] Music, if it does nothing else, arouses feelings and associated physiological responses, and these can now be measured. Bernstein recognizes the importance of ambiguity in musical expression, leading to suspense, the latter provoking "strong tensions and powerful expectations."[22] The response to a piece of music need not be conscious, Meyer notes, but those trained in music tend, because of the critical attitudes they have developed in connection with their own artistic efforts, to become self-conscious of their aesthetic experiences, to objectify their meaning, and to consider them objects of conscious cognition.[23] Although Meyer is uncomfortable with the idea of music as a universal language, given the transcultural and transhistorical variants of style, he nevertheless reflects that "these languages have important characteristics in common . . . Most important is the syntactical nature of different styles . . . the organization of sound terms into a system of probability relationships, the limitations imposed upon the combining of sounds, etc. . . . In this respect, musical languages are like spoken or written languages which exhibit common structural principles."[24]

As to rhythm, Meyer notes the value of motor responses to music, both in the player and the listener, and states that "the ultimate foundation of rhythm is to be found in mental activity."[25] Rhythm comes from the mind, through the body, and motor behavior is important in the appreciation of music—hence the foot tapping and the dance.

Meyer also discusses the relevance of memories for the affective musical experience, noting that these are evoked by either conscious connotation or unconscious image processes. It is these imaginings that are the stimuli for the affective responses, not the direct musical stimuli themselves, unless the latter are intellectualized and are exclusively musical, in which case "the affective experience will be similar to the form of the musical form which brought it into being." For the ordinary listener, however, there may be no necessary relationship between the emotion and the form and content of the musical work, since "the real stimulus is not the progressive unfolding of the musical structure but the subjective content of the listener's mind."[26]

Music in the Brain

The cerebral representations of music have been explored in recent years, especially with new brain-imaging techniques. However, as with spoken language, earlier data came from observations and personal testaments of people with brain damage, especially strokes.

Loss of the ability to understand or perform music acquired with brain disease is referred to as amusia. This is dissociated from aphasia, and several patients with strokes have experienced aphasia but have retained musical abilities, able both to sing and to recognize melodies.[27] The most celebrated case is probably that of Maurice Ravel (1875–1937), who had an aphasia, probably secondary to a corticobasal degeneration. He retained the abilities to recognize melodies and his sense of pitch and rhythm but could no longer read music.[28] However, he continued to compose: his *Bolero* was written during the years of his illness, and the piano concertos were completed after that.[29]

Vissarion Yaklovlevich Shebalin (1902–63), a Russian composer, was studied by the neuropsychologist A.R. Luria. At the age of fifty-one Shebalin had a stroke, from which he recovered with minimal neurological impairment, but a second stroke six years later left him with a dense aphasia. For the remaining years of his life he continued to compose, however, apparently without any decline of standards and in a style similar to that which he had developed before his illness. Dmitry Shostakovich (1906–75) described Shebalin's Fifth Symphony as a "brilliant creative work, filled with highest emotions, optimistic and full of life." The symphony, composed during his illness, was "a creation of a great master."[30]

Charles Baudelaire (1821–67), the French poet most renowned for his collection of poems, *Les Fleurs du Mal,* took a fall in March 1866. In the following days he developed lapses of verbal inattention, using words inappropriately, and as his illness progressed to a full stroke he experienced aphasia and a right-sided paralysis. He made some sort of initial recovery but then relapsed, and was never well again. He retained an appreciation for music, however, and could still sing.

In one study of twenty-four patients with Broca's aphasia, twenty-one could sing, six of them excellently. There are also reports of aphasic and apraxic conductors who continued to successfully lead an orchestra and a report of a blind organist who, after developing Wernicke's aphasia, lost the ability to read and write in Braille but continued to read and compose music in this medium.[31]

Thus there seems to be some good clinical evidence that patients with left hemisphere lesions and aphasia retain musical abilities, complementing retained poetical skills as noted in chapter 3. It is therefore of considerable interest that there are many reported cases of patients with right hemisphere lesions who have developed amusia, although their interpretation is quite unclear, each case seemingly so different. The most substantial study was carried out many years ago, without the sophistication of our modern methods of neurological analysis. Howard Gardner's conclusion, following his review of the available case studies, is that "the general preservation of melodic capacity and perception in aphasic—(i.e., usually left-hemisphere patients), together with the monotonous quality of voice and song in right-hemisphere patients, indicates a strong right-hemisphere bias for at least the melodic component of music."[32]

This conclusion, reached a number of years ago, has been echoed and supported by a contemporary who, following review of the available case literature, states that in right-handed people, reported cases of amusia without aphasia most often involve the right cerebral hemisphere.[33] Such patients report difficulty in recognizing musical sounds, with loss of rhythm, and music sounds to them monotonal.

However, more sophisticated methods reveal that, as for language, the cerebral basis of musical appreciation and expression is rather more widespread.[34] Furthermore, the perception of music is not the same as the emotional response to it, the latter certainly engaging a widespread neuronal network but particularly related to limbic and subcortical structures, as discussed in chapter 2.

Studies of the Cerebral Basis of Music

Very young infants seem to possess musical perception, recognizing melody and differentiating rhythms, as any mother can confirm.[35] Lullabies are delivered in slow, emotive tones and become part of a ritualized and repeated mother-infant pattern of communication, promoting bonding and security. It is not what is said by the mother that is relevant but rather the prosody and the emotional expression with which it is said. As Storr has written of this interchange, "The most important components are . . . metre, rhythm, pitch, volume, lengthening of vowel sounds, tone of voice and other variables . . . all characteristic of a type of utterance which has much in common with poetry."[36]

Electroencephalographic recordings of infants have shown that the left hemisphere is activated by recordings of speech and the right by music.[37] Infants as young as six months prefer consonant sounds to dissonant ones, and by eight months they exhibit a left ear (right hemisphere) superiority for music; and children as young as seven can distinguish well-formed from poorly formed musical sequences.[38]

There is now considerable evidence that the right hemisphere has the lead over the left for musical ability in adulthood. Studies of direct brain stimulation, for example, of patients undergoing neurosurgical procedures, mainly for epilepsy, have yielded rather contradictory results regarding laterality but suggest that areas of the brain close to the right superior temporal gyrus are related to musical perception and memory.[39] In a review of the studies of patients with so-called musicogenic epilepsy, in whom seizures are reflexively provoked by musical stimuli, the neurologist Grigor Wieser and colleagues have noted an association with temporal lobe epilepsy, with a bias toward the right.[40] In one of their patients, studied with single-photon-emission computed tomography (SPECT), right temporal lobe changes of perfusion were noted when the tracer was injected during the musically induced seizure. Similar findings have been reported by others.[41]

Some of the dichotic listening studies have shown that the left ear (right hemisphere) is superior to the right for identifying affectively toned music (minor as opposed to the major mode). In one study that evaluated presentation of music and poems to the right and left ears, both were reported to be more pleasant in the left.[42]

Using a cognitive test of musical abilities, known as the Seashore Test, Brenda Milner examined patients with epilepsy who had had either the left or right temporal lobe damaged and then removed to relieve them of their seizures. Milner reports impaired ability to remember melodies after right-sided damage and operations.[43] The sense of rhythm was also disturbed. In people with no musical training, right temporal lobectomy has been shown to be associated with impairments of rhythm and sensitivity but not tonal imagery, and damage to the area of the right superior temporal gyrus has been shown to impair melodic perception, although in some studies, impairments were seen also in those with left-sided damage to equivalent areas.[44]

Musical imagery, the ability to replay music in the head, has been shown to be impaired in patients with epilepsy following right but not left temporal lobec-tomies; and Robert Zatorre and colleagues, using PET in healthy controls, have found activation primarily of right hemisphere areas, notably in the right tem-poral and frontal lobes, with such tasks.[45] In related experiments, the same re-searchers found that the primary auditory area of the right cortex plays an im-portant role in pitch discrimination and organization; they noted strong (but not exclusive) associations between listening to melodies and activation of areas in the right superior temporal gyrus, in front of the primary auditory cortex.

The right frontal cortex has been shown to be involved in memory for pitch, while timbre perception depends mainly on the right temporal lobe. Interestingly, alterations of temporal processing in timbre discrimination tasks reveals that the left hemisphere is better at the manipulation of rapid temporal coding (tens of milliseconds presented sequentially), while the right is better with slower changes (hundreds of milliseconds).[46]

In the above studies, the data point to a dominant role for the right hemi-sphere, especially regions of the frontal and temporal cortices, in several aspects of musical appreciation. Not all the findings are in agreement, and in some of the studies bilateral changes are noted, albeit to a lesser degree on the left side than on the right. This may relate to the date-limited number of studies, to the differ-ences in imaging paradigms, and to the type of tasks given. Song, for example, with its verbal overtones, will reliably activate temporal areas in the left brain as well as the right. In any case, higher-order complex cognitive tasks, such as lan-guage and music, are not going to be discretely localized within the brain but will involve a complex array of circuitry in nonlinear distributed neuronal networks. However, the resolving position seems to be that the corresponding areas of the right and left hemispheres that subserve musical functions have different re-sponses to differing aspects of music activity; in studies carried out on perform-ing musicians and professionals, this contrast is further revealed.

Positron-emission tomography studies of performing pianists have been in-vestigated.[47] Playing the work of Johann Sebastian Bach activates the right tem-poral lobes, whereas playing scales is more likely to activate the left side. In one study, musicians and nonmusicians were compared for different cerebral activa-tions for various components of music, including pitch, rhythm, and meter. For pitch, superior temporal areas were activated on the right in nonmusicians but on the left in the musicians, although the middle and inferior temporal areas were activated on the right in both groups. The left medial frontal cortex was activated only in the nonmusicians during a musical tempo discrimination, while the same group activated the right inferior frontal cortex during meter discrimination.[48]

These studies are taken from a number that have appeared in the past two decades which, following from the ideas of Meyer noted above, suggest an effect of musical education on the lateralization of functions with regard to musical perception, with professional musicians revealing a bias to alteration of activity in left hemisphere structures.[49] It remains unclear whether these changes are the result of plasticity of the brain with learning or are neuroanatomical variants, since structural differences in the size of various neuronal elements have also been noted when the brains of professional musicians have been compared with those of amateurs. In musicians these include an increase in the size of the corpus callosum anteriorly, especially in those who started musical training before the age of seven, an increase in the size of the precentral (motor) gyrus on the right, which correlated negatively with the age of onset of training, and an increase in the size of the left-sided planum temporale in those musicians who possess absolute pitch.[50]

In a corresponding fMRI study, it was shown that the musicians with and without absolute pitch and nonmusicians alike activate the left superior temporal lobe on perceiving phonemes; for tones, however, the musicians with absolute pitch activated the same areas, while the other two groups showed either symmetrical or right-sided activation.[51]

Peter Schneider and colleagues, in a recent study using magnetoencephalography, find that Heschl's gyrus is significantly more active in professional musicians than in nonmusicians when listening to tones; and using MRI, this brain area was found to be larger in musicians, and both activity and size correlated with a measure of music aptitude.[52] The implication from these studies is that the planum temporale on the left side, which has long been thought to be associated with human language ability, is related not only to the spoken language but also to higher-order musical processing in certain types of musical talent.[53] These studies also suggest the commonality of brain anatomical structures for language and music. Moreover, there seem to be structural differences in the neurons of the areas subserving audition between the hemispheres. Those on the left are more myelinated, the pyramidal cells are larger, and the cortical columns are more widely spaced. What this may indicate about function is speculation, but it supports a dichotomy, revealed through the other work reviewed, between the two sides of the brain in relation to language processing.[54] What is clear from the ever growing research in this area is that in comparison with propositional and categorical speech, musical processing is very much the province of the right hemisphere, especially in the ungifted, ordinary listener, while in those with special skills the laterality is different in several respects.

Music and Poetry

Few studies of the link between music and poetry have been conducted from a neuroscience point of view. Fred Lerdahl has pointed out that such studies as exist usually compare music and syntax, rather than what would seem the more obvious comparison, music and prosody. He applied musical analytic methods to model the sonic organization of poetry and noted the commonalities of durational patterns, prosodic structure, stress, metric grids, melodic contour, and timbral prolongations. He predicted that the brain areas processing such elements would be the same for music and language, recognizing that others, which are generally regarded as purely linguistic structures (syntax, semantics, phonological distinctions, and the like), would use different cerebral circuits. He supported this prediction by citing the evidence, some of which has been reviewed already, of the divergence between the effects of lesions in the two hemispheres, with an emphasis on the right hemisphere subserving the common elements. He suggests that

> these exclusive and common structures are a consequence of human evolution. In this view, the roots of music and language are the same, in the form of premusical and prelinguistic communicative and expressive auditory gestures involving shapes of duration, stress, contour, timbre and grouping: these elementary shapes lie at the basis of expressive utterance in language and of musical expression (an idea that goes back at least to Rousseau). With evolution came specialisation: music and language diverged in their most characteristic features, pitch organisation in music and word and sentence meaning in language. Poetry straddles this evolutionary divergence by projecting, through the addition to ordinary speech of metrical and timbral patterning, its common heritage with music.[55]

Emotional Response to Music

A commonly reported response to listening to music or poetry is a shiver or a tingle down the spine. This is momentarily euphoric and is a physiological response to the perceptions. Some people experience a lump in the throat or goose pimples, and in many the response is associated with tears. In music such release seems related to particular structural events in the music, especially those that

create and resolve tension or when unexpected events happen sooner than anticipated.[56] These phenomena, which seem innate, have been examined by Zatorre
and colleagues, who asked volunteers to listen to favorite pieces of music (without words) while being scanned with PET; their "shivers" were rated subjectively
for intensity. During these experiences, subjects' heart and respiration rates and
muscle tension increased, and changes in blood flow in several brain structures
were recorded. These were mainly limbic related and included increased activity
in the right thalamus and orbitofrontal cortex, the anterior cingulate cortex, the
left ventral striatum, and the insula bilaterally. Interestingly, blood flow decreased
in both the left and the right amygdala and in ventromedial prefrontal cortex and
in the precuneus regions bilaterally. Furthermore, activity in the right parahippocampal gyrus was correlated with activity in the right precuneus, an area of the
brain known to be linked to memory, selective attention, and self-awareness.[57]

These results suggest that the forebrain reward systems were activated (ventral striatum), with an integration with cognition (frontal cortex). However, the
emotion experienced was different from the emotion of anxiety or fear, a theme
taken up later in relation to the appreciation of tragedy, reflected in the amygdala
response. In fear situations the signal from the amygdala is increased, the opposite of that reported with this experience.

In studies in which emotional responses to pleasant and unpleasant music
were observed, Blood and colleagues compared PET image differences in listening to consonant and dissonant sounds. Increasing dissonance was associated
with increased activation of the right parahippocampal gyrus and the precuneus,
while increasing consonance was reflected by bilateral activity in the orbitofrontal
cortex, the right subcallosal cingulate, and the frontal polar cortex.[58]

Thus emotional responses to music involve predominantly, but not exclusively, right-sided neuronal circuits, with reciprocal connections between temporal and frontal structures. Some key areas that integrate memory, emotions, and
cognition are involved (amygdala, ventral striatum, parahippocampus, precuneus, and frontal cortex), as is the cingulate gyrus, so important for mammalian
play and bonding activities.

Studies of the cerebral circuits of musical appreciation, memory, and performance have been few when compared with those of language, but there does
seem to be some harmony in the data. There are inherent difficulties in interpreting reports on patients with strokes, many of which are dated and used techniques, such as dichotic listening, that are now deemed unreliable. Modern investigations have broken down music processing by the brain into different

components, such as the processing of pitch or rhythm. However, the more recent brain-imaging data have yielded interesting information that complements the clinical findings and allows certain conclusions to be drawn. There clearly is no singular part of the brain, or one hemisphere, that modulates music. As is true in spoken language, both hemispheres play a role in the appreciation of music, which in the intact brain are complementary.

Most reports emphasize the importance of the right hemisphere in responding to music, unlike spoken language, especially for some components of musical processing, although the anatomical specificities have yet to be worked out in detail. Training and professionalism and a critical appreciation of music may alter the structural circuitry of musical representation, emboldening the contribution of the traditional language areas of the left hemisphere. This is in keeping with our current views on hemisphere differentiation, with perception being more holistic and less analytic on the right side. Form and content in music, above all the arts, are not separable, unless the form becomes analyzable at the expense of the emotional content, hence perhaps the shift from the right to the left hemisphere in the critical analysis of music by professionals.

Areas of the brain such as the right superior temporal gyrus are involved in the perception of pitch and timbre and appreciation of melody, which interact with the parahippocampal gyrus and areas of the frontal cortex and precuneus in memory-associated circuits, but some of these limbic areas also relate to the affective processing of music. Furthermore, music recruits the neural circuitry of the brain's reward systems (also activated by drugs of addiction), which forms part of a complex neuronal system that underpins normal social conditioning and bonding, as well.

Most people seem to accept that music is a universal human attribute and that it has a neurobiological basis. The octave is an acoustic fact.[59] This not only implies the revealed close ties to brain structure and function but also suggests an evolutionary value, with an identifiable phylogenesis. Music has structural affinities with poetry, and, taken in conjunction with the literature reviewed in chapter 4, it is here suggested that action of the nondominant right hemisphere is a prerequisite for musical perception and appreciation and for the "other way" of using language, poetry.

As to whether or not music can be considered a language, the last words here are given to a musician, Leonard Bernstein, who concludes, "In any sense in which music can be considered a language . . . it is a totally *metaphorical language*."[60]

CHAPTER SEVEN

Neurotheology I

Epilepsy

The past decade or so has seen the development of a new neuroscience discipline, neurotheology. Neurotheology seeks the cerebral basis of religious experiences, a wish of William James come true, even if perhaps a hundred years later, but now advanced by the new methods of both brain imaging and external stimulation of the human brain with noninvasive techniques. These studies have allowed the normal brain to be visualized in various emotional states, including those of religious excitation, and, with subtle stimulation of the brain with magnetic pulses, the evocation of various feelings, including those associated with religious experiences. The spirit of neurotheology is by no means new, however, and physicians have written about the subject in one way or another since ancient times.

The condition most often discussed in this context is epilepsy. It has featured in several earlier chapters of this book, and James associated it with the "acute fever" of religion. Although James never developed the theme any further, it was clearly for him a condition worthy of study.

Epilepsy and Psychiatric Illness

Many studies have explored the relationship between various types of epilepsy and psychopathology, and the area has remained one of considerable controversy. One line of inquiry shows that the history of epilepsy is closely associated with that of psychiatry, and both have bygone links with gods, demons, and the supernatural.[1] The ancients regarded epilepsy as sacred, and it was referred to as such by Hippocrates (460–377 BC) in his famous text, "On the Sacred Disease." The Greeks reasoned that epilepsy must be divine because only a god could throw a man to the ground, render him senseless, and then restore him to normality. However, Hippocrates opined that there was nothing sacred at all about epilepsy and that it was instead a brain-related disorder. Hence came one of the most important statements of neuropsychiatry of all time, Hippocrates' apothegm, already quoted but worth repeating: "Men ought to know that from the brain, and from the brain only, arise our pleasures, joys, laughter and jests, as well as our sorrows, pains, griefs and tears . . . and by this same organ we become mad and delirious, and fears and terrors assail us." For Hippocrates, the brain was the seat of both the falling sickness and madness, and both were related to disordered phlegm.[2]

The Bible gives the following account of epilepsy and its cure:

> Master, I have brought to thee my son, *for he is a lunatic and sore vexed* [and] hath a dumb spirit; and wheresoever he taketh him, he teareth him: *and bruising him hardly departeth from him;* and he foameth and gnasheth with his teeth, and pineth away . . . And they brought him unto Him; and when he saw him straightway the spirit tare him; and he fell on the ground, and wallowed foaming. And He asked his father, how long is it ago since this came unto him? And he said, Of a child. And ofttimes it hath cast him into the fire and into the water to destroy him: *And Jesus rebuked the unclean spirit, and he departed out of him* . . . and he was as one dead . . . But Jesus took him by the hand, and lifted him up; and he arose.[3]

In ancient Rome, epilepsy was known as *morbidus lunaticus,* the semantic binding with the moon implying a periodic affection (a lunar tic) embracing epilepsy and other forms of mental illness. Shakespeare may have had insights of his own:

Iago: My Lord is fall'n into an epilepsy:
> This is his second fit: he had one yesterday.

Cassio: Rub him about the temples.

Iago: No forbear
> The lethargy must have his quiet course:
> If not, he foams at mouth: and by and by
> Breaks out to savage madness . . .[4]

Although Hippocrates had shown the way, it was only with the Enlightenment that disease generally began to shed its associations with sin and transgression and somatic theories of causation became tenable. In the nineteenth century, with the rise in the number of hospitals being built, especially asylums, many people with epilepsy came under the observation of physicians who had a special interest in disorders of the brain. Neuropsychiatry was born, the parent but not the guardian of both neurology (the study of the brain and its diseases) and psychiatry (the study of the mind and its disorders). Much of the writing at that time that linked epilepsy and mental illness came from France and Germany, and a classification of the psychiatric syndromes of epilepsy began to crystallize.[5] Those disorders that were directly linked in time to the epileptic seizure were referred to as ictal, while those usually more enduring disorders that were bound with the epilepsy but not directly associated with the seizure were referred to as interictal. It is important to repeat here that epilepsy is not the same as seizures; seizures are but one manifestation of the underlying neurochemical, neurophysiological, and often neuroanatomical disturbance of the epileptic process.

The most important neurologist who wrote about epilepsy in the nineteenth century was not French or German but was from Yorkshire, England: John Hughlings Jackson, whose contributions to an understanding of the nervous system have already been noted. As neurologist at the National Hospital for the Paralysed and the Epileptic (now the National Hospital for Neurology and Neurosurgery), he had the opportunity to study many patients with epilepsy. However, he had interests beyond neurology, especially in philosophy and in what today is called cognitive neurology. Hughlings Jackson brought some fundamentally new insights to neurology with his ideas on how disease may affect cerebral function. Central to these was to consider the evolution of nervous function and to suggest a hierarchy of such functions. He saw the brain as developing in both space and time, rather than as the static organ lying on the pathologist's dissecting table. The brain, he proposed, is hierarchically organized, not simply a collection of reflexes, and re-representation is present at all levels of the hierarchy. With any lesion of the brain he saw two effects, one owing to the destruction of tissue, leading to negative symptoms, the other owing to release of subjacent activity of other healthy areas of the brain, causing positive symptoms.

Seizures can arise from any part of the brain, and their origin often can be localized. Those originating from the medial temporal structures are referred to as partial and sometimes as temporal lobe, or even limbic, seizures. This epilepsy is localization related (focal or partial), it is often associated with structural lesions in the limbic brain regions, and it can be difficult to treat. Patients with this form of seizure disorder have ongoing, repeated, and persistent abnormalities in limbic-related circuits. On occasion, these crystallize into the singularity of the seizure, but in between such neurophysiological events they remain ever present, not dormant, to influence limbic functions.

Thus the classification of the psychiatric aspects of epilepsy, initially developed by the continental asylum doctors of the nineteenth century, divided the behavioral consequences of seizures into those that are ictally driven and those that are interictal. Since that time there have been many studies of the interictal psychopathologies, fewer of the ictal associations.[6]

In general, the most common psychiatric problem reported in epilepsy is interictal depression. This may be associated with disturbances in the temporal lobes, but depression is a treatment-emergent effect caused by some of the antiepileptic drugs patients take and also by the sheer misery of having a persistently demoralizing condition. However, of more relevance for this text are the observations that interictal schizophrenia-like states are overrepresented and typical bipolar disorders are rare among people with epilepsy.[7] The lifetime prevalence of the former varies with the population examined but may be as high as 10 percent of people with epilepsy, far in excess of the prevalence of schizophrenia in the general population. The psychosis is more frequently noted in association with difficult-to-control seizures that arise from the temporal lobes. Furthermore, for a long time an association has been noted between the schizophrenia-like psychoses of epilepsy and left-sided temporal lobe epilepsy. The symptoms of this condition are much like those of schizophrenia in the absence of epilepsy, and in one review, almost twice as many patients had a left-sided (43 percent) as opposed to a right-sided (23 percent) seizure focus. The emphasis on maximal metabolic changes in the left side of the brain in this condition has been further confirmed with some of the modern brain-imaging techniques, including PET and MRI spectroscopy.[8]

The ictally driven psychoses are quite different. Of the two main forms, only the postictal psychoses need concern us here.[9] These are usually states of over-excitement, and the clinical pictures are often manic or hypomanic in character, with an intense suffusion of feeling. Typically, a person with epilepsy will have a cluster of seizures and then, perhaps a day or even two days later, will develop the abnormal mental state (perhaps as Othello). This is often associated with intense religiosity. These postictal states tend to be short lived (in contrast to the interictal states), lasting hours or days but rarely weeks.

The relationship between the type of epilepsy and the laterality of the reported abnormalities in these psychotic states is of particular interest. The postictal manic and hypomanic pictures are much more likely to be seen with right-sided temporal lobe epilepsy, one variety of secondary mania, in contrast to the leftward bias for the interictal schizophrenia-like states. Although this is an area of continuing controversy, as more sophisticated methods of brain investigation have developed, these findings seem to hold up.[10]

Epilepsy and Religion

The literature on the connection between epilepsy and religion, at least to the end of the nineteenth century, has been well reviewed by the medical historian Oswei Temkin. Many well-known historical mystics and prophets are said to have had epilepsy, the implication being that somehow divine invocation proceeds from the falling sickness. The ability to prophesy became entwined with this story. In the sixteenth century, Antonius Guairenius commented on one case as follows: "I have seen a certain choleric young man who said that during his paroxysms he always saw wondrous things which he very much wished to set down in writing. For without doubt he expected them to come to pass. For this reason the ancients called this disease divination."[11]

In Arabic "the diviner's disease" is a synonym for epilepsy, physicians having noted that patients with epilepsy often had fabulous visions, which they compared with those of diviners and soothsayers. According to Temkin, epilepsy, syncope, and divine rapture coalesced in the Neoplatonic philosophy of Agrippa (1486–1535), who wrote a text entitled "On Rapture, Ecstasy, and Divination in Those Who Are Seized by Epilepsy and Fainting and in the Dying."[12] Attacks of epilepsy somehow resembled rapture, and from them prophesies could emerge.

The nineteenth-century German physician Paul Samt (1844–75) provided detailed descriptions of more than forty cases of patients with epilepsy and insanity. Many not only thought they were in heaven but also gave their physicians divine status. Samt indeed referred to the God nomenclature that patients used in describing their surroundings. He speaks of "poor epileptics who have the prayer book in their pocket, and the dear Lord on their lips."[13]

Temkin relates a description given by the nineteenth-century physician Richard von Krafft-Ebing (1840–1902): The patient had epilepsy, and his seizures were usually followed by a so-called twilight state with confusion. However, several times a year he would become excited, condemn his godless environment, mistake those around him for devils, thrash out, and wish to be crucified for the true faith. At the height of his ecstasy he saw God face to face and declared himself Christ, God's true warrior, prophet, and martyr. The patient did not lose any memory of these attacks, and afterward remembered his divine visions and did not wish to correct them. As Temkin pointed out, this and countless other clinical descriptions bear a close resemblance to the medieval and Renaissance tales of prophesying patients with epilepsy.[14]

Descriptions of patients with epilepsy whose religious feelings have been notably strong can be found in the writings of several authors in the period before the second half of the nineteenth century. The religious mystic Swedenborg was born into a deeply religious family; he studied at the University of Uppsala, being mainly interested in mathematics. In 1744 he changed his career and life and became involved with the spiritual world and its understanding. He discoursed with angels and became chronically paranoid, suffering from hallucinations and delusions, ultimately declaiming that Jesus Christ had made his Second Coming through him to found the Church of the New Jerusalem.

Swedenborg lived a solitary existence, barely washing, obviously eccentric, but writing profusely. At one time, while in London, he proclaimed that he was the Messiah and locked himself away, emerging from his self-imposed incarceration two days later with foam around his mouth. His case was written up by the famous English psychiatrist Henry Maudsley (1835–1918), who referred to Swedenborg as a learned and ingenious madman and suggested that he had probably had epilepsy.[15] The theme was later taken up by Elizabeth Foote-Smith and colleagues, who interpreted many of the details in Swedenborg's writings as symptoms of temporal lobe epilepsy, including his descriptions of ecstasy, which would be compatible with ecstatic auras: "I had also in my mind and my body a kind of consciousness and indescribable bliss, so that if it had been a higher degree, the body would have been as it were dissolved in mere bliss." He described an episode that these authors suggest resembled the description of a generalized tonic-clonic seizure: "There came over me a shuddering, so strong from the head downward and over the whole body with a noise of thunder and this happened several times . . . I then fell asleep." He later recalled, "Words were put into my mouth. And Oh! Almighty Jesus Christ, that thou . . . dained to come to so great a sinner. Make me worthy of thy Grace." Following this he continued in prayer. This event, which occurred in March 1744, was a turning point in his biography and was the beginning of a lifelong experience of consorting with spirits and angels.[16]

Foote-Smith and Smith postulate more extensive elements of the Gastaut-Geschwind syndrome within Swedenborg's personality, in addition to his religiosity, not only with a deepening of all of his emotions but also with regard to his hypermoralism, his humorless sobriety, his mood lability, and his hypergraphia. They point out that his *Arcana Coelestia* consisted of more than two million words. Swedenborg himself claimed that much of what he wrote was dictated by spirits, and what the spirits were dictating came from God.[17]

Swedenborg founded a religious group called the Church of the New Jerusalem. His illness was also considered as epilepsy by another early contributor to the literature on religiosity, Dr. J. C. Howden. For Howden, Swedenborg was one of several founders of religions to have had epilepsy; he included Mohammed and Ann Lee, the founder of the Shakers, in this list.[18]

Toward the end of the nineteenth century there was a considerable expansion of both the clinical and experimental neurosciences, and the historical associations between epilepsy and religion attracted the attention of psychopathologists with an interest in these matters. An analogy was drawn between the epileptic attack and the moments of inspiration of genius, and, interestingly in this context, pride of place was given to a number of famous geniuses who were said, on account of their inspirations, to have had epilepsy. One author, Cesare Lombroso (1836–1909), famed for his attempts to unite the theory of moral degeneration with physical stigmata and bodily measurements that might reveal underlying psychological traits such as criminality, considered that epilepsy in somebody who was a genius represented a "morbus totius substantiae," a disease of his whole substance.[19] According to another, in states of mania

everything appears to them changed; they think they are in heaven . . . At the same time numerous hallucinations appear. Something is burning; birds are flying about in the air; angels appear; spirits throw snakes in the face of the patient; shadows come and go on the wall. The patient sees heaven open, full of camels and elephants, the King, his guardian angel, the Holy Ghost. The devil has assumed the form of the Virgin Mary. The ringing of bells is heard, shooting, the rushing of water, a confused noise; Lucifer is speaking; the voice of God announces to him the day of judgement, redemption from all sins.[20]

Lombroso writes about nineteenth-century contributions, developing some of these themes also found in John Ferguson Nisbet's *The Insanity of Genius*. Lombroso writes about the "epileptoid nature of genius" as follows:

According to the entirely harmonious researches of clinical and experimental observers, this malady resolves itself into localised irritation of the cerebral cortex, manifesting itself in attacks which are sometimes instantaneous, sometimes of longer duration, but always intermittent, and always resting on a degenerative basis—either hereditary or predisposed to irritation by alcoholic influence, by lesions of the skull etc. In this way we catch a glimpse of another conclusion, viz., that the creative power of genius may be a form of degenerative psychosis belonging to the family of epileptic affections.[21]

Lombroso notes the many geniuses who had been "seized by motory epilepsy" and discusses "the hypothesis of the epileptoid nature of genius itself." Apparently, the convulsions were expressed infrequently, and he suggests that such people have had some kind of "equivalence" of the epileptic seizure (here, the exercise of creative power). He sees the epileptic seizure as an analogy for the moment of inspiration; "this active and violent unconsciousness in the one case manifests itself by creation and in the other by motory agitation."[22]

Lombroso cites as examples the "confessions" of several men of genius, including Fyodor Dostoyevsky and Louis Goncourt. It is well known, he notes, that Dostoyevsky described moments of "the presence of eternal harmony":

> This phenomenon is neither terrestrial nor celestial, but it is an indescribable something, which man, in his mortal body, can scarcely endure—he must either undergo a physical transformation or die. It is a clear and indisputable feeling: all at once, you feel as though you were placed in contact with the whole of nature, and you say, "Yes! This is true." When God created the world, He said, at the end of every day of creation, "Yes! This is true! This is good!" . . . And it is not tenderness, nor yet Joy. You do not forgive anything, because there is nothing to forgive. Neither do you love—oh! This feeling is higher than love. The terrible thing is the frightful clearness with which it manifests itself, and the rapture with which it fills you. If this state were to last more than five seconds, the soul could not endure it, and would have to disappear."[23]

Dostoyevsky himself likened his states of ecstasy to the experiences of Muhammad, and he included characters with epilepsy in several of his novels, notably, Prince Myshkin, in *The Idiot*. Lombroso also suggests that Saint Paul had a seizure on the way to Damascus, in which he fell to the ground unconscious. He then had a hallucination of Jesus, who spoke to him. After these experiences, he became "one of the most fervid Christians."[24]

The relationship between epilepsy and religion has been reviewed several times.[25] Jeffery Saver and John Rabin list the following religious people about whom it has been said, at one time or another, that they had epilepsy: Saint Paul, Muhammad, Margery Kempe, Joan of Arc, Saint Catherine of Genoa, Saint Teresa of Avila, Saint Catherine dei Ricci, Swedenborg, Ann Lee, Joseph Smith, Dostoyevsky, Hieronymus Jaegen, Vincent van Gogh, and Saint Thérèse of Lisieux. Their religious contributions, and their differential diagnoses, as given by these authors, are shown in table 7.1. Most were suggested to have had partial seizures, complex in form and compatible with temporal lobe epilepsy.[26] If accurate, echoing the views of others, this list includes the founders of several substantial religious movements.

Ken Dewhurst and Bill Beard described six patients who had postictal religious conversions following a series of temporal lobe seizures, essentially forming part of a postictal psychosis. One patient had his first conversion experience

> in 1955 at the end of a week in which he had been unusually depressed. In the middle of collecting fares [he was a bus conductor] he was suddenly overcome with a feeling of bliss. He felt he was literally in heaven . . . On admission to hospital he said that he had seen God and that his wife and his family would soon join him in heaven; his mood was elated, his thought disjointed and he readily admitted to hearing music and voices. He remained in this state of exultation, hearing divine and angelic voices for two days.

A second patient

> stopped taking his antiepileptic medications. Within six weeks he was having fits every few hours; he had become confused and forgetful. At this point he suddenly realized that he was the Son of God; he possessed special powers of healing and could abolish cancer in the world; he had visions, and believed he could understand other people's thoughts. He described his conversion thus: "It was a beautiful morning and God was with me and I was thanking God, I was talking to God . . . I was with God."[27]

Hearing the voices of God, Christ, or the archangels is a frequent auditory hallucination in such states, often accompanied by visions of the same, patients also having associated delusions. A fear of impending death, with fearful visions or delusions, is also a common feature of the clinical picture, which has been noted and well described in the scientific literature for more than 150 years.

Such religious states occur in some other psychiatric disorders, especially schizophrenia, in which condition they are reported in about 3 percent of patients. They are commoner in mania, but no figures are available. This contrasts with such religious experiences in about 25 to 30 percent of postictal psychoses.[28] In these states there is a reported association with the mood of elation but also with the déjà vu phenomenon, a symptom that is clinically a pointer to involvement of the right temporal lobe.[29]

Personality Changes in Epilepsy

It will be recalled that the Gastaut-Geschwind syndrome defines a change of personality in people with epilepsy, most often associated with chronic temporal lobe epilepsy, of which one of the cardinal features is hyperreligiosity. With such predispositions, the state of a psychosis is not reached, but patients may adopt a

TABLE 7.1

Suspected Epilepsy in Historical Figures

Person	Description of Spells	Frequency	Likelihood of Epilepsy	Differential Diagnosis[a]	Religious Aspects
St. Paul (?–65)	Conversion on road to Damascus: sudden bright light, falling to the ground, hearing the voice of Jesus, blindness for 3 days with inability to eat or drink Ecstatic visions	Unknown	+	Complex partial seizure with generalization Psychogenic blindness Burns of cornea or retina Vertebrobasilar ischemia Occipital contusion Lightning stroke Digitalis poisoning Vitreous hemorrhage Migraine equivalent	Father of Catholic Church Possible ecstatic aura, interictal hypermoralism, hyperreligiosity, hypergraphia
Muhammad (570–632)	Pallor, appearance of intoxication, falling, profuse sweating, visual and auditory hallucinations	At least several	+	Complex partial seizures	Islamic prophet
Margery Kempe (ca. 1373–1438)	A cry, falling with convulsive movements, turning blue, nausea, psychotic behavior	Recurrent	+	Epilepsy Hysteria Postpartum psychosis Migraine	14th-century Christian mystic and autobiographer
Joan of Arc (1412–31)	"I heard this Voice [of an angel] . . . accompanied also by a . . . great light. . . . There is never a day when I do not hear this Voice; and I have much need of it."	At least daily by the time of her execution in 1431	+	Ecstatic partial seizure and musciogenic epilepsy Intracranial tuberculoma	Extraordinary, deeply held, idiosyncratic religious beliefs motivating martial prowess in the defense of Orléans
St. Catherine of Genoa (1447–1510)	Extreme sense of heat or cold, whole-body tremor, transient aphasia, automatisms, sense of passivity, hyperesthesia, regression to childhood, dissociation, sleepwalking, transient weakness, transient suggestibility, inability to open eyes	Unknown	+	Complex partial seizure Hysteria	Christian mystic

Name (dates)	Clinical features	Frequency		Diagnosis	Description
St. Teresa of Ávila (1515–82)	Visions, chronic headaches, transient loss of consciousness, tongue biting	1 major loss of consciousness spell; frequent headaches	++	Complex partial seizure / Hysteria	Catholic saint
St. Catherine dei Ricci (1522–90)	Loss of consciousness, visual hallucinations, mystical states	Every Thursday at noon with recovery by Friday at 4:00 P.M.	+	Complex partial seizure	Catholic saint
Emanuel Swedenborg (1688–1772)	Acute psychosis; foaming at the mouth; olfactory, gustatory, and somatic hallucinations; ecstatic aura; falling; loss of consciousness; hallucinations; convulsions; postictal trance states	Recurrent	++	Complex partial seizure / Mania / Schizophrenia	Founder of Church of the New Jerusalem
Ann Lee (1736–84)	Visual, auditory hallucinations	From childhood until at least 1774	+	Epilepsy	Founder of the Shaker movement
Joseph Smith (1805–44)	Speech arrest, fear, "pillar of light," hearing voices, "when I came to . . . I found myself lying on my back looking up at heaven"	One clear conversion event (1820)	+	Complex partial seizure	Founder of Mormonism
Fyodor Mikhailovitch Dostoyevsky (1821–81)	Sense of bliss, then a cry, a fall, generalized tonic-clonic seizure with frothing at the mouth and injuries. Postictal intense depression and guilt, lasting several days	Every few days to every few months	+++	Complex partial seizure with generalization / Primary generalized seizures / Hysteria	Influential Russian novelist Ecstatic auras: "I have really touched God. He came into me myself; yes, God exists, I cried, and I don't remember anything else." Interictal religiosity, increasing with age
Hieronymous Jaegen (1841–1919)	Mystical experiences, visual hallucinations, headaches	Unknown	+	Complex partial seizure / Migraine	German mystic

(continued)

TABLE 7.1
Continued

Person	Description of Spells	Frequency	Likelihood of Epilepsy	Differential Diagnosis[a]	Religious Aspects
Dr. Z. (Arthur Thomas Myers; 1851–94)	Pallor, vacant look, perseveration of "yes" to any remark, tongue smacking, déjà vu, right-sided motor signs, postictal passivity	Mulitple episodes 1871–94	+++	Complex partial seizure Left temporal lobe lesion on autopsy	Late-life interest in afterlife, reincarnation; prominent in the Society for Psychical Research
Vincent van Gogh (1853–90)	Sense of vertigo, tinnitus, hyperacusis, xanthopsia, restlessness, delirium	About a dozen spells between the ages of 35 and 37	+	Complex partial seizure with postictal psychosis Ménière's disease Digitalis intoxication Meningoencephalitis luetica Schizophrenia	Renowned painter Hyperreligiosity
St. Thérèse of Lisieux (1873–97)	Violent trembling, visual hallucinations, wounding by a "shaft of fire," mystical conversions	Several spells after age 9	++	Complex partial seizure	Catholic saint

SOURCE: Based on Saver and Rabin (1997), 501–2.
[a]All diagnoses listed in this column have been advanced in the medical literature.

religious lifestyle, often contrary to their previous habits. Their mental state may sometimes flower into a psychosis with a bout of seizures, after which they report most intense religious experiences. Sometimes they kindle a belief, over time, that they have epilepsy for a specific purpose, namely, that they are special and have been chosen to suffer with it, that epilepsy is God's gift to them. This can sometimes be dangerous because they then may harbor the belief that God will cure them if he wants to. They deem their antiepileptic drugs unnecessary and may stop taking them, the result being an exacerbation of seizures and the potential flowering of the psychosis. If the clinical descriptions and biographies presented in this chapter have any validity, they illustrate the development of such chronic hyperreligious states over time, and several of the personalities discussed would today be recognized as exemplars of Gastaut-Geschwind syndrome.

Institute of Neurology Studies

At the National Hospital for Neurology and Neurosurgery in London, where Hughlings Jackson and his successors began studying people with epilepsy 140 years ago, many patients with the characteristic personality changes of Gastaut-Geschwind syndrome or with typical postictal psychoses have been observed. In recent years, several studies have specifically examined aspects of religiosity and the often associated hypergraphia.

In one of the first, six patients with temporal lobe epilepsy and hypergraphia were observed; data were collected and combined with those from fifteen other published cases.[30] The six subjects wrote long, often detailed descriptions of their lives, and several were constructing religious texts, similar to the Bible or the Koran. Poetry writing was a common feature. Often present were a meticulous attention to detail and an associated mood disorder, mainly of euphoria, the latter often linked to the hypergraphia. One patient, a journalist, was hypergraphic in the course of his work, but postictally, associated with a change of mood, he started writing in an entirely different style, with philosophical content, in complete contrast to his everyday journalism. In the series, hyperreligiosity or comparable metaphysical beliefs were reported in nine cases, and seven had episodes of déjà vu. No patient had a left-sided focus for the epilepsy, and a statistically significant excess of right temporal abnormalities was noted.

The full syndrome is described here by David Bear:

A 56-year-old woman experienced a foul odor, followed by focal movements of the left face and arm, which on occasion generalized to a tonic-clonic convulsion. The surface EEG and recordings from indwelling electrodes implicated a right temporal lobe spike focus localized to the amygdala. The patient had composed thousands of pages of handwriting, distinguished by somber personal reflections, religious exegeses, and angry diatribes against former physicians, police and politicians. Her writing was especially noteworthy because she suffered painful, deforming rheumatoid arthritis which required the use of finger and wrist supports. In her diaries she comments "my hands are so sore but I have to just write." In addition to the unmistakable religious fervor of the writing, she traveled with satchels of audiocassettes containing her own sermons on biblical themes.[31]

In a more recent study at the Institute of Neurology, Anthony Freeman and I investigated the phenomenology of these states, especially the religiosity, in more detail, attempting to better understand the underlying brain associations.[32] Measurement of such phenomena as religiosity and hypergraphia is difficult, with few available validated rating scales and mainly a tradition of clinical observation to guide hypotheses. One scale used was developed by David Bear and Paul Fedio, at the U.S. National Institutes of Health, precisely to fill this gap. It assesses eighteen personality traits, many linked in the literature with Gastaut-Geschwind syndrome. One of the subscales relates to religiosity, another to hypergraphia. The scale comes in two versions, one for the patient to fill out, the other for a caregiver, a relative, or another person who knows the patient well.

The scales were initially given to patients with temporal lobe epilepsy unselected for any psychiatric problems, and the early studies confirmed that the patients endorsed more of these personality items than did people without epilepsy. In Bear and Fedio's original study, religiosity scores were higher in patients with temporal lobe epilepsy, even when compared with patients with mixed psychiatric disorders (and no epilepsy). However, there has been some controversy about the specificity of the findings for the temporal lobe epilepsy—in part, because of difficulties in studying patients with other forms of epilepsy.[33] The Institute of Neurology study used the Bear-Fedio scale in addition to other scales that assess aspects of individual religious experiences and behavior.

We used two scales: INSPIRIT and the Hood Mysticism Scale. The INSPIRIT is a questionnaire that asks about spiritual or religious beliefs and experiences, including time spent on various religious practices and how close people have felt to powerful forces of one kind or another. There are also direct questions about belief in God and about experiences that may have reinforced such beliefs.[34] In our study, INSPIRIT was modified to allow for reporting of a wider range of religious experiences than in the original and better descriptions of the nature of them. The Hood scale, based on Ralph Hood's readings of James's varieties, taps into the quality of a person's religious experiences. This scale evaluates two major factors: general mystical experience and religious interpretation.[35] Three experimental groups were defined. The first comprised twenty-eight people with temporal lobe epilepsy and a clinically identified prominent religious devotion. The second consisted of twenty-two people with temporal lobe epilepsy who had no religious affiliations; and in the third group were thirty regular churchgoers without known epilepsy. The purpose of the study was to examine in more detail the psychological profile of those patients with epilepsy who exhibited hyperreligiosity and, by comparing them with the epilepsy control sample, to explore the underlying epilepsy variables that may be related to the religious experiences. By examining a group of worshipers who did not have epilepsy, we hoped to capture phenomenological differences between them and our epilepsy sample.

The results of this study are revealing. We were able to reconfirm the original findings of Bear and Fedio, showing that the temporal lobe hyperreligious group not only endorsed the religiosity subscale, as expected, but also exhibited other elements of Gastaut-Geschwind syndrome. Notably, the hyperreligious group had high scores on the subscales of emotionality, philosophical interests, anger and sadness, dependence, and hypergraphia. They also were rated by a significant other to have more paranoia and mental viscosity (sticky thinking, with some slowness of cognition) than the nonreligious sample. Thus the profile that emerged in the religious patients with epilepsy was true to the original clinical descriptions of Gastaut-Geschwind syndrome and emphasized hypergraphia, philosophical interests, and emotionality linked with the hyperreligiosity. Among the patients with temporal lobe epilepsy, those with hyperreligiosity more often had a history of episodes of psychosis and exhibited more bilateral electroencephalogram changes than the nonreligious group.

The backgrounds of the ordinary churchgoers were different from those of the epilepsy patients (more females, of an older age, more likely to be married, and with a higher educational level and occupational status), but their religious behaviors also differed. The patients with epilepsy and hyperreligiosity were more likely to belong to a religion not regarded as mainstream (such as the Church of England or the Catholic Church); Seventh-Day Adventism was popular.

The INSPIRIT listed a number of experiences and asked how often the respondent had felt each of them. The hyperreligious group endorsed the following responses more often than the control epilepsy group: feeling "as though you were very close to a powerful spiritual force that seemed to lift you outside"; feeling "an awareness of an evil presence"; having had "an experience of a miraculous event"; having had "a sensory or quasi-sensory experience of a great spiritual figure" or "an experience of a great spiritual figure" (such as Jesus, Mary, Elijah, Buddha or Allah); having had "an experience with near death or life after death"; having had "an experience of being punished in some way by God"; and having had "an overwhelming experience of fear."

On the Hood Mysticism Scale, the main features that identified the hyperreligious epilepsy sample were the "noetic," "temporal-spatial," and "ineffable" qualities of their experiences. *Noetic* here means that the experience itself is perceived as a valid source of knowledge, with an emphasis on experiences that are nonrational, intuitive, and insightful but not purely subjective. Ineffability is the quality of being inexpressible in ordinary language. The temporal-spatial dimension of the experience indicates the extent to which time and space are modified. There is a loss of a sense of self while retaining consciousness, and typically the experience is one of happiness. The full profile of the hyperreligious patients is shown in table 7.2. The patients with bilateral temporal lobe electroencephalographic changes in particular scored higher on "sense of presence of evil," "experience of a great spiritual figure," "experience of angels," "sensory or quasi-sensory experience of angels," "near death experience," "overwhelming fear," "complete joy and ecstasy," "being punished by God," and "loss of self-control."

No differences were noted in the overall profiles of religious behaviors when the churchgoers without epilepsy were compared with the hyperreligious group, that is, in terms of having any kind of religious experience and the frequency and duration of such experiences. Both groups endorsed having experienced many such events, but clearly the quality of the experiences differed.

These results lead to some relevant conclusions regarding the overall theme of this book. First, temporal lobe epilepsy can be associated with an identifiable

TABLE 7.2
Defining Characteristics of Patients with Temporal Lobe Epilepsy and Hyperreligiosity

A sense of a presence of evil
Being very close to a powerful spiritual force that seems to lift you outside
A sensory or quasi-sensory experience of a great spiritual figure
An experience with near death or life after death
An experience of being punished in some way by God
An overwhelming experience or fear
Complete joy and ecstasy
Experiences of a noetic and ineffable kind
Loss of sense of self while conscious
Experiences of modifications of time and space
Sense of joy and bliss
An experience of a miraculous event

constellation of behavioral dispositions, referred to as Gastaut-Geschwind syndrome. These behaviors have been identified for years but are now better documented with rating-scale assessments. Second, patients with hyperreligiosity often have experienced postictal psychotic states, a fact that underscores the potential links between their psychological profile and that of an epilepsy-related psychosis; as has already been noted, hyperreligiosity is often seen in the context of such a psychosis. With regard to the actual religious experiences, the epilepsy sample reported more experiences of the feeling of the presence of some external being, either of evil or of great spirituality, associated with feelings of death or dying and intense fear. The experience is ineffable and noetic, not simply an awareness. An identification of and with that essence is present, and ecstasy and miracle are features of the descriptions.

Here are some descriptions of the actual experiences of hyperreligiosity:

Patient 1 said, "I had three experiences in all, two were similar, and the third completely different. The first two, although frightening, were joyful and happy and excitable. The last was terrifying, and when it ended I thought I was dead. During the first two I had hallucinations and heard voices—I thought at the time that I was spoken to by God, I felt elated. During the first attack I thought I was John the Baptist. During the second I simply believed I was spoken to by God. Both attacks lasted more than half a day. During the third attack, I believed God saved my life. I felt as if I had died, but come back . . . I felt God was with me taking care of me."

Patient 2 said, "I became a Christian after attending a healing meeting where I believe I heard the voice of God calling to me saying 'Come to me and I will heal you.' From that point on everything started to change." The patient then had epilepsy surgery. "I personally believe that God was in the theatre watching over me and changing my life. It seemed as if I woke up, a new creation, with a fresh start in life."

Patient 3 said, "I had experienced what could only be described as a spiritual need that led to the elevated feelings of a spiritual emergency, in which the experience was somewhat holy even though I was not delusional at all."

Patient 4 said, "I suffered hallucinations that the woman across the ward from me was the devil and had come to take me to hell. As I recall, this happened three times—there was in my mind an analogy with the denial by Peter of Christ three times." Just after the six-hour birth of her son, she "suddenly decided that he was Jesus Christ and my husband and I were Joseph and Mary. According to my husband this delusion passed over the next few weeks."

Patient 5 wrote, "I am the Lord thy God, thy God, who took thee out of the house of Israel and out of the land of Egypt."

Patient 6 wrote, "I am writing all this" (J'écrit tout cela), then began again, "God with my right hand is writing all this" (Dieu avec ma propre main écrit tout çela).

The texts of patients 5 and 6 are shown in figures 7.1A and 7.1B.

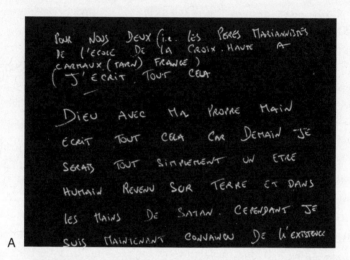

A

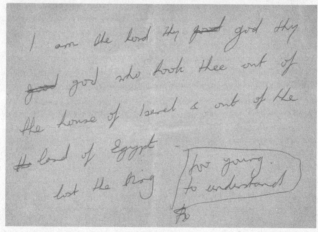

B

Figure 7.1. *A*, This patient had a compulsion to write and was bilingual. However, he crossed out "J'écrit tout cela" and replaced it with "Dieu avec ma propre main écrit tout cela." *B*, The patient writes, "I am the Lord thy God Thy God who took thee out of the house of Israel and out of the land of Egypt." This is representative of many religious texts from people with epilepsy.

Many of our patients wrote of their strong religious convictions, but often they preferred to talk about their experiences rather than write them down. One patient suddenly thought she was John the Baptist and went into the streets proclaiming it. Another recalled holy spirits entering the room he was in and flying around; this experience was associated with a vision of a cross on the wall in front of him. Yet another woke to find himself in heaven—a considerable surprise to him, as he was an atheist.

Some care must be given to the interpretation of the results of this study, especially with regard to comparisons between hyperreligious patients with temporal lobe epilepsy and churchgoers without epilepsy, in part, because of the demographic differences. However, while a number of features have been noted that distinguished the experience of the two groups psychologically, overall the epileptic patients did not report either more strongly held religious beliefs or more time spent in religious practices; nor, indeed, did they differ in the frequency and duration of their experiences.

From the neurological point of view, it was the patients with temporal lobe epilepsy and bilateral disturbances of function (as revealed through the electroencephalogram) in their temporal lobes who reported the most intense religious experiences, especially endorsing expressions regarding the inner subjective nature of their experiences, their ineffability, and the temporal-spatial component. Of all the subjects studied, these people have the most intense and disturbing religious experiences—some of James's geniuses of the religious line.

Other groups have also studied the links between epilepsy and religiosity. The seminal works of Howden and of Dewhurst and Beard have been noted. In addition, John Csernansky and colleagues looked for correlations between psychopathological and neurological variables in a small sample of patients with epilepsy. They did not find a statistical difference with regard to laterality but favored the left and bilateral abnormalities as opposed to the right hemisphere in association with religiosity. Some others, also using rating scales, have not found such positive associations. These results have been reviewed elsewhere, but they do suggest caution in interpreting the results of the studies presented in this chapter.[36]

Orrin Devinsky, another neurologist with considerable interest in epilepsy and behavior, summarizes a brief review of the topic thus: "Dewhurst and Beard's classic paper provided some of the early support for the modern concept of the temporal lobes as the seat of religious-emotional experiences."[37] Devinsky does not discuss the issue of laterality, but the accumulating data reviewed in this chapter suggest that bilateral limbic disturbances are related at least to the more extravagant visual and auditory ecstasies of patients with epilepsy. Most studies emphasize the link between hyperreligiosity and postictal states, perhaps because of the dramatic and sudden presentations. However, religious conversions and persistence of strong religious beliefs thereafter are well recorded, as are the interictal personality changes evident in Gastaut-Geschwind syndrome.

These states occur in different cultures. Akira Ogata and Taihei Miyakawa identified three cases of religiosity from a larger population of patients with epilepsy in Japan. All had temporal lobe epilepsy, and the religious episodes were postictal, although all had interictal features of religiosity, as well. The authors estimated the frequency of religiosity as a feature of the postictal state as 27 percent. In the interictal state, none of the patients worshiped according to traditional Japanese patterns of belief but instead followed either a form of combined Buddhism-Shintoism, a new sect of Christianity, or an amalgam of folk beliefs.[38]

Epilepsy and Creative Talent

Late-nineteenth-century neuropsychiatrists hinted at a possible association between epilepsy and creativity. Their writings, though perhaps longwinded, make for entertaining reading, and all of the evidence given is empirical.[39] In fact, it seems quite unclear that epilepsy is associated with any special creative talent, and rarely is it compatible with genius. Thus on the lists of "famous" people who apparently had epilepsy and succeeded mightily, including the possible religious mystics already quoted, creative artists do not figure highly.[40] Often noted are van Gogh, Dostoyevsky, and Gustave Flaubert. There is some support for an epilepsy diagnosis in the case of van Gogh, but alternative explanations for his illness have been given, notably, bipolar affective disorder, although the role of heavy absinthe consumption, especially in provoking his seizures, has also been suggested.[41]

Several members of van Gogh's family are known to have had epilepsy, and he himself was treated at Saint Paul de Mausole asylum at Saint Remy de Provence for epilepsy, having been admitted a few weeks after the celebrated psychotic episode in which he cut off his left ear following an argument with his fellow painter Paul Gauguin. His physician at the time, Dr. Peyron, considered van Gogh to be subject to attacks of epilepsy and treated him with bromides, the standard medication for the illness in those times.

In fact, van Gogh had several brief psychotic episodes, and it was reported that during them he would get extraordinarily excited. After cutting off his ear, he was found unconscious and was first admitted to hospital. His attacks continued, his behavior during them extremely frightening, and he was eventually transferred to the asylum at Saint Remy. The character of the attacks was typical of postictal psychoses. The onset of van Gogh's episodes was sudden, and they would gradually resolve, but over quite a short period of time—days, or less than two weeks—which would be quite unusual for an attack of mania. The episodes were heralded by some disorientation and loss of concentration. Van Gogh himself said, "I have had in all four great crises, during which I did not know the least what I said, what I wanted, and what I did. Not taking into account that I had previously had three fainting fits without any plausible reason and without retaining the slightest remembrance of what I felt."[42] Van Gogh referred to these episodes as grand crises; it appears that not only was he amnesic for these episodes, but also he experienced associated hallucinations and bizarre religious and paranoid delusions.

Of more interest is the possibility that van Gogh kindled a Gastaut-Geschwind syndrome. There was evidence not only of hyperreligiosity but also of hypergraphia. Van Gogh's hypergraphia may be inferred in the classic way, from the profuse outpouring of letters to his family and different artists, but also by viewing the prodigious output of his paintings as a variant. In less than two years while he was at Nuenen (1884–86), van Gogh finished 225 drawings, 25 water-colors, and 185 oil paintings. In Paris, between 1886 and 1888 there were about 200 oils, 10 water-colors, and 40 drawings, and at Arles (1888–90) about 185 oils, 100 drawings, and 10 water-colors. In total, his artistic output averaged an oil painting approximately every other day for at least six years. Inspection of the paintings in chronological order reveals the repetitive and seemingly compulsive nature of some of his themes, particularly quasireligious ones, for example, those olive trees.

Van Gogh came from a religious background; both his father and paternal grandfather were ministers. Religion was, therefore, a feature of his life, but religiosity became a feature of his illness. In childhood he was not known for any excessive religious zeal, and it was not until about the age of twenty that he turned increasingly to religion and spent much time reading the Bible. By 1886, this had become an obsession. He considered becoming a minister and received a trial as an evangelist, but he was dismissed for excessive zeal bordering on the scandalous. During this time he gave away his possessions, lived in a hovel, and became unkempt in his personal appearance.

Religious asceticism and martyrdom are essential themes in van Gogh's correspondence from 1875 to 1880. He strongly identified with Christ, taking on a portrayal of the martyrdom of Jesus, and he read the New Testament over and over again. In 1887 he was translating the Bible into French, German, and English in four separate columns of text, along with the Dutch version. On Sundays he went not only to the Dutch Reformed Church but also to three other churches of different denominations.

Van Gogh's religiosity fused with philosophical mysticism, and themes of suffering, death, and heaven appear frequently in his writings and his paintings. He mused on heaven and eternity, hence the paintings of the starry skies and olive trees. It has been suggested that the ear he gave to Rachel the prostitute was intended as a religious gift with symbolic overtones.

Of his attacks, during which he had delusions with a religious content, van Gogh said, "I have attacks such as a superstitious man might have and . . . I get perverted and frightful ideas about religion." He wrote on the walls of his house at Arles, "I am the Holy spirit: I am healthy of spirit."

Given the acute nature and the content of his psychotic episodes in the setting of a history of probable epileptic seizures, it is highly likely that van Gogh suffered from episodes of postictal psychosis. However, it seems that he also had personality traits of hypergraphia and hyperreligiosity, in keeping with the features of Gastaut-Geschwind syndrome.

In the biographical sketch of another artist, Alfred Kubin (1877–1959), the view is expressed that there may be some positive creative benefit to epilepsy, especially temporal lobe epilepsy. The authors suggest that Kubin had attacks reminiscent of complex partial seizures and that somehow the "juxtaposition of already familiar images and ideas" created by the seizure formed the basis of his creativity.[43] However, they do not make a convincing case that Kubin ever had epilepsy.

Similar claims have been made for the Danish religious philosopher Søren Kierkegaard (1813–55). Kierkegaard's written output during his relatively short life was prodigious, and he was intensely religious. He attacked the established church and Hegelian philosophy with equal vigor, convinced that God had appointed him to reveal the true nature of Christianity. He wrote about his flight of ideas, his own compulsion to write, his obsessive need of God to help him with all of his assignments, and of living like a "scribe in His office." He appears to have had aura-like experiences, akin to those of Dostoyevsky, with moments of "indescribable joy," and "attacks" were described in which he would fall to the floor with clenched hands and tensed muscles. Kierkegaard wrote of his own personal suffering as a tension between his mind and his body, and he referred to the "thorn in his flesh," an obvious allusion to the phrase used by Saint Paul, which some have interpreted as a reference to epilepsy. Kierkegaard kept his burden secret and eschewed both marriage and becoming a pastor, possibly owing to epilepsy. However, the jury is still out on his possible epilepsy.[44]

Epilepsy and Poetry

Epilepsy and writing are connected through the clinical phenomenon of hypergraphia. Two of Waxman and Geschwind's patients wrote poetry, and the theme of the hypergraphic outpourings in several patients was religious. However, our considerable experience with the hypergraphia of patients with epilepsy indicates that, sadly, it is rarely creative, and though often mystical, it is perseverative and vague in content.

A brief consideration of the poets said to suffer from epilepsy is warranted. William Lennox and Margaret Lennox, in their mammoth summary of the known facts about epilepsy, mention only a few poets who may have had epilepsy: Algernon Swinburne, Lord George Byron, and Edward Lear. Considering the relative frequency of poetry writing as a literary art and the known prevalence of epilepsy, it would seem, from such a short list, that epilepsy and adequate poetical expression are antithetical.[45]

There is not much to say about Byron's seizures that has not already been published. Lennox and Lennox report that he was said to have had convulsions at birth (in 1788) and had frequent minor attacks and occasional convulsions throughout his life. Byron was born lame; throughout his life he had an abnormally thin leg and a small right foot, and he was described as having a sliding gait.[46]

Byron fell in love at the age of eight, and when, at sixteen, he heard that his beloved was about to marry, he apparently almost had convulsions. He was said to have had a convulsion on seeing Edmund Kean act. These were almost certainly all affective convulsions, what perhaps now would be called pseudoseizures.[47]

It is better established that toward the end of his life Byron had a series of seizures (five tonic-clonic seizures in fifteen days), but he is said to have commented that these were the first seizures he had ever had. On February 15, 1824, Byron, at this time in Missolonghi, asked for cider and swallowed some; then "a great change came over his countenance. He tried to stand up, staggered forward, and fell . . . and he was then seized with violent convulsions, and his mouth was pulled down at one side." An attending doctor recorded that he "foamed at the mouth, gnashed his teeth, and rolled his eyes like one in an epilepsy."[48] This seems to have been the only documented seizure, and he made a good recovery from it; he died in a delirium on April 19 of the same year.

Perhaps the most interesting of the group is Algernon Swinburne (1837–1909). After schooling at Eton, Swinburne went to Oxford but left without a degree. While there he became influenced by the Pre-Raphaelites and was guided into a career in literature by Richard Monckton Milnes (1809–95), later Lord Houghton.[49] Houghton introduced him to the delights of erotic and sadistic literature, which formed a part of Swinburne's own prodigious poetic output.

There is no doubt that Swinburne had seizures, but these were almost certainly linked with his alcoholism. He had his first seizure in 1863, at the age of twenty-six; an excellent account of one of his attacks has been given by Sir Edmund Gosse. While in the reading room of the British Museum,

> Swinburne had fallen into a fit while working . . . and had cut his forehead superficially against the iron staple of the desk. I was walking along a corridor when I was passed by a couple of silent attendants rapidly carrying along in a chair what seemed to be a dead man. I recognised him instantly from his photographs which now filled the shop windows. His hanging hands, closed eyelids, corpse-white face, and red hair dabbled in blood presented an appearance of utmost horror, but I learned a few days later that his recovery was rapid and complete.[50]

Several other friends witnessed these fits, including Milnes and the artist James Whistler, and the descriptions given would seem typical for generalized seizures. The history of alcoholism is quite compatible with these being symptomatic, that is induced, seizures, as opposed to epilepsy. Swinburne was prescribed a "torpor" for his malady.

Edward Lear was born in 1812, the youngest of a family of twenty-one siblings. He was rejected by his parents as a child; his father, having lost his money on the stock exchange, sent him to live with his elder sister Ann. Lear had his first seizures around the age of five or six and had ten to fifteen attacks a month. Another sister, Harriet, also had epilepsy. He referred to his attacks as "the Demon"; they would be complemented later in life with "the morbids," the acute depressive episodes to which he was prone. "It is a most merciful blessing," he wrote, "that I have kept up as I have, and have not gone utterly to the mad bad sad."[51]

Lear's seizures seem to have been introduced by some kind of aura, which allowed him to seek privacy before the attack. In his diary entry for February 14, 1880, he wrote, "It is wonderful that these fits have never been discovered, except partly apprehending them beforehand, I go to my room." He experienced "cataleptic pauses of an hour," and some of his seizures were "violent," leaving him confused for even longer.[52] A severe attack would put him indoors for the rest of the day and leave him with "weary nerves," that is, irritable. He worried about the effect of the seizures on his eyesight: after one episode he wrote, "Knocked out at 5.00 . . . not seeing the hills or the sky." He tried "self control" to stop his seizures but soon came to the conclusion that self-control had little to do with the matter.[53]

Lear was an accomplished artist, both as a natural history illustrator and a landscape painter. He illustrated the poems of Alfred Lord Tennyson, composed songs, and loved children, though he had none of his own. He began writing his poems, especially the nonsense verse, quite late in his life. Although the early limericks probably date to the 1840s, the major nonsense songs were composed in the 1860s and the 1870s, the loved nonsense song, *The Owl and the Pussy Cat*, being written in 1867.[54] His most recent biographer, Peter Levi, is rather dismissive of the verse of his youth ("suburban . . . scarcely distinguishable") and considers Lear "essentially a painter." In his *Art of Poetry*, Levi begins the chapter on Lear: "Edward Lear is not what we normally call a great poet."[55] Although his verse was much appreciated by such people as John Ruskin, Alfred Tennyson, and W. H. Auden, whether Lear was ever a major poet is arguable.

The comic melancholy of the limericks and some of his sad characters reflect surely on his own personality and his sense of rejection, his childlike sense of humor, and his eccentricity. He was a prodigious writer: thirty volumes of his correspondence have survived (he destroyed twenty or more years of his own early diaries), and he complemented his huge output of paintings with (by his own estimate) between twenty thousand and thirty thousand drawings. Hypergraphic he certainly was.

With the exception of Lear, the poets discussed in this chapter almost certainly had seizures provoked by external influences rather than epilepsy. For Byron, it was probably a fever in the context of some systemic illness, and the attacks occurred late in his life, shortly before he died. In Swinburne's case, the attacks were alcohol related, representing withdrawal symptoms after bouts of heavy drinking. Neither would be diagnosed today as epilepsy.

Lear certainly had epilepsy, and it may be that he had partial seizures. His epilepsy, possibly with visual auras, may have arisen in the occipital lobes of the brain rather than in the limbic lobe. He nonetheless described his own peculiarities, which were reflected in his reclusive lifestyle, continually escaping from company and traveling abroad. He had an accompanying affective disorder, although no evidence of any hypomania has been noted. In his poem about himself he refers to his mind as "concrete and fastidious," and he had the insight that he was thought of as "ill tempered"—all possible links to at least some elements of Gastaut-Geschwind syndrome.[56] However, as noted, the quality of his poetry has been cast into some doubt, and certainly it does not rank with the great poetry of the English language.

This chapter has suggested some important links between the brain and behavior. Epilepsy is associated with religious ecstasy and with religiosity in some patients. The most common form of epilepsy with this clinical profile is temporal lobe epilepsy, and the more extreme behaviors are seen in those with bilateral electroencephalographic changes. Postictal religiosity is associated with mania, hypomania, and severe disturbances of affect; it is more likely to be seen in patients with right-sided temporal lobe epilepsy, and the profile of the experience is identical to the expressions recorded in the past of many religious prophets. Epilepsy as a disorder is poorly linked with creativity, especially poetry; it is rarely associated with bipolar disorder; and if patients do develop a chronic psychosis, it is more commonly associated with schizophrenia-like presentations. The pattern of associations already suggested therefore between poetic creativity and neuropsychiatric illness as revealed in bipolar affective disorder and schizophrenia (chapter 5) is repeated in patients with epilepsy. In other words, poetic creativity in patients with epilepsy is rare, as are instances of classical bipolar disorder, while schizophrenia-like states are overrepresented. The literature on epilepsy adds a further link in the chain of biological associations between the right hemisphere affect and religiosity; and the experiences of people with epilepsy in states of postictal psychoses are the linchpin of neurotheology. It is as if the neurophysiological disturbances of the limbic epilepsy hijack the cerebral circuits that underlie religious feelings and expression.

Thus it is possible to bring those people that William James referred to as having "religious fever" under scientific observation and to study some of the geniuses of the religious line. However, temporal lobe epilepsy is only a part of this evolving story. The next chapter explores other neurobiological associations of religious behaviors.

CHAPTER EIGHT

Neurotheology II

Other Neurological Conditions

The previous chapter presented the links between epilepsy and states of religiosity, from those of ecstasy and revelation to more subtle enduring personality changes in the direction of philosophical rumination and religious observance. However, epilepsy is not the only neurological disorder linked with religiosity, although it is the disorder most often discussed and researched in this context.

Neurotheology as a branch of neuroscience has begun to develop only in recent years; the first book dedicated to this subject was published in 2002. However, there are now established university departments that study the science of religion, and neuroscientists have taken up the challenge to investigate not only consciousness in its broadest context but also emotional states, including those associated with religious feelings and practices. Neurotheology stands alongside other topics such as neuroaesthetics as a valid area of neuroscience that can now be explored with, for example, brain stimulation and brain-imaging techniques. These two disciplines represent neuroscience offshoots of what the biologist E. O. Wilson called sociobiology, namely, the systematic study of the biological basis of all forms of social behaviors across the phylogeny, including mankind. For Wilson, religion was one such behavior that was universal, conferred genetic advantage, and, indeed, helped drive evolutionary change.[1]

The book referred to above is a compilation of texts from various authors, many of them published elsewhere in a similar format, with sadly little in the way of new data on show. The first chapter quotes a section of Nietzsche's *The Gay Science* in which the protagonist proclaims, "Whither is God . . . I will tell you . . . God is dead. And we have killed him."[2] The contributions are not simply in praise of an atheism, however, or even a materialistic reduction of the spiritual to neurons and brain circuits. Nietzsche himself was an atheist, but he took religion and God seriously, from his very first writings in *The Birth of Tragedy* to his last work in *Ecce Homo* (Behold the man).[3] Some views of the contributors are considered later in this chapter, and Nietzsche and his writings are discussed in the final chapter. First, some other neurological disorders associated with religiosity are discussed, followed by results from studies of normal volunteers who have been investigated in states of religious devotion.

Although neurological conditions other than epilepsy are associated with states of religiosity, in reality their number is few, and they are little discussed in the neurological literature. The best overall review is that of Saver and Rabin. The authors point out that most religious experiences parallel similar nonreligious experiences, such as joy, love, fear, and awe, and that the emotions associated with the religious experience are ordinary emotions, differing little, if at all, in their tone but substantially differing in being directed toward a religious object.

The expressions of any particular religious language, Saver and Rabin observe, will depend upon the same mechanisms within the brain that relate to the expression of nonreligious language; the authors conclude that the cerebral circuits underlying religious affect and cognition not only are widely distributed in the human brain but also are a part of the cerebral apparatus available to everyone, the ecstatically religious and the nonreligious alike. Thus, they opine, what is peculiarly distinctive to the religious experience is not so much in the realm of affect, language, or cognition but in perception, namely, the direct sensory awareness of God or some other being. Like William James, they do not postulate an identifiable separate organ of religious perception; instead, they attempt to understand the neurological substrates of such experiences as the direct awareness of a sacred or divine presence.[4]

Dementia

The previous chapter on epilepsy noted the links between temporal lobe limbic structures and religious experiences, and the personal descriptions of patients with epilepsy who are hyperreligious have revealed the intensity of these sensory apprehensions. Saver and Rabin's review concentrates mainly on a similar epilepsy-related literature. With regard to other neurological conditions, frontotemporal dementia is almost the only other one discussed.

Dementia refers to a number of neuropathologies in which there is an acquired loss of intellectual abilities. It has many causes, from the static, such as a head injury or injury to the brain from loss of oxygen, to the progressive. The latter dementias, sometimes referred to as parenchymatous dementias, usually arise in middle to late life and present with a slowly progressive loss of skills and intellectual capacity, inevitably leading to dependency and death. The best known form is Alzheimer disease, and a second common variety is dementia secondary to cerebrovascular disease. A third form, frontal dementia, has been described for many years and was referred to at one time as Pick's disease, after the neuropsychiatrist Arnold Pick (1851–1924).

It has now become appreciated that frontal types of dementia are much commoner than was previously thought, and the clinical and pathological pictures extend far beyond the condition described by Pick. As a group, the frontotemporal dementias tend to affect the frontal and temporal lobes of the brain, and the presenting features are often behavioral rather than cognitive in the first instance. The clinical picture will vary, depending on which parts of the brain are first affected by the pathology and on the rate of progression of the disease.[5] In some patients, unilateral frontal or temporal lobe pathology occurs initially; the temporal variant has been well described by Bruce Miller and colleagues from UCLA. Hyperreligiosity is one feature of temporal lobe pathology.

Patient RTLV1 was a fifty-nine-year-old man who made errors with calculations over two years, wore unmatched shoes and socks, and tucked his jacket into his pants. Initially easygoing, he became stubborn and irritable. A religious awakening led him to spend hours in church; he argued with his wife and friends regarding his new religious ideas. His verbal output was fluent. A CT brain scan revealed mild atrophy, most marked in the right temporal lobe. A SPECT scan showed decreased cerebral blood flow in the anterior temporal regions, greater on the right. After he died, pathology was asymmetrically distributed, confirming the predominantly right temporal neuronal loss and gliosis.[6]

A second patient in the series "spent the day copying verbatim from the Bible," and although investigations revealed bilateral temporal lobe abnormalities, she was left handed, and the side of traditional language dominance was unclear. In their summary of the clinical presentations, the authors report that three out of five patients with the right-sided form of frontotemporal dementia had either increased religious ideas or heightened philosophical thinking.

A familial form of frontotemporal dementia has also been described. Seven members of a family were identified with linkage to chromosome 17. The patients experienced personality and behavioral deterioration, in particular, with signs of Parkinsonism and, initially, release of abnormal behaviors, with disinhibition. Hyperreligiosity was noted in three of the seven. The behavior pattern was consistent with a frontal lobe dementia, and on pathological examination all of the brains examined (six) showed moderate to severe frontal and temporal lobe atrophy.[7]

Saver and Rabin, in their discussion of the links between dementia and religious behaviors, make the point that in contrast to frontotemporal dementia, in Alzheimer disease, along with the decline of many lifelong interests, religious concerns and practices also decline.

Saver and Rabin attempted to find a unified hypothesis of the neurology of religious experiences, largely relying on the epilepsy and dementia literature. They considered the primary substrate to be within the limbic system and to be part of a distributed neural network marking events with either positive or negative valence. Acting as an intermediary between affects and cognitions, this cerebral system may mark experiences as depersonalized or derealized, as crucially important and self-referent, as harmonious—indicative of a connection or unity between disparate elements—and as ecstatic and profoundly joyous.

This theory stands in contrast to but alongside alternative hypotheses that emphasize the importance of the nondominant hemisphere in the modulation of holistic, nonverbal experiences, with the left hemisphere translating the experience of the nondominant hemisphere into an analytic and verbal version, which is inherently incomplete since the experience that is reported is ineffable.

The perceptual and cognitive contents of the numinous experiences are seen in Saver and Rabin's scheme as similar to those of ordinary experience, but they are tagged by the limbic system as of profound importance, united into a joyous oneness. In their view, the descriptions of these experiences resemble the descriptions of ordinary experiences, but the distinctive feelings appended to them cannot be captured fully in words. They refer to "limbic markers," which can be named but cannot be communicated in their intensity, resulting in a report of ineffability.

What is striking about frontotemporal dementia and the described clinical features is the length of time of the clinical history in some patients, often extending up to ten years before presentation to neurologists. Their overall ability to function socially remains intact, even if somewhat constrained, artistic skills being retained or even enhanced. Disinhibition with social impropriety and offensive behavior are more a feature of the right temporal variant, and the authors conclude from their own observations that "the right hemisphere, at least the orbito-frontal and temporal aspects, may be necessary for mediation of socially appealing behaviour in humans."[8] Saver and Rabin go on to note, however, that since patients with epilepsy who have one or another of their temporal lobes removed at operation to help their surgery do not develop these severe behavioral syndromes, the impaired behavior in their cases probably related to bilateral temporal lobe involvement.

Although these authors' interpretation of bilateral involvement may be correct, their observations about the effects of temporal lobectomy are not, as the following case studies of ours suggest. Patient TLE 1, a female, began to have seizures at the age of twenty-six. She had déjà vu auras and then developed complex partial seizures and sometimes secondarily generalized attacks. Her EEG showed a right temporal lobe abnormality. She was mildly religious but never went to church, and there was no psychiatric history before the operation, which was a right temporal lobectomy. The pathological study revealed amygdala and hippocampal sclerosis.

Immediately after her operation the patient experienced the feeling of God's presence. She also had an auditory hallucination saying, "It's not time yet." She confessed that the experience was a revelation and that she believed that God was protecting her. She started attending church, often twice a week, and now goes to prayer meetings and meditation classes. A trip to Lourdes has been planned. She continues to feel the presence of God, and when it is strong, for example in church, the experience is associated with feelings of euphoria and a racing pulse. She remains free of epileptic seizures.

Patient TLE 2, a thirty-two-year-old man, had febrile convulsions as a child and at age seven began to have spontaneous seizures. These were partial and generalized in nature, and EEG studies showed bilateral temporal disturbances, more on the right, and an MRI scan revealed an abnormality in the subcortical region of the right frontal lobe, probably vascular in origin. He displayed minor signs of frontal lobe disturbance before the operation, mainly in the form of a preoccupation with sexual themes. A frontal lesionectomy was carried out and the pathology revealed a dysembryoplastic neuroepithelial tumor as the cause of his seizures.

Over the months after his operation he developed signs of a psychosis, with predominant religious preoccupations. He was ambivalent about a choice of religion between Buddhism and Christianity, but he received messages from God and had seen writing on a wall saying, "Jesus Saves You," which he believed had special reference to himself. His psychosis is well treated by antipsychotic drugs, but hyperreligiosity has become a permanent feature of his mental state. This patient incidentally is also a talented musician, whose compositional powers if anything have improved following the operation.

Head Injury

The following case history is of interest because the patient developed an altered mental state in the absence of epilepsy, as a complication of a head injury.

Patient HI 1, a fifty-year-old man, was involved in a road traffic accident, suffered a head injury, and had prolonged retrograde and posttraumatic amnesias. He was taken to the hospital, where he remained confused for several days. After discharge, his wife noted that his personality had completely changed: he was more irritable and aggressive, his memory and concentration were poor, and he became intensely religious. He started going to church every week, which he had not done before, and he started to read the Bible every night. This latter behavior was all the more interesting because, on account of his cognitive difficulties, he could not well grasp the contents of what he was reading. An MRI scan showed cerebral damage to the right frontotemporal regions, compatible with the head injury.

Studies of Religious Experience in People without Neurological Disease and Normals

Religious moments, inspirational and personally meaningful, are reported in a high proportion of normal people, perhaps as high as 50 percent. Most religious discourse relates to feelings about God or gods, about beliefs in an afterlife or in reincarnation. In one survey in North America, 95 percent of people queried confessed to a belief in God, and 71 percent to a belief in an afterlife.[9] In spite of the ubiquity of such sentiments in all social groups, few studies have addressed their potential neurological associations or those of their behavioral counterparts, namely, the neural events and circuitry that may relate to behaviors of devotion.

There are many studies of relationships between personality style and religious behavior but few consistent results.[10] If anything, religiosity in the general population correlates negatively with such measures as psychoticism, and measures of obsessionality may be an exception. Several authors, including Freud, have drawn attention to some similarities between the obsessional rituals of the very devout and obsessive compulsive behaviors, and relief from anxiety on completing the compulsive acts is a common feature of both.[11] Repetitive stereotyped behaviors can be easily observed by the curious, for example, at the Wailing Wall in Jerusalem or at international airports. Obsessive traits are much more common in the very religious, and religiously tainted thoughts are a common feature of obsessive-compulsive disorder. Although somewhat adrift from the central themes of this book, these observations in normals and in those with obsessive-compulsive behaviors beg for an underlying neurobiology. It so happens that there have been many studies carried out looking at neurophysiological and neuroanatomical correlates of obsessive-compulsive disorder, and the weight of evidence points to alterations of function in frontal-basal ganglia, cortical-subcortical circuits.[12] The right hemisphere is again overrepresented in this literature. Yet another piece of the puzzle is the association of an obsessional rigidity of thinking (sometimes referred to as viscosity) as part of the described Gastaut-Geschwind syndrome of people with temporal lobe epilepsy.

Studies of Religious Experience in Normal Volunteers

Only one study has examined the cerebral accompaniments of prayer. Nina Azari and colleagues set out to test the hypothesis that religious experiences are not primarily emotional—as suggested by William James—but rather are cognitive and attributional. Attribution theory, which derives from social psychology, suggests that social situations are explained by the characteristics of the individuals interacting and the nature of the social environment. There are interpretations and explanations in attributions, involving needs for meaning; individuals may attribute causality to a wide range of events, natural or supernatural. In this view, the experience is not a felt immediacy, which would predict activation of limbic areas, but is viewed instead as a cognitive construct that activates "brain areas mediating reasoning."[13] Azari and colleagues examined twelve healthy German adults, six of whom were self-identified as religious. All of the latter had fundamentalist beliefs, had reported conversion experiences in the past, and interpreted the biblical text literally as the word of God.

All subjects read the first verse of the Psalm 23 (religious), a nursery rhyme (happy), and some instructions from a local telephone book (neutral). The religious subjects were asked to induce a religious state while reading the psalm. They were imaged using PET, while reading silently and while reciting the texts. The authors report that all religious subjects attained the religious state best while reciting.

The areas of the brain activated by the religious experiences were cortical, especially the right dorsolateral prefrontal, the dorsomedial frontal, and the right medial parietal cortex (precuneus). No activation of the limbic structures was observed during the religious states, although in the happy state in the nonreligious sample, the left amygdala was activated. The authors interpret their results as supporting the view that religious experience is a cognitive process in which prefrontally localized cognitive schemas, which "manage" memories stored in posterior brain regions, interact with activity in the dorsolateral prefrontal cortex.

A problem with the interpretation of the study, especially with regard to the failure to activate limbic structures in the religious states, was that the subjects reported a decreased negative affect during the experience, which would, in theory, mitigate against limbic arousal. Clearly, the states evoked in these volunteers are qualitatively different from those discussed in the neurological populations quoted above, and in epilepsy the emotional arousal encountered in the acute states, at least, is very powerful. The study is important, however, in highlighting the cognitive components of religious states and the role of the parietal cortex, especially in the nondominant hemisphere.

Michael Persinger and colleagues have carried out many studies of volunteers using a special technique for stimulating the brain. His investigations cover more than two decades of scientific research into the links between the brain and religious experiences. He has also concerned himself with associations between symptoms and signs of temporal lobe disturbance and religiosity and the role of the parietal cortex in such events.[14] In general, about 22 percent of his subjects have reported intense religious experiences.

Persinger notes that paranormal experiences are frequently associated with a sensed presence, involve the acquisition of information by a sense not regarded as normal, and contain distortions of time. Death or dissolution of the self are common themes, and embraced under the rubric paranormal are religious experiences, including sensing the presence of God, as well as other spiritual events such as haunts and alien abductions. As others have done before him, Persinger takes epilepsy, and, in particular, temporal lobe seizures, as a starting point: "There appears to be a continuum of temporal lobe sensitivity along which all human beings are distributed."[15] Using rating scales that measure temporal lobe experiences (temporal lobe sensitivity), he found that those individuals with the highest sensitivity also have more paranormal experiences, exhibit more frequent alpha rhythm over the temporal lobes on the EEG, and score higher on eccentric thinking and hypomania ratings, using the Minnesota Multiphasic Personality Inventory, than those who score in the lower ranges of temporal lobe sensitivity. Temporal lobe transients (waves of amplitude at least twice that of general activity—events Persinger confusingly refers to as spikes) were significantly more common in those with high temporal lobe sensitivity, and they correlated with religious belief or dogma clusters or "feeling of presence" cluster on his measures. One published study used EEG to examine a group of ten student poets. The six who reported having had religious experiences displayed the highest scores on the temporal lobe symptom clusters but no difference in spike counts when compared with nonpoets.[16]

In another Persinger study, volunteers who identified themselves as religious, as well as churchgoers, scored higher on temporal lobe symptomatology than the nonreligious, and those reporting religious experiences were reported to be more likely to keep diaries and to enjoy reading and writing poetry.[17]

In a series of studies, Persinger stimulated the temporoparietal regions of the brains of volunteers using low-frequency, weak magnetic fields in the region of one to five microteslas in strength. This evoked in most normal people a feeling of a sensed presence. The experience was more often elicited from those who had elevated scores on the measures of temporal lobe sensitivity. Interestingly, they were evoked most easily when stimulation was applied for a period of twenty minutes, after which "a bilateral burst-firing pattern . . . was applied over the temporal poles for an additional 20 minutes." The optimal parameters for obtaining the experiences were those which he claimed imitated burst-firing patterns of amygdala and hippocampal neurons. Persinger goes further to suggest that the experience of paranormal events, which are reported by many people, reflects spontaneous fluctuations in the earth's magnetic field.[18]

He also suggests, with little supporting anatomical evidence, that the deep personal significance given to paranormal events is a predictable property of a labile amygdala, the paranormal events somehow substituting for epileptic seizures. This is reminiscent of observations in patients with epilepsy whose seizures, in the course of their clinical history, transform into behavioral equivalents or whose seizures can be suppressed by antiepileptic drugs—only to find that they develop a behavioral problem, sometimes of psychotic proportions.[19] At one point Persinger actually refers to microseizures in the temporal lobes as normal events, which lead to the coherence of activity in brain structures that are not usually correlated.

The sensed presence, Persinger speculates, is "the right hemisphere equivalent of the left hemispheric sense of self"—the latter being a verbal construct. This idea is based upon concepts that the sense of self is an emergent property of language, thus implicating the left hemisphere, and that there is likely to be an equivalent homologue for this in the right hemisphere. Anything that facilitates interhemispheric intercalation, including intrinsic electrical activity, allows brief intrusions of the activity of one hemisphere into the other, interactions that are not normally represented. These right hemisphere intrusions to consciousness are experienced as paranormal events and may lead to sudden moments of enlightenment or even religious conversion. However, in Persinger's scheme, other brain processes are involved, including a perceptual reorganization involving the prefrontal areas, with an additional gradual modification of stored episodic memories. Brain plasticity and synaptic reorganization underlie these events.

Persinger's results bear consideration but also require much caution. His data have not been independently replicated. A related series of studies, however, has shown that patients with affective disorders and those with bipolar disorders during their illness phases have increased so-called temporal lobe experiences, albeit using a different scale from that used by Persinger.[20] His equating of temporal lobe EEG changes in normal people with the underlying processes of epilepsy is highly questionable, as are some of his neurophysiological arguments. The neurophysiology is simply not that well worked out (for example, how the amygdala and hippocampi actually function and integrate or how the hemispheres cohere with each other in relation to ongoing conscious and unconscious events). That microtesla stimulation of the brain can evoke paranormal experiences remains an intriguing observation but, some might suggest, one of unproven validity.

However, in the context of the theme of this book, these studies could be significant. Persinger's discussion of the neurophysiological basis of these religious experiences emphasizes the nondominant hemisphere, the medial temporal structures and their cortical connections, and the links with the epilepsy data. He also has concerned himself in his research and theories with disorders of mood and the neurobiology of creativity, especially the writing of poetry. He concludes that religious experiences are evoked in normal brains by small electrical events in temporal lobe structures. The propensity to have such experiences and the associated electrophysiology is variable within any population, however, and is perhaps found more frequently in those who create poetry. Persinger notes that religious experiences can be tuned by enhancing the activities of the right hemisphere, for example, by singing, and that religious ceremonies are constructed to mold these conditions. In a summary that refers to the right hemisphere intrusions noted above, he harks back to some of the suggestions that are also made earlier in the present volume: "The primary difference between the dissociative, creative poet, who transiently experiences these intrusions, and the patient with a chronic left temporal lobe focus is best described by Laing. Whereas the poet can conceptualise about the universe or God and remain intact, the schizophrenic confuses and ultimately loses the boundaries."[21]

Institute of Neurology Epilepsy Study

Of several hypotheses that have now evolved regarding the cerebral substrates of the religious experience, the roles of the nondominant hemisphere and of some limbic lobe structures seem to have emerged as both testable and valid within the context of the growing understanding of brain structure and function, especially with regard to emotion. Furthermore, epilepsy has been shown to be an interesting and reliable model of a neurological disorder associated with religiosity. It was with this background that my group at the Institute of Neurology measured the volumes of the hippocampus and the amygdala using MRI in patients with epilepsy whose interictal behavior was rated using the Bear-Fedio Inventory.

Thirty-three patients with refractory epilepsy were examined, and the volumes of their limbic structures were compared between those who scored high or low on three subscales of the inventory: religiosity, writing, and sexuality.[22] Mean right hippocampal volumes were significantly lower in patients who met the criteria for hyperreligiosity than in those not rated as religious. While in itself this finding was interesting, confirmation of the association emerged when the actual scores on religiosity were correlated with hippocampal size. There was a significant negative association between religiosity scores and hippocampal size, on the right side only. This correlation was found for both patient self-ratings and on the independently obtained caregiver ratings: the smaller the right hippocampus, the greater the expressed religiosity.

The only other study of which the authors of the paper are aware that supports a more direct link between the hippocampus and at least some aspects of Gastaut-Geschwind syndrome is the published case of Kumagusu Minakata, a Japanese genius of natural history and folklore, famous in Japan for the immense range of his work. He wrote an enormous number of papers, his script was performed in miniscule letters in compact space, he was hyposexual, and he had peculiar ethical concerns with an extraordinary interest in religious matters. When his brain was subjected to MRI at postmortem, right hippocampal atrophy was reported. Minakata did not report seizures in his life, but the Japanese authors of the paper speculated on the possible diagnosis of temporal lobe epilepsy.[23]

Neurotheology

The four main contributors to the field of neurotheology, and well represented either in the book devoted to the subject or with their own books, are Rhawn Joseph, Matthew Alper, James Austin, and Andrew Newberg.[24] Newberg and his colleagues have studied the states of the brain during meditation with SPECT scans. Subjects were scanned when they reached a state of indescribable "timelessness and infinity"; in other experiments, Newberg and colleagues have examined nuns in prayer. Their results suggest that during such heightened religious states, parts of the parietal lobes were underfunctioning, and there was a reciprocal inverse correlation between increased activity in the frontal lobes and the parietal perfusion. Increased activation was also seen in the cingulate gyrus bilaterally and in the thalami. The part of the parietal cortex involved they refer to as the orientation association area (posterior superior parietal lobule, Brodmann's area 7, precuneus), and they suggest that there is an orientation association area in each hemisphere, the left creating the brain's spatial sense of self, the right creating the physical space in which that self can exist. They suggest that the hypoperfusion in the orientation association area results in a decrement of sensory information arriving at the parietal cortex, leading to a blurring of the boundaries of the self; the less this activity, the more intense the religious experience. They, too, emphasize the greater contribution of the nondominant hemisphere to this process and speculate that hyperstimulation of the posterior superior parietal lobule underlies what they call Dionysian aesthetics.[25]

Newberg and colleagues appeal to an evolutionary explanation for the development and survival of religious sentiments, supporting the theory that evolutionary pressures led to the adoption of preexisting cerebral circuits for spiritual feelings and behaviors rather than to the development of new cerebral structures or circuits for such developments. Newberg's own caution is that there is no way to determine whether the changes in the brain that are seen to be associated with spiritual experiences mean that the brain is causal of the experiences.

Joseph's view is suggested by the title of his book: *The Transmitter to God*. His neurological thesis also heavily emphasizes the limbic system, especially the hippocampi and the amygdala. The latter, he claims, is especially responsive to sensory cues of some religious symbols such as crosses and is the brain structure that makes it possible to experience spiritual and religious awe but also all the terror and dread of the unknown; however, it is also responsible for the capacity to transcend the known.[26] His arguments are generated from an immense amount of anthropological data and much neurological speculation. With Cro-Magnon, some thirty-five thousand to a hundred thousand years ago, came complex religious ceremonies and artistic representations of animals but also of goddesses. The world of these peoples was permeated by the spirits of the living, the dead, and the yet to be born; they believed in an afterlife, and they buried their dead with artifacts. Gradually, over thousands of years, small groups became more socially advanced and cohesive, and cities and civilian life emerged as religious customs became stabilized, often involving violence and sexuality.

Underlying these social and cultural developments was a developing neurobiology involving the amygdala and the hypothalamus, both being "pleasure centers" containing opiates and the hypothalamus being involved in the sexual response. "The activity of the amygdala, hippocampus and the temporal lobe activity are richly interconnected and appear to act in concert in regard to mystical experience."[27] According to this theory, the amygdala subserves aggressive behavior—explaining blood lust and war in the name of God. Joseph also notes that religious experiences and texts often involve fear, fear being particularly linked to activation of the amygdala, and that the right hemisphere is more involved with subliminal experiences and human dreaming.

As have other writers, Joseph identifies several religious leaders as having, if not epilepsy, at least evidence of limbic system instability, including, on his list, Abraham, Lot, Ezekiel, and Jesus Christ. His main thesis, however, is that "every individual appears to be naturally 'wired for god' and thus capable of receiving the word of God . . . The Kingdom of God is within you." In some people, hyperactivity in those brain regions that accomplish this transmission leads to enhanced capabilities. He goes further to suggest that the presence of God actually triggers hyperactivity in the limbic areas, especially, therefore, in those selected to be his prophets and messengers. Genes coded for spiritual experience have been present for eons, and "the Earth was genetically seeded to grow humans who would become increasingly intelligent, and increasingly spiritually inclined."[28]

Joseph is an ebullient writer and presents many elements from a wide variety of sources to support his overall thesis. However, much of what he claims is hardly supported by scientific evidence, and much of the latter that he quotes is similar to that quoted by Newberg and his colleagues, who themselves are quoted by Joseph abundantly and with approval. As one commentator on Joseph's propositions has noted, "Despite intriguing findings concerning neurobiological correlates for certain types of intense religious experience, broader neurotheological interpretations of the findings are unwarranted. They involve speculation that not only strays away beyond the facts but crucially ignores or contradicts much recent work in cognitive and developmental psychology and cognitive anthropology."[29]

Matthew Alper begins his search for the "God" part of the brain with evolutionary theory, his discovery of the writings of Immanuel Kant, and Kant's distinction between noumena and phenomena. Alper observes, following the writings of authors such as Carl Jung, Joseph Campbell, and Mircea Eliade, that every known culture has perceived reality as having two realms, the physical and the spiritual, and he suggests that "spiritual consciousness" comes from an inherited, neurophysiologically based function, which he refers to as "the God part of the brain." Human beings are wired, as he says, to ascribe spiritual status to all things, and this brain function overrides our critical reasoning—witness the universal belief in God or gods in the absence of any empirical evidence.[30] (In this instance, not seeing is believing.) His underlying neurology is partially dependent on the research of Joseph, Alper, Boyer, Austin, and Newberg, key features in his neuroanatomy being the amygdala and the temporal and parietal lobes.

A Note on Meditation

In reviewing states of the nervous system, other than those associated with epilepsy, that relate to religious experiences, this chapter has not mentioned a number of papers on mental states such as meditation or near death experiences (although Persinger and colleagues have studied subjects who practice transcendental meditation, and the study of Newberg has been noted and quoted). Scores on Persinger's scale measuring complex partial seizure symptoms are high among subjects who successfully meditate. Furthermore, increased activity in the frontal lobes has been shown in meditation, in both fMRI and PET studies.[31]

A considerable tome has been devoted to the subject: *Zen and the Brain,* by James Austin. The Zen of this book is an ancient sect of Mahayana Buddhism that uses meditative techniques from the art of yoga. For Zen and its followers, meditation is the path to enlightenment that describes a special way of knowing; many would regard it as fundamentally a religious path. However, unlike most of the experiences referred to in this book, God or the gods do not seem to feature in Zen. Human beings and the universe are seen as one whole—everyone is part of the Great Self, although one goal seems to be to shake off the body, leave it behind, and achieve a complete Cartesian separation of the mind from its somatic burden.

Austin's thesis, in a book that is a bewildering *olla podria* of neuroscience and the life and times of Zen and its practitioners, is that the experience of the Great Self comes from the brain and that training in Zen leads to the release of preexisting neurophysiological functions, in other words, normal brain events, which become reassembled into novel configurations. He concedes that it is not easy to characterize the mystical experience nor to clarify the exact overlap between this and other kinds of religious experiences. The recorded physiological and neuroanatomical responses that have been associated with meditation are exhaustively reviewed in the book, but the author acknowledges the difficulty in drawing conclusions from a mass of anecdotal and often uncontrolled data. Austin's text is, in fact, part autobiographical account of the author's own introduction and experiences with Zen and part instruction manual.

Austin is interested not only in what the cerebral substrates of the meditative experience may be but also in how states of internal absorption take over and modify the individual brain. His neuroanatomy of the Zen experience involves widespread neuronal circuits with especial reference to the reticular activating system, the cingulate gyrus, the amygdala, the hippocampus, the thalamus, the hypothalamus, the limbic system, and the cerebral cortex—in fact, virtually the whole brain is included. Enlightened states, however, occur at rare moments when psychophysiological responses that are intrinsic in the brain converge.

Austin's book, which overflows with speculation, hypotheses, and conditionals, also gathers into its theories opioids, monoamines (and dopamine surges), gamma amino butyric acid, and glutamate transmission. The author suggests, for example, that there may be a conjunction of acetylcholine and glutamate transmission, activating functional interactions among major nuclei in the thalamus and their cortical counterparts, especially in frontotemporal and parieto-occipital regions of the brain and, at the same time, a dumbing down of many temporal lobe limbic, central gray, and medial orbital frontal lobe activities. Such a neurophysiological-anatomical configuration is associated with the Zen experience, with its negative connotations of loss of certain emotional and cognitive attributes, while at the same time emphasizing the attentional aspects of the state.

It is not clear, as noted, that such moments are the same as those that are of interest to the theme of this book. Austin is concerned with states such as *kensho*, "a flash of mental illumination, a unique form of comprehension . . . consciousness shorn of its entire baggage of self."[32] *Kensho* is seeing into the essence of things and is a prelude to *satori*, a deeper, more advanced state of insight and wisdom. Such states seem to be transient, however, and apparently few people are capable of having multiple experiences. Furthermore, they arise after months or years of work at the techniques, far removed from either the spontaneous ecstasies associated with epilepsy or the religious experiences of the average churchgoer or temple worshipper.

Much of the neurobiological literature on meditation is derived from observations of the surface EEG, which, frankly, is rather unrevealing, either about meditation or about the state of the brain during meditation. There seem to be thousands of ways and types of meditation, and in many people it is not clear how this may differ from, for example, states of simple relaxation. This is not to deny links between religious practices and meditation; it is rather to reiterate that meditation itself is qualitatively different from the religious ecstasies that have been central to most of the investigations reviewed in this and the previous chapter. Timeless, infinite, merging-with-everything-like experiences may have a transcendent quality and may be a part of the overall religious sentiment, but the vivid ecstatic religious experiences that have been central to the investigations here seem to be different. In addition, transient states of meditation are not the same as enduring personality features, which are portrayed in the intense religious life of some of the patients and personalities noted throughout this book.

The research presented in this chapter indicates that there are few neurological disorders other than epilepsy that are associated with hyperreligiosity. The main one is frontotemporal dementia, and, as with the epilepsy studies, the weight of evidence favors bilateral limbic involvement but with an emphasis on the right, nondominant hemisphere. The cases cited in this chapter also note that removal of the right temporal lobe can release religious ideation and behaviors. This fact, added to the phenomenology of the described states, with the strong sense of presence of another in extracorporeal space that is a common denominator of patient experiences, implies involvement of other cerebral structures, and several authors have drawn attention to parietal lobe involvement. The volunteer studies strongly support this interpretation, especially the data from Nina Azari, Andrew Newberg, and Michael Persinger. Persinger's work supports an association between religiosity, euphoria, and a tendency to write and to enjoy poetry and emphasizes the nondominant hemisphere, the temporal and parietal lobes, and the bilaterality of electrophysiological arousal for maximal effect. These data complement the results discussed in chapter 7 accumulated from the study of patients with epilepsy and hyperreligiosity.

The forces of natural selection that shape our behaviors are addressed by nearly all contributors to this field. Humankind is young, from an evolutionary point of view, but the human brain derives from eons of selective pressures. The genetic contributions to our behaviors, including religious behaviors, simply cannot be ignored. Indeed, several studies investigated the genetics of religiosity, the most convincing being those of identical twins reared apart, for whom the environmental influences on their behaviors will be different. Monozygotic twins, who ostensibly have the same genetic apparatus, have been compared with dizygotic twins, reared apart, on a variety of rating scales of religious belief and behavior. It has been shown that monozygotic twins are more alike than dizygotic ones, and it has been calculated that some 50 percent of the observed variance in religious experiences and beliefs is genetically rather than environmentally influenced.[33] The molecular biologist Dean Hamer recently published his book *The God Gene: How Faith Is Hardwired into Our Genes,* in which he claims not only that spirituality is adaptive from an evolutionary point of view but also that the gene (or genes) related to it is linked to those that regulate the neurotransmitters that control mood. Hamer used a 240-question Temperament and Character Inventory, constructed, in part, by the psychiatrist Robert Cloninger, to measure spirituality. He then examined the DNA of his sample and sought correspondences between genes and the spirituality trait. The identified gene relates to monoamine transporter function (vmat2).[34]

What can be said of neurotheology? Thomas Aquinas (1224–74) stated that the existence of God is self-evident and that those things are said to be self-evident to us "the knowledge of which is naturally implanted in us."[35] Of course, he was not espousing a neurobiological view, but his words may, in the light of current knowledge, be interpreted in such a way. Religious know-how seems to be part of our human nature, and for Joseph and his followers, this gives a highway to God; the limbic system is our transmitter and receiver of the divine signals. Others prefer a more neutral stance, especially in view of the limited data so far accumulated. Neuroscience, as a scientific discipline, must adopt this neutral stance to any investigations and subsequent results carried out in the area of brain and behavior, irrespective of the subject matter, and religious experiences and behaviors cannot be immune from such inquiries. Unfortunately, at the present time there are many people around who would still send Galileo to the Inquisition and who are so "astonished" by the bare facts of neurological expositions that they can only resort to the failed historical methods of suppression, denial, or rejection of the findings and implications of such scientific explorations.[36]

At present there are few hard and fast data to call upon in the area of neurotheology, and most writers on the subject recycle the same results from a small number of disparate investigators. However, evidence is slowly accumulating for some understanding of the cerebral associations of religious experiences: that such experiences are embodied in the brain and that the key circuits involve the temporal and parietal lobes especially of the nondominant hemisphere. Future work will either support or refute these findings, but neurotheology, like its related discipline neuroaesthetics, will increase its field of influence over the next decade:

> Know then thyself, presume not God to scan,
> The proper study of mankind is man.[37]

CHAPTER NINE

God, Music, and the Poetry
of the Brain

It is time for a recapitulation of the various themes that have been running through this book and to attempt a synthesis. The first point to reiterate is the contrast between the eons of evolutionary history and the brevity of existence of *Homo sapiens*. In contrast to the birth of the universe some billions of years ago, *H. sapiens* appears but a few hundred thousand years old and has been speaking for an even shorter period—a mere blink in evolutionary time. No one knows how and exactly when our capacity for language came about or whether its arrival was sudden or gradual, from gesture or from the cognitive equivalent of the big bang. It does seem that some precursors of *H. sapiens*, certainly the Neanderthals, were well adapted and thrived in their communities, produced artifacts, and were eliminated (almost certainly brutally) by the success of the *H. sapiens*, equipped as they were with highly efficient weapons of language and a language of weapons. Artifacts, aesthetics, and art developed as products of the evolving cognition in which symbolism totally dominated.

In the great civilizations that developed in China, India, Egypt, and Greece, mythologies developed and deities multiplied. But from the multitudes monotheism, the concept of the one and only God, emerged. Humankind became separated from nature, symbolism triumphed, and the gap was filled, at least in part, by religion and art.

Figures from different surveys vary, but according to a Gallup poll taken at the end of the twentieth century, around 97 percent of Americans believed in God, 90 percent prayed, 41 percent claimed to have had a religious experience, and, among Protestants and Catholics, some 80 percent believed in an afterlife, 79 percent in miracles, 63 to 73 percent in heaven, and 47 to 61 percent in hell.[1]

Other polls note that only 11 percent of Americans accept the standard view of evolution and that 47 percent believe that God created human beings in their present form within the past ten thousand years.[2] Additional statistics show that about 2 percent of Americans believe they have been kidnapped by an extraterrestrial force, 48 percent believe that Earth has been visited by UFOs, and 27 percent think that aliens have visited the earth. That mumbo jumbo has conquered the world is obvious, but the question here, as in the title of Francis Wheen's book, is how.[3] The answer, sadly, resides in the developed inadequacy of our cognitive structures and systems, which are simply not as rational as we would like to believe and which are driven far more by emotion than most commentators are willing to concede.

The Greek gods were a reflection of the human mind, and like those that created them, they were capricious, divided, and behaved badly. A radical shift in religious thinking occurred with the development of monotheism, in which one God was seen either as an all-embracing but ineffable concept or as the God who created man after his own image and thus bore the very image of man. Humankind, being born of that image, should have been perfect, especially in mind and knowledge, but there were ways for man to fail, either by being born defective (with original sin) or by being born perfect and then falling into sin. Whichever fate, the goal of life became to redeem the individual from such imperfection, variously with the help of the priests or a holy book or both. Perfection was given by rationality, ultimately via the Cartesian method, itself able to prove the existence of God, and by proportion, symmetry, and the balance of life, reflected in much of religious art. As Nietzsche revealed to us, fear of the truth (exemplified by Platonism) and of pessimism spurned the highest artistic inversion of the truth and spawned civilizations devoted to a life in God. The religious interpretation of existence, he opined, is not natural, it is rather antinatural, leading us away from life in this world—a negation and self-hating of the human species.[4]

An early scientific understanding of the deception emerged with philosophers such as David Hume (1711–76) and Kant, from whose writings the foundations of an antirationalism were laid, the underlying principles of which have to a large extent been borne out with the progress of the theories of evolution and neuroscience. Truth cannot be mined purely empirically; the existence of what Kant referred to as the synthetic a priori ensures that the order and regularity of appearances and events in our lives are our creations; truth is relative—more or less.

Recapitulation

Certain themes explored in chapter 1 formed the basis for subsequent explorations of the neurological basis of religiosity. William James suggested a potential for a science of neurotheology when he discussed the associations between the geniuses of religion and certain disease states, notably, affective disturbances, and in his works he implied links between poetry, music, and religious feelings. The underlying evolutionary pressures for the development of religious behaviors have been stressed by several writers, including Freud, Jung, and Wilson, and as Boyer has more recently pointed out, for humans to think scientifically actually is an unnatural default: religious inclination is the natural mode of our thought. The tendency for myth making is embodied in the human brain, and one interpretation of this is that the expressions of such chthonic archetypes are neurophysiologically ingrained.

In chapter 2 the importance of the right hemisphere for emotional expression was introduced, a line of thinking going back at least to Hughlings Jackson but one that escaped the attention of neuroscience in any significant way until recently. The new neuroanatomy was outlined, with particular attention to circuits rather than centers and to cortical-subcortical integration. Recent research, given important technological advances such as brain imaging, has now begun to explore in more detail the neglected functions of the right side of the brain and reveal its capacity to modulate language in such a way that we have to completely reappraise our views of brain-language relationships. The overriding of cognition by emotion was emphasized, and the neuroanatomical misunderstanding that the limbic system is somehow limited in its influence on the neocortex of the human brain corrected: on the contrary, the limbic lobe represents a considerable portion of the adult human brain, and its influence should be considered far greater than has generally been understood.

The importance of the right hemisphere for language was developed in chapter 3, and some special ingredients of language that relate to prosody and certain elements of poetic expression were highlighted. The language of the right hemisphere is that of uncertainty, metaphor, prosody, and emotional tone. It is the language of music. The language of the right hemisphere involves features recognized as poetic that have been used, since the early religious invocations of almost preverbal humankind, to express human feelings. It is not the language of science; it lacks the detail and propositionizing qualities of the more logical, categorizing, left hemisphere–driven speech. The metaphors of the latter are much more codified and fixed; they reveal less flexibility, and they function in an entirely different way. It was noted, however, that in human communications both cerebral hemispheres must operate together, cooperatively. The right hemisphere adds to the arid language of the syntactical left hemisphere a playful, emotional melody, resulting in the prosody of normal speech. The balance between the two sides of the brain is crucial in determining the musical and poetic variety of our resulting expressions. Without the right hemisphere, the isolated left hemisphere provides only the dull syntax of precision and seems intolerant of rich metaphor.

These distinctions were explored further in chapter 4, where two fundamentally different ways of using language were noted, the propositional and the poetic, and the possibility of different ways of understanding the meaning of truth, based on hemispheric and linguistic differences, was introduced. Like all classifications, the boundaries drawn between poetry and prose are to a large extent artificial; that said, poetry has some defining characteristics that distinguish it from prose, making it a special form of communication. In particular, rhythm, meter, and metaphor were identified, as was the physicality of it all; the similarity of these structural ingredients of poetry and those of music was noted. This theme, of the musical nature of poetry and the poetic nature of music, has been presented over centuries of comment and has again recurred often in this book.

These links were further investigated in chapter 5 through examination of the breakdown of language in various neuropsychiatric illnesses, from aphasia to schizophrenia. In this regard some associations were suggested: that between bipolar disorder and verbal creativity, especially poetic creativity, and the rather inverse relationship between epilepsy and creativity, especially focal epilepsy. Bipolar disorders are rare in epilepsy, and there are few poets with epilepsy in the established canon. The theme of the Gastaut-Geschwind syndrome and hypergraphia was also introduced, with its associations with both disturbances of the right hemisphere and religiosity. There are few schizophrenic poets, and those that have been identified, such as John Clare or Friedrich Hölderlin, saw their creativity wane with the waxing of their schizophrenia.

Support for the contention that understanding the functions of the right hemisphere is central for an understanding of poetic expression thus came from three different disorders that have afflicted humankind since time immemorial, namely, schizophrenia, epilepsy, and manic-depressive illness. In the first two in the chronic state, bilateral pathology is seen, with an emphasis on the left hemisphere and downward regulation of brain activity, while in the third, the emphasis is on upward regulation of activity in the right hemisphere.

Chapter 6 described the cerebral representations of music. Again, there seems to be an emphasis on right hemisphere activity. It was noted that music has been associated with poetry since time immemorial and both represent kinds of language. The underlying neuroanatomy related to some of the emotions associated with listening to music includes such subcortical structures as the ventral striatum, the very same structures involved in the neuroanatomical circuitry of reward and closely linked to basal ganglia structures that drive motor (emotion) output.

The next two chapters addressed neurotheology, highlighting the findings in epilepsy. The honing down of the data suggests a biological link not only between epilepsy and religiosity but between temporal-limbic epilepsy with a right-sided emphasis and the attending religious emotions. The studies with volunteers linked more extensive areas of the brain with this circuitry, including the parietal cortices (with again an overriding right-side dominance), and the precuneus was identified as potentially important.

Poetry and Religion

The final link in this story is that between poets, poetry, and religion. There are obvious affiliations between the languages of poetry and religion, not only at a theoretical level but also through obvious examples of psalms, hymns, and spiritual poetry and as revealed in the biographies of many poets. A list of some of the more notable religious poets and some of their experiences is given in appendix 2. It is not my intention in presenting this list to suggest that all great poets were overly religious; clearly they were not, Shelley's atheism being an obvious example, that of Thomas Hardy and A. E. Housman being less well known. Furthermore, the religious poets named, with singular exceptions, did not write only religious poetry. However, it does seem that many poets are or have been deeply religious people, and several of those quoted have at some time in their lives undergone a religious conversion. Much religious writing, from hymns to the Bible, achieves poetic value, and certain schools of poetry, such as the metaphysicals, were deeply religious.

A key element of poetry, the use of metaphor, unites the languages of religion and poetry. Without necessarily referring back to formalized religion, poetry engenders in people a mystical, preverbal, intensely personal spiritual feeling that is often difficult to articulate (as discussed in chapter 4).

The claims of special associations between religiosity and poetic biography, based on the selected life histories, is, of course, open to many criticisms. In particular, there is the problem of the denominator: From how many poets have those few selected for discussion in appendix 2 been taken? In any case, there are so many religious people in the world that a collection of religious poets would not add up to much of statistical significance. However, the association between religiosity and poetry goes much deeper, to the very roots of creativity and the language of poetry itself.

Religion, Art, and Poetry

The close bonds between art and religion can be observed at any art gallery or heard at a musical concert. The psychoanalyst Otto Rank (1884–1939) has pointed out that in the evolution of the human mind, the development of art and religion closely paralleled each other.[5] Early art forms must have derived from the need of primitive man to form concrete representations of the soul, based on a realization of death, and a need to believe in immortality. Gods became icons, eventually beautified representations of ideals, which lead to the development of aesthetics. Primitive art arose out of a collective, and Rank speculates that the development of art actually contributed to the development of formalized religion:

> The close association, in fact fundamental identity, of art and religion, each of which strives in its own way to make the absolute eternal and the eternal absolute, can be already seen at the most primitive stages of religious development, where there are as yet neither representations of gods nor copies of nature . . . The transition from animism to religion (that is, from the belief in the soul to the belief in God) was possible through art, because in art lay the only mode of exhibiting the soul in objective form and giving personality to God.[6]

The development of myths likely similarly arose from such immortality wishes and was translated for the collective into poetry. The creative myth was transformed by metaphor, the essential poetic ingredient. Poetic inspiration in this scheme harks back to the very origins of language and hence also to religion—in this journey, the poet became a hero.

It seems that all of the world's great religions have a collection of sacred poems as a basis for their beliefs and practices. The early Greek tragedies were performed in the context of religious ceremonies, with priests in attendance; and religious myths served as their themes.

The idea that poetry was an inspiration from the gods was developed by Plato. Divine power inspires poetry but eliminates reason, so the poet was seen, in Plato's conception, as a potential madman. However, in those times, the poet who sung about the gods was often considered to be singing as a god; he became an inspired oracle, one of the most enduring images being reflected by the head of

Orpheus, which continued to prophesy long after his dismemberment by the Bacchae.[7] As George Santayana (1863–1952) puts it, "The religion of the Greeks was . . . nothing but poetry . . . [and] the poetry is not mere poetry, but religion." The poetry itself justified the facts of ancestral worship and personal involvement; it gave a "glimpse of the divine."[8]

Poets at one time were perhaps thought to be prophets, a theme that persisted long after the divinations of the early Greek philosophers. Giovanni Boccaccio (1313–75) considered poetry a form of theology, whence came its prestige. For Sir Philip Sidney (1554–86), poetry was not only the supreme verbal art, it also had divine sanction. Nearer our time, it is said that the poet Alfred Austin (1835–1913), on being criticized for the grammatical content of some of his work, commented that he dare not alter his words as they came from above.[9]

In fact, many creative people have been reputed to have said that their religion was central or helpful to their creativity.[10] Franz Joseph Haydn (1732–1809) attributed the conception of his *Creation* to religious inspiration.[11] When Robert Schumann (1810–56) thought he was having an attack of madness he would compose religious music. In the words of William Blake,

> Hear the voice of the Bard,
> > Who present, past, and future sees
> Whose ears have heard
> The Holy Word
> > That walk'd among the ancient trees.[12]

The concept of the muse, so central to creativity, was also linked to religion. Dante Alighieri (1265–1321) first saw his Beatrice at a wedding feast when he was only nine years old, she being seven. Beatrice was eventually immortalized as a heavenly protectress in his Christian epic, *The Divine Comedy*, in which she appears as a Platonic ideal of both beauty and divinity.[13] The deeply religious young Petrarch (1304–74) first spied his Laura in a church. She was inspirational for his famous *Canzoniere*, the poems that describe his journey from the love of Laura to his love of the divine. The poet Robert Graves pondered that "the muse is a deity, but she is also a woman" who is never completely satisfied: "A poet cannot continue to be a poet if he feels that he has made a permanent conquest of the Muse, that she is always his for the asking." Graves felt that the most important religions are based on worship of a goddess.[14]

Critical Studies

There has been little critical attention to the religious nature of poetry, it is rather assumed in most commentary on poetry. Santayana states that the poet "dips into the chaos that underlies the rational shell of the world . . . He paints in again into the landscape the tints which the intellect has allowed to fade from it"; poetry and religion are part of the "life of reason." He refers to a higher function of poetry, beyond mere versifying, that is associated with creative reason. For him, the highest poetry is that of the prophets and those who interpret them. Poetry, by portraying the ideals of experience and destiny, and when raised to its highest, is "identical with religion grasped in its innermost truth."[15]

The poet and critic I. A. Richards rather explicitly refers to the connections between poetry and religious experiences: "Very often the whole state of mind in which we are left by a poem, or by a piece of music, or, more rarely perhaps, by other forms of art, is of a kind which it is natural to describe as a belief . . . [that] is a consequence not a cause of the experience, [and] is the chief source of the confusion upon which Revelation Doctrines depend."[16]

Richards notes that scientific beliefs in general are about "*that* so and so" and can be precisely stated, whereas the beliefs generated by poetry are akin to those of children or primitive peoples. The latter beliefs tend to be parasitic: they readily attach themselves to things and are then referred to as knowledge, albeit a different kind of knowledge from scientific fact. Hence the revelation, "Beauty is truth, truth beauty"—a Platonic invocation of the purity of ultimate truth.[17] In this regard, Richards quotes Percy Dearmer's *The Necessity of Art:*

> Beauty is eternal, and we may say that it is already manifest as a heavenly thing—the beauty of Nature is indeed an earnest to us of the ultimate goodness which lies behind the apparent cruelty and moral confusion of organic life . . . Yet we feel that these three are ultimately one, and human speech bears constant witness to the universal conviction that Goodness is beautiful, that Beauty is good, and Truth is Beauty. We can hardly avoid the use of the word "trinity," and if we are theists at all we cannot but say that they are one, because they are the manifestation of one God. If we are not theists there is no explanation.[18]

There can be no other closer evaluation of the kinship of the inspiration of both poetry and religious belief than that.

Northrop Frye sums up the relationship as follows:

Poets are happier servants of religion than [of] politics, because the transcendental and apocalyptic perspective of religion comes as a tremendous emancipation of the imaginative mind. If men were compelled to take the melancholy choice between atheism and superstition, the scientist, as Bacon pointed out long ago, would be compelled to choose atheism, but the poet would be compelled to choose superstition, for even superstition, by its very confusion of values, gives his imagination more scope than a dogmatic denial of imaginative infinity does.[19]

Frank Brown, in his study of the critical writings of John Wheelwright (1897–1940) and the poems of T. S. Eliot, specifically discusses the association between the languages of poetry and religion, and he dwells particularly on the relevance and commonality of metaphor for both.[20] The essential role of metaphor in poetry has already been discussed in chapter 4. Brown compares and contrasts the metaphorical language of poetry with the conceptual language of theology, while Wheelwright distinguishes what he calls "steno-language" from "depth language."[21] In the former, meaning is restricted to logical content, while in the latter it "move[s] beyond narrowly empirical conceptualisation." Obviously, "depth" language in this context is the language of poetry; and if the stance is taken that a person's world is somehow confined by language, then the "world mediated through 'steno' discourse is never the same as the world mediated through poetry and myth"—poetry is beyond the reach of reason.[22] By using metaphor, poetry gives a different kind of knowledge, which transcends that of steno-language by revelation through linguistic transformations interacting between thought and feeling. Poetry gives a sense of the transcendent, the sacred, and the religious, and for Brown is a way to discover truths unavailable through other forms of discourse. Its truths were therefore somehow seen as superior to the truths of science and rational discourse.[23]

Brown builds on this system to suggest the religious meaning of some poetry: "One somehow comes to know more of what and who one is as a whole and perhaps to sense more deeply one's relationship to a larger Whole . . . In transforming in a significant, if subtle, way one's mode of knowing, poetic metaphor alters and expands one's ever finite understanding of oneself and of the realities within and by which one lives." This is "somehow related to whatever religious significance our modes of understanding and being (or becoming) may manifest." He thus draws an analogy between the poetic metaphor and "the deeper elements of scriptural witness and human existence that various languages of religious belief seek to interpret." Poetry can effect personal transformations that are like, or may be, religious transformations. "Poetry joins ritual, music, dance, and other 'arts' to become one of the truly primary languages of religious belief."[24] The poet

Stephen Spender (1909–95) has expressed his experience thus: "In poetry, one is wrestling with God."[25]

One problem with much of the discussion on the religious nature of poetry, of which the above is only a sample, is that it unfortunately reflects a rather narrow definition of religion and of the religious experience. It is clear that the poetry of many of the writers quoted in this chapter was not religious poetry that was doctrinal or devotional; they often expressed a much broader concept of the religious. With such maneuvers as the conflation of secular and divine love, the romantic illusions of the transcendent pathetic fallacy, and the revelations of mysterious experiences, many poets can be seen as "religious" in an inspirational sense, including those who are not normally considered as such in a more restricted sense. A broad definition would include many, but the examples of D. H. Lawrence (1885–1930) and Walt Whitman (1819–92) serve to make the point.

Thus the religious nature of poetry can be seen in ways other than purely devotional or as an attempt to esteem the presence of God or the gods. In *Poetry and the Sacred,* Vincent Buckley acknowledges that many poets refer to the creation of poetry as a religious act, even though the poetry itself is not necessarily devotional. However, the realization that much of poetry is sacred leads him to suggest that poetry may represent an atavistic survival of certain types of psychic structure. Buckley quotes the following from Mircea Eliade:

> Yet this experience of profane space still includes values that to some extent recall the nonhomogeneity peculiar to the religious experience of space. There are, for example, privileged places, qualitatively different from all others—a man's birthplace, or the scenes of his first love, or certain places in the first foreign city he visited in youth. Even for the most frankly non-religious man, all these places still retain an exceptional, a unique quality: they are the "holy places" of his private universe, as if it were in such spots that he had received the revelation of a reality *other* than that in which he participates through his ordinary daily life.[26]

A poet "tests" such privileged places for their sacredness and re-creates "holy places of his private universe." In so doing, the poet experiences the "ontological shock" in the discovery of the "inscape," or the "essence" of things.[27]

The Right Hemisphere, Affect, and Poetry

One of the most interesting developments in neuroscience in recent years has been the growing appreciation of the role of the right, so-called nondominant, hemisphere in human behavior, and in this book, its relationship to certain language and music abilities has been repeatedly emphasized. Furthermore, there are clues from both a neurological but also a philosophical perspective that before conscious verbal expression there exists a *Vorgestalt*. Psychoanalytically framed authors such as Ernst Kris and Lawrence Kubie have worked with concepts such as the preconscious, at once symbolic and nonverbal, surely also interlinked with the preverbatim. Kris, arguing against the concept that artistic talent implies some fragility of the mind, is sure that art is linked to the intactness of the ego. His concept of regression in the service of the ego implies an active seeking of elements of the primary process so as to fashion it, not to be dominated by it.[28]

Kubie also modifies Freudian theories. He emphasizes the interplay between conscious and unconscious forces and refers to a preconscious, which is allegorical, symbolic, and nonverbal and acts as a way station between the conscious and the unconscious. Here, every coded signal has overlapping meanings, but this coded language is the essence of creativity. For Kubie, mental illness is, therefore, in opposition to creativity.

Thus the preverbatim has been understood to be richly metaphorical, affect laden, and textured with biographical memory. What cerebral circuitry underlies this preconscious, preverbal potential poetical repository? The contention here is that the right hemisphere must play a major role.

So what is that special ability leading to a facility for truly creative poetic talent? There is some evidence that the cerebral processing involved in various artistic endeavors is different. This book has mainly addressed poetry and music, but others have tackled a broader spectrum of artists and talented people. The psychopathological associations are different, as has been reviewed. Ludwig summarizes it thus: "Overall the findings suggest that members of those creative art professions that rely more on precision, reason, and logic (e.g., architects, designers, journalists, essayists, literary critics) are less prone to mental disturbances, and those that rely more on emotive expression, personal experiences, and vivid images as sources of inspiration (e.g., poets, novelists, actors, and musical entertainers) are more prone."[29] It will be recalled that Ludwig finds no relationship between creativity of any kind and schizophrenia. It seems a reasonable proposition that different forms of creativity relate to different underlying cerebral processes, reflected in differing psychopathological associations. With some notable exceptions (Leonardo da Vinci, Michelangelo, Blake, and Wagner, to name a few), truly talented people tend to be talented in certain areas and not in others. Poets may be good poets, but they are not generally good scientists or architects.

With regard to poetry, the associations that have any strength are with mood disorders, especially a tendency to cyclothymia or frank manic-depressive illness. Jamison has done the most to revive the notion of the association between such psychopathology and creativity. She notes, however, that persons with manic-depressive illness are not unwell most of the time, and in the climbing phase of a manic bout, mental tempo speeds up, associations are enriched, and output increases.[30] Furthermore, according to Andreasen, it was during periods of normal mood that the writers she studied were most creative.[31] In their own studies, Ruth Richards and Dennis Kinney have found increased everyday creativity among psychiatrically normal relatives of bipolar patients, while in bipolar patients, only mild elevations of mood facilitated creativity. The authors conclude that "there is no one single pattern to the relationship between mood and creativity."[32]

Severe psychiatric illness seems incompatible with poetic creativity. The breakdown of language use in schizophrenia fails the poetic inspiration: the verse empties rather than fills with meaning, metaphors become concrete, expression flattens. Certainly in the early stages of language breakdown, some startlingly original linguistic buds may flower; odd but exciting metaphors may invigorate the verse. The poet's existential agony over his or her developing mental breakdown may break through the lines, torturing the poem and the reader alike with the painful reality of impending madness. However, such poetry soon ceases to communicate, and the talent withers. There is nothing romantic or creative about schizophrenia—or epilepsy, for that matter. These shocking disturbances of the brains and minds of the gifted and the ungifted alike release nothing but an insidious dilapidation of subtle mental harmonics.

Perhaps the link between poetry and bipolar disorder gives a clue, not because the alterations of the mental state that are associated with it facilitate output and enhance well-being but because it reveals something about the underlying neurobiology of poetic language. Poetic language is the language of the special faculties of the right hemisphere, and the associations between manic-depressive illness and poets and their poetry reveals just this biological association. The link with bipolar disorder is not just that at some point in the hypomanic cycle the illness facilitates productivity; rather, the association actually reflects on the underlying involvement of the right hemisphere in the modulation of those aspects of language necessary for poetic creativity. Poetic language is a marker of brain-behavior associations, a window into the role of the right hemisphere for certain aspects of language.

Consciousness

In recent times, the field of consciousness, as opposed to unconsciousness, has become an active and respectable area of neuroscience. Julian Jaynes, in one of the earlier of the new generation of books about the nature and meaning of consciousness, adopts an evolutionary perspective on the rise of consciousness. Language was a latecomer to the primate scene; intentional calls developed into the use of nouns and then commands. The words themselves created new perceptions, which led to cultural changes, which, in turn, fed the development of new words and worlds. Rather as Bruno Snell has argued, Jaynes also suggests that the *Iliad* reflects a state of mind of the protagonists fundamentally different from that of later generations—and he refers to this progenitor of modern consciousness as the bicameral mind.[33] The two hemispheres of the brain, Jaynes argues, were independent; there was no sense of a personal ego, no sense of self but a God-centered consciousness, which at some point fell afoul of evolutionary progress. The characters of the tales of the *Iliad* reveal a lack of subjectivity and introspection; the stories are all about action, but the actions are not consciously driven, they are directed by the gods.[34]

Jaynes rather fancifully suggests that the heroes actually heard the voices of the gods giving them instruction. The gods, he implies, were actually man's volition, but only recently have we recognized our inner voices as coming from ourselves rather than from the gods. According to Jaynes, these voices were organized in the right hemisphere, in the equivalent of Wernicke's area, and transmitted over the corpus callosum and anterior commissures of the brain to the auditory areas of the left hemisphere. With the development of hemispheric laterality specialization, "the language of men was involved with only one hemisphere in order to leave the other free for the language of the gods." With the rise of subjective consciousness, the bicameral mind broke down, instruction came from without and not within, and the written code and the development of narratives came to dominate. "And once the word of God was silent, written on dumb clay tablets or incised into speechless stone, the gods' commands or the king's directives could be turned to or avoided by one's own efforts in a way that auditory hallucinations never could be."[35]

With regard to poetry, in Jaynes's theme, "The first poets were gods. Poetry began with the bicameral mind. The god-side of our ancient mentality, at least in a certain period of history, usually or perhaps always spoke in verse. This means that most men at one time, throughout the day, were hearing poetry (of a sort) composed and spoken within their own minds."[36] Such ancient poetry was close to song.

However fanciful Jaynes's theories may have been, they have been partially revived by Mithen's ideas about the singing Neanderthals, and they did lead Jaynes to suggest that not only song but also poetry may be a right hemisphere function. More specifically, he associates poetry with the posterior part of the right temporal lobe.

Carl Sagan, also adopting an evolutionary perspective, highlights the importance of both hemispheres acting collaboratively in the creation of human cultural pursuits: "We might say that human culture is the function of the corpus callosum."[37] He remarks that the verbal abilities of the left hemisphere have obscured our appreciation of the intuitive right hemisphere—like our inability to see the stars in the sunlight—but poetry revives when the darkness descends. The overriding dominance of left brain functions in human culture, especially since the introduction of written script, and their part in its erosion have become common currency.[38] Consciousness precedes speaking phylogenetically and ontogenetically, and the writer simplifies any experience he or she is dealing with.

Physicality, Inspiration, and the Limbic System

The physicality of listening to music, poetry, and religious incantations, the physiological changes and the shivers down the spine, are often associated with tears. The limbic lobe, the neurological substrate for processing memory and where the representations of the exterior and interior worlds of an individual organism come together, can be conceptualized as the neurological fulcrum where past meets present and from whence emotional tone is reciprocally fed back to incoming sensations. It is the part of the brain that integrates and identifies the self as an "I" and is closely associated ontologically with the development of social behaviors: recall that MacLean's three cardinal mammalian behaviors are associated with the limbic system—nursing and maternal care, maternal-infant audiovocal communication, and play. MacLean further suggests that the origins of human language were most likely in infant-mother interactions, babbling based on vowel-consonant combinations beginning about eight weeks after birth. He singles out the separation cry—a slowly changing tone with a prolonged vowel sound (*aaah*), a distressing cry linked with the most painful emotion, separation, but associated with great craving to communicate—as deeply significant for mammalian development.[39] It is probably relevant in this context that the brain areas associated with primate calls, such as the cingulate gyrus, are close to sites that, on stimulation, release autonomic activity, including changes of breathing and heart rate, sexual arousal, and automated oral behaviors.

The great evolutionary step, then, was the transfer of such a limbic-based language, referred to by MacLean as prosematic (rudimentary sign), to cortical control. Terrance Deacon points out that the prosodic aspects of speech, linked to right hemisphere functions, have features akin to primate vocalizations. "Exaggerating the representation of this background function (i.e., monitoring prosody) to the right hemisphere, and phonemic and word analysis to the left during development, may similarly provide a means for processing these sources of information in parallel with minimal cross interference. Consequently, the right hemisphere may become more intimately associated with midbrain homologues of innate call circuits that still exist in the human brain."[40] These prosodic elements of speech rely more on laryngeal and lung activity, as opposed to the glottis and mouth, and they influence speech over a longer time interval than the rapid control exerted over speech by the left hemisphere. In the course of primate evolution, the larynx has descended in the throat and the pharynx has enlarged correspondingly, increasing the range of sounds produced, especially vowels. Thus rhythm, volume, tone, and musicality all involve cooperation between limbic and cortical circuits but most likely also involve a predominance of right hemisphere activity. Deacon singles out the cingulate area as an integrative cortex, between the frontal cortex and the circuit of Papez, that is involved in primate vocalizations and social adaptations and that could be important in the development of volitional control over vocalizations.[41]

The phylogenetically oldest areas of the brain from which vocalizations can be evoked with stimulation are structures in the midbrain that receive neuronal projections from higher brain areas involved in vocalizations and connect to the cranial nerve nuclei that control the muscles also used in vocalization.[42] In nonhuman primates, the only cortical area involved in vocalization is, in fact, the cingulate gyrus, destruction of which in the human brain leads to the condition of akinetic mutism and stimulation of which leads to vocalizations.[43] Chapter 3 noted the variability and individual differences of language localization in the brain and also the growing evidence of the role of the frontal lobes in language capability. The cingulate gyrus is a part of the frontal circuitry, and in human language skills its linguistic function is harmonized with and subordinated to the prefrontal and other cortical areas involved in the generation of language.[44]

Thus one theory of the development of human language as we know it today is linked to the development of brain areas that are closely associated with the regulation of autonomic activity and intimately involved in the regulation of maternal-infant behaviors, especially distress calls and play. The phylogenetically older vocalizations and expressions, therefore, retain their associations to human language, especially through limbic–right hemisphere connectivity.

Finally, play is saturated with metaphor, the creation of other worlds with alternate meanings, and it often involves ritual. For the adult, the play is a staged event of poignancy, historically emerging from tragedy and rich in metaphor and make-believe. Storr places great emphasis on the close similarity between play and creativity, and in MacLean's scheme play is a cingulate-mediated activity. Storr quotes the following with approval: "The experiences of early childhood are firmly recorded in the lower centres of the *old* brain and exert a profound effect upon subsequent behaviour . . . They are like the patterns of behaviour that are inherited as instincts, or are acquired as the result of imprintation."[45] Play is usually thought of as the pastime of children, but, of course, it is something that occupies adults as well; and it has, since the origins of culture, been central to social communal activity.

Tragedy

Within the history of our cultures lie not only religion, music, and poetry but also the art of tragedy. So much has been written about the meaning of tragedy that to attempt any new interpretation seems somewhat churlish. Nonetheless, the question as to why we go to the theatre or cinema to experience tragedy, for our enjoyment, remains an unanswered and interesting question. The genre reflects separation and loss, and the evoked sensations are autonomically driven: the outcome, when successfully performed, is tears.

The history of tragedy is entwined with that of poetry and music through the festivals of Dionysus, and the effects of tragedy on the individual were first examined by the Greek philosophers. Aristotle introduced the idea that good tragedy provokes the emotions of pity and fear but the ultimate effect is to provoke a catharsis of the emotions. The effect, as Chaucer also saw, depends on the fate of the tragic hero:

> Tragedie is to seyn a certeyn storie,
> As olde bokes maken us memorie,
> Of him that stood in greey prosperitee
> And is y-fallen out of heigh degree
> Into miserie, and endeth wrecchedly.[46]

Tragedy in this context is seen as a change in the hero's state from prosperity to adversity, determined by the general and external fact of mutability. As George

Steiner reflects, tragedy reminds us that in human affairs, the spheres of reason, order, and justice are limited. Tragedy springs from outrage at the conditions of life and the possibilities of disorder.[47] In classical tragedy, human disaster is the subject of fate, whereas modern tragedy plays more on the failings of the human character. For both, however, necessity is inherent in the plot, as is conflict.

As briefly discussed in chapter 4, Aristotle tried to define formulas for the successful writing of tragedy, and within the prescriptions were his definitions of poetry. For Aristotle, the emotions are not so much stirred as discharged, an almost medical connotation akin to purgation.[48] This view, while invoking the physicality of the effects of tragedy, is seen as contrary to an alternative, namely, that tragedy does, indeed, arouse the emotions but that its power derives from the incorporated emotion. This was Plato's view and the basis for his objection to the presence of poets in his ideal Republic: they might arouse the mob by stirring up unruly passions.

Others have suggested that through the act of catharsis, of emotional cleansing, the observer becomes a participant and is enlightened by the knowledge of suffering gained and the wisdom achieved. This is akin to, but separate from, the discovered knowledge of the tragic hero himself—*anagnorisis*—a key to tragic interpretation. The hero's personal insight into his destiny, and his suffering through knowledge, become a part of our own enlightenment and our recognition and assimilation of the tragedy of our own vulnerability and death.

For most commentators, tragedy embodies tensions between contraries. For Aristotle the contraries are pity and fear; for George Steiner, tragedy reflects a fusion of grief and joy.[49] Others refer to tragedy inducing a sense of the sublime, or of aesthetic pain, with a combined emotion of debasement and at the same time awe, elevation, or grandeur. However, the suggestion is made in this book that the tragic feeling arises not from such a combination of known feelings but from a different emotion, one that intimately concerns the self. This is sometimes given names such as tragic qualm or tragic grief. To observe a calamity in real life is upsetting and may evoke pity, or sorrow, empathically felt. To be placed in personal danger may lead to feelings of anxiety and fear. The evoked emotion from witnessed stage tragedy is different, essentially an old affect, generated from the tensions in the play and resolved by the closure of the plot. James Joyce actually refers to "the tragic emotion," which he imagines as a face looking two ways, toward terror and toward pity; it is a static emotion, unlike desire or loathing, which demanded kinesis.[50]

Of all the human passions, fear, anger, and bereavement stand out as universal. They are deeply entwined in the stories of the Greek tragedies but are also bound to one another. Fear generates anger, and both anger and fear are core emotions in bereavement. As outlined, fear and anger are limbic, especially amygdale-driven, emotions; as for grief, the neurobiology of bereavement has not been studied. Fear has an evolutionary history far older than humankind. All mammals know fear, and fear and anger relate to social dominance, the former to loss of dominance and the latter to its attainment. Grief and mourning, on the other hand, have a cognitive component that overrides fear and anger, since grieving is about loss; and because it is about loss of a person or persons to whom one is attached, empathy is involved, as is recognition of the future and the potential of others to mourn for oneself. In preliterate societies, the development of empathy and the ability to appreciate that other individuals have minds (the theory of mind) must have been crucial to the driving of primate and then human evolution.

Through the medium of early religious ceremonies and rights, fear became shared, and fear of death came to be mollified by the potential of the afterlife. Mourning was part of this process. A new type of consciousness emerged with the development of language, and "I," "now," and "here" reified the individual's location in time and space. Artifacts representative of our cognitive projections were created, and this new form of creativity blossomed into art, initially of a religious nature, enabling a binding of the individual to the past and the future.[51] In tragedy, fear, anger, and bereavement combine, from the grief of Agamemnon to that of Lear, and loss is central to the emotion.

This brief discursion into tragedy is given to allow the links between music and poetry to be followed from an aesthetic point of view and to introduce one of the most original thoughts ever brought to the subject, expounded in Nietzsche's *The Birth of Tragedy*. Nietzsche's own life probably bore the tragic flaw—*hamartia*—of an inherited neurological illness, he himself falling into madness in January 1889, embracing a horse to protect it from the cruelties of the carriage driver. Although it is often stated that he died of the effects of tertiary syphilis, this is quite incompatible with the known prognosis of the disorder at that time, with a life expectancy of no more than three years, whereas Nietzsche did not die until 1900, at the age of fifty-six. Furthermore, he developed none of the paralytic signs usually found in the disorder, remaining ambulant until almost the very end. His father died at a young age, from a disorder referred to as softening of the brain—most likely a dementia, genetically, then, handed down to his next of kin—the Greek tragic ideal embalming Nietzsche, embowering him in his own tragedy.[52]

The genre arose in the theatre of Dionysus, with an introduction of the chorus and the Dionysian dithyramb. Great stories were recounted, many based on the Homeric legends, in which through the fate of the tragic heroes, the relationship between the gods and humankind, and the power of both human and divine will, were revealed to the audience. Good and evil were portrayed alongside human error and weakness. The gods intervened in human affairs, possessing the minds of men, sometimes to help mortals but often to hinder their progress. Themes of fate and metamorphosis, reflecting and deflecting the lives of the humans, were predominant. The gods strove to understand the irrational behavior of humankind—though often in vain—but also tested the individual's resolve.

The chorus in the tragedy reflected to the audience the action of the play, providing a commentary on the plot, noting the impending tragedy and the ultimate *anagnorisis*. It is thought that in the earliest performances the chorus recited the tragedy; later, actors appeared, performing with the chorus.

Nietzsche developed the theme that tragedy emerged out of the spirit of music. Although his *Birth of Tragedy* can be criticized as rather unacademic and essentially can be seen as a panegyric to Richard Wagner, it is a historical analysis based on the distinction between the worship of the gods Apollo and Dionysus, the former representing the written rational world (reason), and in the arts represented by sculpture, Dionysus epitomized in dance and music. In tragedy Apollonian beauty fuses with Dionysian sadness, as Dionysian wisdom is symbolized through Apollonian artifacts. While Nietzsche's ideas were startlingly original, they almost certainly arose from prolonged discussions he had with Wagner over many hours at the latter's house at Tribschen, and there were hints of rather less well developed but similar themes in the earlier German philosophical literature and in the works of the poet Hölderlin. Although the writing is complex and depends heavily on the works of the philosopher Arthur Schopenhauer, whose ideas he would soon abandon, the overall scheme is enlightening and thought provoking.[53]

Thus Greek tragedy is about the sufferings of Dionysus, the god with the power to inflict madness, who himself was made mad.[54] He was subject to *sparagmos* and *omophagia* and was identified with animals (the goat) and potency (orgies). However, he represented no particular emotion but, according to one biographer, "represented a force that is beyond human control but that we cannot shut out: the force that takes possession of our minds or places us outside ourselves, in 'ecstasy.'" Lillian Feder argues that the myths of this ancient cult reveal a prototype of early human consciousness, a reflection of the growing self-consciousness of the human mind, and the struggle between violence and creation that spawned the development of human social awareness.[55] The myths reflect a need to control these humanoid drives, and they became intertwined with the development of early languages, religion, and art.[56]

Apollo represents the rational, the boundary setting, "the glorious divine image of the *principum individuationis*."[57] Apollonian art is the art of the line; it is found in sculpture and in Doric art. Dionysian art is music. They are seen as opposites, yet in tragedy, the highest representation of art, they must come together and harmonize: "We must see Greek tragedy as the Dionysiac chorus, continually discharging itself in an Apolline world of images."[58]

Nietzsche argues that since God is dead and life made intolerable with pain and suffering, consolation can come only from creativity and art, in particular, music. Hence his famous apothegm, "The existence of the world is *justified* only as an aesthetic phenomenon."[59] Art is a stimulus to life, it is part of "saying Yes to life" (*Ja sagen*). In this context, then, tragedy for Nietzsche has an aesthetic value. It is not wisdom or catharsis that is achieved but an affirmation of life in the context of death. Interestingly, in some later writings, Nietzsche refers to the creative act as associated with "the cerebral system bursting with sexual energy," and in *The Birth of Tragedy*, the concept of *Rausch* (intoxication) finds frequent reference. The physiological interpretation is implicit.

Nietzsche blamed the disappearance of tragedy from the Greek stage on the rise of a Socratic culture seeking truth through knowledge, driven by dialectics and what he called scientific optimism. Socrates and Plato repudiated tragedy, and for Nietzsche the Socratic dialectic was simply too optimistic, in its view that rational minds could solve the problems of existence, and is therefore inherently antitragic. Dionysus was laid to rest, Apollo became ascendant, and the systematizers and classifiers took over.[60] Nietzsche refers to the intellectual descendant of Socrates as "at bottom a librarian and a corrector of proofs, wretchedly blinded by the dust of his tomes and by printing errors."[61] Rationality rather than instinct came to dominate our culture; and for Nietzsche, decadence set in not with Dionysus, to whom it was generally credited, but with Socrates and his ilk. Socratic consciousness and Platonic dogmatism supplanted Homeric action; the hero died not of tragedy but of a failure of logic.[62] Socrates, who was put to death for corrupting the youth of Athens, was seen by Nietzsche as life denying, because his way of seeing things not only made individuals subservient to a set of external rules, thereby fostering a slave mentality; what was worse, they were rules for which there could be no validation.[63]

Myths are symbolic communications that invest stories with gods and other supernatural beings and ordinary people, who play out questions of who we are and where we come from in a different time and place. They have to do with the origins of life, with eternity, with the beginning and end of time, with destiny, with mutability, with journeys to be undertaken, with tasks to achieve, and with heroes. The psyche is much more complex than Descartes's *cogito, ergo sum*; and it is no *tabula rasa*. While human consciousness relies heavily on language, it is by no means coextensive with it. Some suggest that these myths emerged from an unconscious repository of the developing mind, reflected in Jung's archetypes or, as Christopher Booker calls it, the collective unconscious. In his excursion through the world of stories, Booker identifies a limited number of basic plots to which myths (almost) conform, and tragedy is central.[64]

The contrast between Apollonian and Dionysian modes of thought, if seen in a psychological sense, is an obvious and insightful forerunner of the now developed contrasts between the different styles of thinking of the right and left hemispheres, as discussed in chapter 3. In fact, Nietzsche himself referred to such a bicameral system. In *Human, All Too Human* he states that culture must lead to "two chambers of the brain, as it were, one to experience science and the other non-science: lying juxtaposed, without confusion, divisible, able to be sealed off; this is necessary to preserve health. The source of power is located in one region; the regulator in the other. Illusions, partialities, and passions must provide the heat, while the deleterious and dangerous consequences of overheating must be averted with the aid of scientific knowledge."[65]

Nietzsche's themes were taken up by others, notably Thomas Mann in such novels as *Death in Venice* and *Dr. Faustus*. In the former, the protagonist's visual eye for the beautiful Tadzio contrasts with the spreading cholera epidemic and Aschenbach's gradual psychological decay. In *Dr. Faustus,* it is the disease (syphilis) contracted by Adrian Leverkühn in a moment of *Rausch* that represents the loss of control or an escape from the classical (bourgeois) social mores of his existence—the story being that of the life of a "bold Dionysiac genius."[66] These themes permeate the works of Hermann Hesse, especially his contrasts between the rational intellectual Narcissus, detached from the world in prayer and meditation, and the poet-artist-dreamer Goldmund.[67] Hints are also found in the plays of Henrik Ibsen.[68]

Another writer who has taken up the theme of Dionysus and Apollo in the development of Western culture is Camille Paglia. Giving but little credit to Nietzsche, she contrasts Apollo, the lawgiver and representative of sculptural integrity, with Dionysus, god of fluids, of *sparagmos*, of pleasure and pain—objectification and identification, respectively. Her thesis is that the Apollonian and the Dionysian are two great principles governing the sexual persona in art but also in life, and she has noted the developments in neurobiology.

> Apollo, is the hard cold separatism of Western personality and categorical thought. Dionysus, is energy, ecstasy, hysteria, promiscuity, emotionalism—heedless indiscriminateness of idea or practice. Apollo is obsessiveness, voyeurism, idolatry, fascism—frigidity and aggression of the eye, petrifaction of objects. Human imagination rolls through the world seeking cathexis. Here, there, everywhere, it invests itself in perishable things of flesh, silk, marble, and metal, materializations of desire. Words themselves the West makes into objects. Complete harmony is impossible. Our brains are split, and brain is split from body. The quarrel between Apollo and Dionysus is the quarrel between the higher cortex and the older limbic and reptilian brains.[69]

Alice Flaherty is a writer who discussed her own affective disorder. In her book about writer's block, *The Midnight Disease*, she details her postpartum mood disorder, which had both manic and depressive features. During her manic phases she had hypergraphia, and she acknowledges it as an unusual brain state. On the meaning of life, she has this to say:

> I propose that meaning in the sense of importance, has a great deal to do with valence, the pleasure-displeasure, good-bad dichotomy, that is the most basic aspect of emotion. This sense of meaning has its origins in the limbic system, as opposed to the linguistic meaning encoded primarily in the cerebral cortex . . . The interaction [between these different forms of meaning] reflects what has been called the tension in language between the dictionary and the scream. Without the former we would have no ability to communicate; without the latter, the need to express needs, we would have no drive to write . . . Narrative not only ties events into a chain that makes cognitive sense, it is also an important way of creating a feeling of meaning.[70]

Flaherty here, like Paglia, contrasts the neocortex and the limbic lobe. Both writers, from their own points of view, acknowledge that the limbic components of the human nervous system are as important in driving our cultural behavior as they must have been for those mammals with much less well developed neocortical mantels. The long-lasting lingering limbic links to the right hemisphere firmly bind and bond us to our evolutionary past and, I suggest, dominate our cognition to an extent that has been completely underestimated. For us, language precedes reason, and our language is derived from the heritage of the primitive protolanguage of our biological ancestors.

Religion, Poetry, Music, and the Brain

The nonscientists quoted here are all approaching a neurophysiological view of some links between different brain systems and both creativity and art. The various chapters of this book have attempted to put the neurological perspective rather more precisely and, with some research backing, outlined some of the links between the brain and human cultural achievements, including those linked with religious feelings. No attempt has been made to identify some specific brain center, some God-spot, where God is thought to dwell or where our soul resides awaiting its transportation. There is no such center; in fact, no brain centers for anything are known. We simply do not understand how the brain works, and to kid ourselves otherwise is only an example of our brains kidding ourselves. Neuroscience at present seeks explanations in terms of circuits, and some approach adopting this line of thinking may be relevant to the endeavor to understand religious feelings.

The human brain is more than bicameral and has constituents that have been accumulating and coalescing for millions of years. The basal ganglia, archicortex, and paleocortex (limbic structures) drove our ancestors from their swampy Dionysian past to the dawn of civilization, with the aid of the neocortex, which is itself bicameral, though early in evolutionary development each hemisphere probably had virtual equipotentiality in control over the individual's environment. Life was driven by emotion, but the brain continually made decisions, based on moment-by-moment comparisons of the immediate dangers and needs, demanding a successful outcome for survival. At some point the cortex became, to use Corballis's expression, lopsided, language as we know it flourished, and the dichotomies between the hemispheres evolved. It seems that the links from the limbic structures to the right hemisphere may have remained or developed to a greater degree than those to the left hemisphere, and much evidence has been put forward in this book and other works that the right hemisphere is dominant for emotion, the declaration of which requires verbal (both hemispheres) and nonverbal (motor-limbic–basal ganglia) expression.

Emotion and its release are central to religious feelings and to the pleasures of music and poetry. The thread that unites them, as presented here, is the neurobiology of the nondominant hemisphere, and the exploratory needle is language and its breakdown in neuropsychiatric illnesses.

There is growing evidence that the limbic structures of the right hemisphere are somehow involved with religious experience. The epilepsy and dementia studies implicate the hippocampus, the amygdala, and the frontal lobes, but it is possible to go a bit further. While the most intensely religious experiences seem to need bilateral recruitment of at least the amygdala and perhaps the parietal cortex, the necessary contributions of the right hemisphere are implicated in the findings of investigators such as Persinger and in other evidence as reviewed in chapters 7 and 8. The persistent declarations of those having religious ecstasies involve experiences that classically seem to suggest parietal lobe distortions of personal space, especially the sense of the presence of the other.

For William James, this sense of presence was a fundamental feature of spiritual life. There have been no explorations of parietal activity of patients in such ecstatic states, but more recent investigations of the functions of that part of the brain are revealing ever new interesting features. More recently, the precuneus has been the subject of much attention and has relevance for this developing theme. This area of the brain is one that shows high metabolic activity when the brain is "resting" and is thought to be involved in the neural networks of self-consciousness. It is highly interconnected with limbic output structures and the medial frontal cortex, it plays a role in music appreciation, and it is activated in episodic memory retrieval.[71] Thus it is suggested that religious feelings are reflections of at least nondominant hemisphere function, the ineffable nature of religious experiences being a given of the rhythmic, prosodic, but preverbal abilities of that hemisphere. It is proposed that the limbic-cortical connections combine to infuse autonomic activity with cortical representations of the *Vorgestalt* giving altered sensations of the self and personal space and evoking feelings of the sublime.

Music has long been linked with religious ceremony, dancing, and intense emotional feelings and expression. The right hemisphere seems predominant for these experiences, although, as with religious feelings, it does not act alone. The accumulating opinion seems to be that the right temporal-limbic cortex is of prime relevance for musical appreciation, with notable exceptions (discussed in chapter 6), and in more recent studies, the cingulate cortex and the subcortical accumbens have been shown to be involved with the process of the positive, sometimes ecstatic feelings. These brain structures, which come into play in reward-guided behavioral choices, have now been shown to be important for the development of conditioned behaviors and in the crystallization of social and sexual bonds, which surely helps explain the importance of music for the stimulation of group cohesion, from the beginnings of the social gatherings of Neanderthals to the present.

The third function mediated by the nondominant hemisphere is that of poetry, which I contend is at some level different from prose and requires a different cerebral representation. The evidence suggests that those aspects of language so precious for poetry are linked with activation of the right and not the left hemisphere; a study of the breakdown of language in aphasic and aprosodic syndromes and in those creative writers who have developed schizophrenia or epilepsy supports this finding. The clinical associations between poetry and hypomania are another reflection of these biological associations. They link the primitive drive to create with the development of a limbic-dominated affect-laden linguistic expression of the right hemisphere. Language, religion, poetry, and music are all intertwined with the evolutionary neurobiology of the human brain. Prosody, that aspect of language that is now regarded as primarily a right hemisphere achievement, includes pitch, tone, melody, cadence, timbre, stress, accent, and pauses—the essential elements of both poetry and music. Prosody derives from the elements of a more primitive vocal system, one attuned to the expression of distress and the cries of danger and separation.

These biological associations explain not only why poetry and music have the power to move us emotionally but also why so much art has been religious art, why so many poets have been religious or have undergone religious conversions, and why the act of inspiration that accompanies creativity is so difficult to capture verbally. This all reflects on the capacity and functions of the right hemisphere of our wonder full human brains to modulate these associated kinds of experience.

The leitmotif of hemispheric differences should not be surprising in view of the growth in the neurosciences in recent years, yet there has been a curious neglect of study of the right hemisphere and its functions and an even greater failure to probe into the neurological underpinnings of our cultural behaviors. The reasons are many, but these two deficiencies in the research go hand in hand, since the functions of the right hemisphere are those that pertain to so much of our cultural heritage but from which we must remain hidden, lest Dionysus carry us away.

Areas of the brain such as the cingulate gyrus, which for Papez was the cortical reception area for emotion, and the accumbens and associated limbic forebrain, which literally drive our emotional motor activity, are central to these behaviors. The accumbens, basal ganglionic in structure, closely associated with the dorsal striatum, and tightly bound with the amygdala, represents a funnel for emotional expression, from the release of anger and aggression to the dances of Dionysus as unveiled by celebrants from Zarathustra to Zorba. The *ganz andere,* and that unquenched ontological thirst of religious need Eliade refers to, are ineffable because their neuroanatomical associations do not directly involve the propositional left hemisphere of the brain. Poetry is to prose as dancing is to walking: it is not the distance traveled that matters, but how it is done.

Among our range of feelings, generated and modulated largely by subcortical and limbic structures and the right hemisphere, resides the ability to experience the numinous. This has arisen as a part of our evolutionary heritage, as part of the biosocial development of humankind, and is variously expressed in music, poetry, and religious sentiment. The latter have been encapsulated by the formalities of structured (left hemisphere–driven) constraints such that even in our secular times, many espouse a belief that only practicing religious people are capable of religious feeling. The arrogance of this stance is a remarkable tribute to a continuing ignorance of, in particular, epistemology and neurobiology. To quote Coleridge,

> Hast thou ever raised thy mind to the consideration of existence, in and by itself, as the mere act of existing? Hast thou ever said to thyself thoughtfully, *It is!* Heedless in that moment whether it were a man before thee, or a flower, or a grain of sand. Without reference, in short, to this or that mode or form of existence? If thou hast attained to this, thou wilt have felt the presence of a mystery, which must have fixed thy spirit in awe and wonder.[72]

This passage expresses the ability to have sublime contact with the self and to have knowledge of the self in the world we inhabit, and it is to be contrasted with the hijacking of our precious inheritance of these chthonic feelings by a formalized Socratic deviation from the natural by systematizers and formal religions. As Nietzsche has put it, "The meaning of the religious cult is to determine and constrain nature for the benefit of mankind, that is to say to impress upon it a regularity and rule of law which it does not at first possess."[73]

Poetry and Why We Love to Cry

Listening to poetry being read or music being played is a physical experience that releases a coordinated expression from the autonomic nervous system. Underlying this response is an urge to movement through rhythm, the cornerstone of poetry and music. Rhythm, essential for prosody, generated by right hemisphere intentions and played through the basal ganglia, has been a feature of poetry from songs of the ancient Greeks to the free verse of modern times.

Rhythm is a biological given of our bodies and our autonomic functions, from breathing and heartbeat to the rhythm of our brains.[74] Music and poetry have definable forms (as discussed in chapters 4 and 6) that give an underlying structure to a work, onto which is added, in poetry, the brilliance of content and the creations of the prosodic *Vorgestalt*. This engaging energy of the harmonious function of the cerebral hemispheres acting together seems essential for the creativity of poetic expression—in Nietzsche's terms, Apollo and Dionysus in unison. The autonomic arousal, leading to and from inspiration, evokes in us a release of our own individual creative act. It is here suggested that this arousal is for us a different feeling from the usual autonomically driven experiences we are accustomed to having in our day-to-day lives.

It has been said that we feel pleasure viewing tragedy on stage, in part, because we know what is going on; we know that the actions on the stage are untrue—that they are not, in a literal sense, happening to us. That is somehow comforting. However, what the tragedian or any artist does is not portray the literal truth. The tragic poet takes the shocking, the terrible, and the sublime in life, works on them, and re-creates. The transmitted experience then becomes, in part, our creation.[75]

The effect of tragedy is not, therefore, one of catharsis, nor is it one of arousing everyday passions; rather, tragedy reveals and releases for us an entirely different emotional experience. This is not to suggest that every time we hear a particular piece of music or read a poem we have a new emotional experience—the repertoire of the central nervous system is somewhat limited. The contention, however, is that the experience is different from everyday emotions, such as fear or anger, and is one that is new for an individual when he or she first comes to experience the joy of being moved by a work of tragic art. It is different because of the cerebral circuitry associated with this emotional state—is different from, for example, the neurological substrates of fear—and which for the individual is ineffable but rewarding.

For Nietzsche, Greek tragedy had its origins in the fusion of the Apollonian (individuality) and the Dionysian (with the singing of the chorus) and died with the eclipse of Dionysus. However, Nietzsche saw such fusion as the basis for all art.[76] The Dionysian, in his view, exposes the joy behind the Apollonian beauty, the content within the form. Like the Greeks, we are faced with many questions about, and the possibilities of, the absurdity of our existence, and that tragic effect serves as "a metaphysical comfort . . . We really are, for a brief moment, the primordial being itself."[77] The arousal experienced is at once painful and pleasurable, but the final epiphany emerges from closure—a release from dissonance and a return to the dominant. Tragic joy is beyond fear and pity; it is a different realm of experience, one that echoes back to the emotional vibrations of our ancestral past. It is *ganz andere*.

Why emotional tearing should be linked with these emotional experiences is unclear. It is another uniquely human attribute, but how or when it arose as a specific aesthetic response is not known. MacLean traces it to the discovery of fire, as a response to smoke. The use of fire and smoke was a common feature of early ceremonies and linked with cremation. Crying was certainly mentioned in the *Odyssey:* The sacred singer Demodocus sung about the Trojan War and told tales that made Odysseus weep uncontained tears.[78] This was a personal weeping for the tragedy of the loss of his friends and companions during the war. Odysseus blamed the gods for the whole catastrophe, for weaving tragedy into men's lives but also, then, for the songs of future generations. Those songs became the Dionysian theatre, the communal song, the hymn, the poem, and the core of tragedy.

The evidence from epilepsy suggests that crying is a limbic-related response. There is a certain kind of seizure, albeit not common, in which patients either laugh or cry, referred to as gelastic and dacrystic seizures, respectively. The epileptic abnormality in gelastic seizures involves cortical areas, especially the frontal and temporal lobes and the cingulate gyrus, and the hypothalamus.[79] Dacrystic attacks, interestingly, are reported much less frequently than gelastic episodes and have been reported mainly with medial temporal origins for the epileptic focus; most reported cases occur in the right hemisphere.[80]

Certainly, both laughing and crying have intimate social functions and are crucial in infant-maternal and later developing social relationships. Crying communicates intense emotional states quite directly and explicitly and usually leads to a positive change of mood: people generally feel better afterward, although not because of decreased arousal or tension or the physiological measures thereof. It is perhaps the feeling retained after the act, which lingers for a while, like the flavor of an interesting food on the palate, that is significant, especially when the event causing the crying is one representing closure, as is the case in the evoked emotion of tragedy.[81] The physical act of crying is mainly one of inspiration, and it is very destructive of human speech.[82] This suggests that both laughter and crying evolved before propositional language, perhaps serving to bridge a prelinguistic phase of cerebral development to the later stages. Again, this would explain why laughter and tears communicate states of mind that are often difficult to express in words. In religious iconography, tears represent sincere faith, the weeping of religious statues being part of the public paraphernalia of some religious cults, private crying being an offering to God. During crying, we attend to ourselves, and the physicality of what we are experiencing: "the unloosen'd ocean / of tears! tears! tears!"[83] We love to cry because we cry to love.

This book has suggested that poetry is an essential act of communication going back to the origins of spoken language and closely associated with music, religion, and ritual. Our spoken languages evolved over time with the development of propositional language, and there followed a gradual devaluation of experiential knowledge in favor of propositional knowledge. Our self-created conceptual world helps us grasp and have power over the external world, but many people still mistake our *conception* of reality for reality. A part of the problem is the failure to make a distinction between knowing and knowing about. Propositional knowledge is universal, public; it is the language of science and philosophy and of systematizers. It has become astonishingly dominant with the development of writing, of scriptures and of proscriptions. Experiential knowledge, on the other hand, is unique, individual, and less easily expressed verbally. It is emotionally textured, and phenomenal.

Social and human evolution have seen those aspects of left hemisphere language, with its engagement in the world of things (the Apollonian), dominate over the contributions of the right hemisphere. Much experiential knowledge is preverbal, emotive, evocative, personal, primitive, and private, but it is this knowledge that seeks communication through many art forms. Few people have the ability to release this knowledge and deliver the message. In fact, while there are many talented people, genius is rare. Many of us are receptive to such impressions, though, perhaps because we all *know* our own personal experiences.[1]

This raises some interesting questions about the nature of knowledge and how we may know the truth about ourselves, the world, and our place in it. This quest has a long philosophical history and is beyond the scope of this book, but some observations and comments are pertinent. It is a neurological fact that we do not have direct contact with the world that surrounds us or, indeed, with our own corporality. We have access only to representations, information filtered through the fine filigree of the nervous system; we have no direct, true, or necessarily accurate contact with reality. As individuals, then, we can have only perspectives on reality, and so-called objective truths become rather elusive, because they are illusive.[2] Truth for some, Nietzsche, for example, is encumbered with language, a movable host of metaphors, transferred and embellished. Lord Byron has his hero, Manfred, refer to grief as the instructor of the wise:

> Sorrow is knowledge: they who know the most
> Must mourn the deepest o'er the fatal truth,
> The Tree of Knowledge is not that of life.[3]

Poets have long deliberated on the truth of poetry, contrasting it with other forms of truth. George Steiner discusses the concept of poetic truth, referring to statements that may seem false by a test of empirical proof yet have both internal consistency and psychological conviction. In fact, experiential knowledge is presumably available to all sentient beings in the animal kingdom, while propositional knowledge, available only through language, is an evolutionary latecomer. We have access only to interpretations, especially in any historical sense, and we all have to start our search for truth within our own individual world. We deal in phenomena (things as they appear), not noumena (things in themselves), and our brains contribute causality to experience. Nietzsche sums this up by saying, "Against positivism, which halts at phenomena—'there are only facts'—I would say: No, facts are precisely what there are not, [there are] only interpretations."[4] Truth, then, is not some independent unconditioned universal but is inextricably entwined with the life and experiences of the living individual and the world he or she has constructed. William James discusses this in his attempts to explain religious devotion:

> If we look on man's whole mental life as it exists, on the life of men that lies in them apart from their learning and science, and that they inwardly and privately follow, we have to confess that the part of it of which rationalism can give an account is relatively superficial. It is the part that has the *prestige* undoubtedly, for it has the loquacity, it can challenge you for proofs, and chop logic, and put you down with words. But it will fail to convince you or convert you all the same, if your dumb intuitions are opposed to its conclusions. If you have intuitions at all, they come from a deeper level of your nature than the loquacious level, which rationalism inhabits. Your whole subconscious life, your impulses, your faiths, your needs, your divinations, have prepared the premises, of which your consciousness now feels the weight of the result; and something in you absolutely *knows* that that result must be

truer than any logic-chopping rationalistic talk, however clever, that may contradict it . . . The unreasoned and immediate assurance is the deep thing in us, the reasoned argument is but a surface exhibition.[5]

People do not have religious beliefs because they have weighed all the evidence and have reached a logical conclusion; belief is based on different premises. This alternative truth has been discussed by many other philosophers in relation to art and religion, including Martin Heidegger and especially Søren Kierkegaard. Kierkegaard's emphasis on subjectivity and self-commitment require the passionate engagement of the whole personality in belief, and what he refers to as being subjectively in the truth essentially implies that such truth depends greatly on faith.

The radical shift to monotheism delivered to mankind the concept of one God as an all-embracing but often ineffable personification who created humankind after his own image. Humans should have been perfect, the latter given in symmetry and rationality, in Descartes's *cogito, ergo sum,* the *res cogitans* as a reflection of perfection, or at least the possibility of perfectibility. Kant began to dismantle this deception, at a time when the Enlightenment was unraveling the mysteries of the mysterious, reaffirming but also reexamining the works of God. The Romantic vision, of the individual spirit, of the primacy of instinct and action, emerged, embracing not only the overthrow of divine right but also representatives of that divine right.

Kant realized that a philosophy such as Descartes's could not account for what he refers to as a priori synthetic knowledge, which does not derive from direct experience but rather is molded from experience by the mind's endogenous processes. This opened up many problems, but an obvious one was that truth could only be relative and not derived from empirical observation, since for Kant all knowledge has an a priori component, the human mind supplying form to the knowable world. All our claims about the world are dependent on our conceptual gifts. Facts can be agreed upon, as a posteriori events, but truth, what is known by an individual, can only be relative, leading to the potential for as many truths as there are human brains.[6] The conviction of facts emerges from community agreements, but this is not so for truths, which arise from personal conviction.

The philosopher Bryan Magee presents the argument thus: "Propositional knowledge, knowledge by description, is pale, grey, thin, second-hand stuff compared with the knowledge by acquaintance from which it is abstracted. It is the theoretical as against the experienced, paper notes as against gold." Albert Camus is even starker: "Of whom and of what indeed can I say: 'I know that!' This heart within me I can feel, and I judge that it exists. There ends all my knowledge, and the rest is construction . . . The world is neither so rational nor so irrational. It is unreasonable and only that."[7]

Many have argued that monotheism represents one of the greatest dangers to civilization, worse by far, perhaps, than global warming. Gore Vidal refers to it as the great unmentionable evil at the center of our culture, represented by three antihuman religions, Judaism, Christianity, and Islam; and Richard Dawkins, appealing for an approach to understanding that embraces both the natural sciences and evolutionary theory, asks for the eradication of such faith, seeing it as the world's most evil evil.[8] The philosopher and mathematician Alfred Lord Whitehead refers to religion as the last refuge of human savagery. Politics has suppressed religion and divinities several times in history, from those who cultivated the French Revolution to, more recently, various communist regimes. Philosophers such as Hume and Nietzsche and artists from Wagner to Philip Pullman, have powerfully argued for the overthrow of formalized religion. Wagner's *Götterdämmerung* reveals the ambiguous and devious ways of the gods; only through their destruction, along with their home, Valhalla, might humankind be saved. In Pullman's trilogy, *His Dark Materials,* religious organizations are seen as malevolent, cruel, and repressive; God dies, and his armies are defeated.[9] Such profound works present an oppressed universe, one still in search of enlightenment.

Shelley encapsulates it thus:

The name of God
Has fenced about all crime with holiness,
Himself fenced about all crime with holiness,
Himself the creature of his worshippers,
Whose names and attributes and passions change,
Seeva, Buddh, Foh, Jehova, God or Lord,
Even with the human dupes who build his shrines,
Still serving o'er the war-polluted world.[10]

One of the most popular books of the new century, Dan Brown's *The Da Vinci Code,* puts the case bluntly: "*Every* faith in the world is based on fabrication. That is the definition of faith—acceptance of that which we imagine to be true, that which we cannot prove. Every religion describes God through metaphor, allegory and exaggeration, from the early Egyptians through modern Sunday school. Metaphors are a way to help our minds process the unprocessable. The problems arise when we begin to believe literally in our own metaphors."[11]

Yet in spite of so many writers and artists delivering the message, the beliefs persist. One estimate is that in the past ten thousand years, humans have constructed no fewer than one hundred thousand different religions. To predict the future must have been crucial for mammalian survival, as was the establishment of causality. The world came before the human mind; but the mind is obliged to create the world in order to successfully manipulate and dominate it. Furthermore, the developing self-conscious mind is, in part, responsible for creating itself. Kant opened the door to the light—or the storm, whichever way one wants to view it—that revealed the potential for the human mind to be fallible, irrational, and constructive. However, such constructions, as Nietzsche points out, are all there is—only atoms, air, and opinions, as the philosopher Democritus long ago put it. As Kant has observed, what the mind seeks is not intellectual understanding but meaning. Truth and meaning are different concepts for the human mind, and meaning always takes precedence over truth. Central to the construction of meaning is metaphor, providing links between different cognitive domains, and meaning is enriched through poetry and the arts. Mythical and logical thought are not the same, since many aspects of myth are inaccessible to logic and the truths of logic are without precedent in myth.

Nietzsche takes this line of thought even further. Recognizing the insubstantial nature of truth (perspectivism), he asks, Since the truth has to be created, like any other act of creation, where does the drive for truth comes from?[12] One drive is social: communities develop "truths" that attain their own existence by promoting some purpose within the group. The metaphors solidify, and the "truths" are nonconsciously embedded into the social conscience of the society.[13] Religion is, of course, one such truth about which Nietzsche had much to say. However, such truths also involve power, which operates at the social level (authority directs which statements shall be regarded as true and which as false) but also at the individual level. Nietzsche's infamous, yet quite misinterpreted, concept of the will to power can be viewed from a neurological perspective as the need for any individual brain to assemble and reassemble environmental information, received through the senses, into meaningful *Gestalten,* without which survival becomes impossible. At a psychological level, it is not truth but the meaning of or the belief in truth that is vital.[14] It is not the world as a thing-in-itself but the world as our idea (as error) that is so rich in significance, profound and wonderful. Hence the illusion, but also the aesthetic:

> The Apolline impulse to beauty led, in gradual stages, from the original Titanic order of the gods of fear to the Olympian order of the gods of joy, just as roses sprout on thorn bushes.

Nietzsche tells us that fear led to beauty, which in turn inspired the Olympian order. Primitive man, preverbal, bicameral in Jaynes' terms, struggling to make sense of a hostile world but with newly developing linguistic skills, has a dream. In the dream he visits the past, sees ancestors, and imagines future events. The dream informs him of one certain thing, which is the existence of other worlds, to which he can visit nightly. The other place is peopled by those he knew, and strangers he has just met. Magical events take place—what further evidence is needed of the reality of the metaphysical and of the gift of immortality?[15]

Ever since the first primate developed the capacity to grasp an object between thumb and forefinger, to gesticulate and utter, and, later, to pick up an implement and draw, the manifestations of the urge to create are documented in what we refer to as artistic achievements. Alongside the use of stone artifacts came the development of handedness, the restructuring of facial and neck anatomy, the evolution of cerebral laterality, and the beginnings of individuation—the recognition that "I am." It can be no accident that such artistic creations, for at least thirty millennia but perhaps for much longer, have been fantastically dominated by religious iconography and expression.[16] The urge to create must, indeed, be an instinct basic to the operation of the brain in captivating and dominating the environment, and the intertwining of religion, magic, music, and poetry in our cultural history surely must have biological foundations, similar to the biological underpinnings of language itself. The need to make sense of the primordial chaos of early human existence, the desire to seek explanation, reassurance, and relief from fear, all must have promoted an urgent expression of representations that we now refer to as art. Language, music, and poetry must have been essential in this quest for some kind of harmony:

From harmony, from heavenly harmony,
This universal frame began:
When nature underneath a heap
Of jarring atoms lay
And could not heave her head,
The tuneful voice was heard from high:
Arise ye more than dead.
Then cold and hot and moist and dry
In order to their stations leap
And music's power obey.

From Harmony, from heavenly harmony,
This universal frame began;

From harmony to harmony

Through all the compass of the notes it ran

The diapson closing full in man.[17]

Creation itself here is viewed as music, harmony in nature, with man as the paragon.

The evolution of creativity can be seen as a basic neurobiological force, evolving in *H. sapiens* to a need to explore other worlds, through a belief in the gods, and then to a need to represent them and to communicate such beliefs. Visual images were a part of this, but those created images were simply symbolic images, not faithful reflections of reality. They soon came to represent harmony, the urge for an aesthetic ideal, a desire to create the beautiful, the beautiful to serve initially the gods, and then later, in some cultures, the one God. "The artists of earlier times . . . imaginatively developed the existing images of the gods and imaginatively developed a beautiful image of man."[18] Initially, these were anthropomorphic images, mainly of animals; many were totemic, part animal and part human. They came to represent mythologies, which over time were communicated in early epics such as those of Gilgamesh and the tales of Homer.

Although Nietzsche's views have baffled many, his voice is too loud to be ignored, especially in a century when the irrational dominates our everyday lives and order is reported mainly through chaos. Nietzsche, of course, rejected most traditional philosophy, his own seeking neither truth nor reason, and he recognized the false foundations upon which such artifacts were based. He doubted, even more than Descartes, and declared war on the optimism of logic, views that are being vindicated by much of modern neuroscience.[19]

Nietzsche called attention to the death of God. This was but one outcome of his perspectivism, his recognition of the relative nature of morality and of truth. He eschewed a view that a concept of God could explain anything causally, morally, or with certainty. However, he acknowledged people's need to believe in God and the persistence of religious beliefs, even in a world where such concepts as God had lost intellectual currency. Christianity was Platonism for the people, and religion was not about to disappear. The death of God as he saw it was a catastrophe because it affirmed that there was no ultimate morality and that we were, after all, human, all too human.[20] As the numbers of religions noted at the beginning of this chapter show, Nietzsche was right: the beliefs persist, and, like the tides in perpetual motion, they will not be subdued by a Canute.

Religious cults have determined and constrained human nature, impressing on it regularity and a rule of law that it does not inherently possess, and natural emotions have been usurped through the power of symbol and metaphor and the abuse of language. Newspeak, the official language of Oceana in George Orwell's *1984*, was a grammatically correct yet perverted language, developed to eliminate heretical thoughts, and allowed the people to accept as true whatever statements the party put out, no matter how absurd. Private life and thought are eliminated, and with them any semblance of personality. "The political inhumanity of our time has demeaned and brutalized language beyond any precedent. Words have been used to justify political falsehood, massive distortions of history, and the bestialities of the totalitarian state . . . Because they have been used to such base ends, words no longer give their full yield of meaning. And because they assail us in such vast strident numbers, we no longer give them careful hearing."[21]

To be "human, all too human" reminds us that in contrast to an Enlighten-ment view that our perfect brains have the potential to unravel all mysteries, in-cluding the perfection of God, in reality we represent an early evolutionary phase of *H. sapiens,* and we carry the huge legacy of *H. pugilisticus* at the very center of our nervous system. What other explanation can there be for the continuing cat-alogue of deliberate death and destruction that surround us every day and seem no less virulent now than they must have been to our ancestors thousands of years ago? Perhaps our present state is represented by Michelangelo's statue of the slave in the Galleria dell'Accademia, in Florence—struggling and prefigured, with an incompletely developed cranium and a face of abject mystery, buried under the rock of ages past. Instead, like Narcissus, we view ourselves reflected only in beauty, unable to recognize that the image appears only because of the darkness of the pool into which we gaze and the sinister depths that lie beneath (see back and front covers, respectively).

It is suggested here that religions exist because we have an underlying neuro-biology that facilitates and drives religious feelings and beliefs. These are related to paleopsychic cerebral processes emanating from our evolutionary past and the development of our brains over many, many millenniums. In this view, neurobi-ological imperatives outweigh any psychological interpretations.

Our brains function only holistically, and to suppose otherwise is folly. Simi-larly, to think that there are discrete centers in the brain for this and that experi-ence or capacity belies not only our everyday experiences but also modern neu-roscience. However, specialized circuits do exist and can be revealed by such techniques as modern brain imaging. The left and right hemispheres of the brain manipulate information differently, but it is only recently that the important con-tributions of the right hemisphere to our cultural achievements have become clearer. The right hemisphere more than the left is involved with the creation of the sense of self, is dominant for control of emotion and for retrieval of autobiographical memories, and is intimately involved with processing personally bonded features of an individual's world—essentially, that which is familiar and is necessary for the creation and appreciation of poetry and music, and probably other artistic forms, as well.[22]

This book has been rather specifically about the cerebral associations of music and poetry, but others may tackle a similar exercise with the other arts. However, the approach taken here, which has been neuroanatomical, linguistic, and biographical, suggests that there may be differences. The work of Post and others, reviewed in chapter 5, notes different psychopathologies associated with different forms of creativity, and it may be that, on closer inspection, schizophrenia, for example, is found to be not only compatible with but even associated with specific artistic abilities. Certainly, some of the art forms not usually associated with poetry and music contain similar basic elements, which serves to reemphasize the right hemisphere's role in artistic achievements, more generally. There are multitudes of illustrations in architecture, for example. Next time you go to a cathedral, look at the design of the entrance doors and the surrounding architraves. They will often reveal all the elements of poetic complexity, including rhythm and repetition and perhaps even rhyme and ambiguity.

The least claim made is that understanding the functions of the right hemisphere helps us understand our love of music, poetry, tragedy, and religion, all of which, it is here suggested, are culturally and biologically united. To miss the latter association, the evolutionary and biological nature of humankind and its cultures, is one of the fundamental errors of most present-day thinkers, especially the political and social science milquetoasts.

Art is an essential aspect of our lives, not a socially given luxury or an appendage of capitalism. Furthermore, in modern society it could and should have retained its religious bygones, surely a function that stems from the associations outlined here. As Wagner writes in his *Religion und Kunst*, first published in 1880, "One might say that when religion becomes artificial, it is reserved for art to save the spirit of Religion by recognising the figurative value of the mythic symbols which the former would have us believe in their literal sense, and revealing the deep and hidden truth through an ideal presentation."[23] Art works, we know, are fictional, but this means that "the aesthetic appearance—in contrast to that of priestly religion—can never slide into obscurantism"; "the poetic priest is the only priest that never lied."[24] Art is one of the ways that we experience these combined emotions, and particularly with music and poetry we can revive the deepest feelings of our inchoate evolutionary past psyche. In these archives are the archetypes of the Achaeans and the doom of the house of Atreus.

Humankind is distinguished from other animals by several fundamental behaviors, among them the seven *l*s of human life: language, laudation, lying, laughter, lacrymation, lyric, and love.[25] Without death, there is no life; without life, there is no love; without love, no art; without art, no poetry or music. When asked what, in a nutshell, the functions of the right hemisphere are, Cutting replied, echoing Nietzsche's *Ja sagen*, "Life, it is about life."[26] The seven *l*s are quintessentially driven by the right hemisphere, which, when harnessed in creative harmony with functions of the left side of the brain, give rise to the death of dualism and the birth of the duet. When extinguished by the dominant, dominant hemisphere, they become like a sun eclipsed, visible only through special spectacles.

This world is not conclusion.
A species stands beyond—
Invisible, as Music—
But positive, as Sound
It beckons, and it baffles—
Philosophy—don't know—
And through a Riddle, at the last—
Sagacity, must go—
To guess it, puzzles scholars—
To gain it, Men have borne
Contempt of Generations
And Crucifixion, shown—
Faith slips—and laughs, and rallies—
Blushes if any see—
Plucks at a twig of Evidence—
And asks a Vane, the way—
Much Gesture, from the pulpit—
Strong Hallelujahs, roll—
Narcotics cannot still the Tooth
That nibbles at the soul—[27]

Brief Biographies of Some Poets with Bipolar Disorder

William Cowper

William Cowper (1731–1800) started writing his first serious poetry at the age of forty; fourteen years later, he was the best-known living English poet. His mother died shortly after his birth, and he was sent by his father, a rector, to a boarding school, where he was fearfully bullied.[1] The first signs of his developing illness occurred while he was a student, in 1753, when he was "struck with . . . a dejection of spirits"—a feeling that, after a while, suddenly lifted while he was looking at the sea. In a moment, his heart became "light and joyful."[2]

His next episode was in 1763. He became insecure, his sleep was disturbed, he developed headaches and ideas of reference,[3] guilt, and suicide; he thought people could hear the voice of his guilty conscience, he became withdrawn, and he lost his concentration. He could no longer remember the Creed and sought religious council from a cousin, who was a preacher. In October 1763, after three suicide attempts, he was admitted to the Collegium Insanorum, run by Dr. Nathaniel Cotton, where he remained for nearly two years, guilt ridden and suicidal, with intense religious preoccupations.[4] His melancholia lifted, apparently following a revelation from the New Testament, and he had a hypomanic upswing, talking about his discovery in an "eagerness of spirit." He composed hymns, some of which revealed his elevated moods, others his guilty despair.[5]

Cowper's next mental breakdown, in 1787, seems to have lasted about six months. There were further episodes in 1790 and 1793.

The course and diagnosis of Cowper's illness has all the hallmarks of a cyclical affective disorder, and he was clearly of melancholic temperament. He reflected on a "gloominess of mind which I have had these past 20 years," and scarcely a morning went by when he did not awake with a melancholic dread of the impending day.[6] The episodes of severe illness were intermittent, but he wrote poetry for the better part of half a century. His last poem, *The Castaway*, has been rated as one of the best in all eighteenth-century verse.

Robert Lowell

The case of Cowper is illustrative of several biographies that support the over-all theme of an association between poets and bipolar disorder. However, biographies from past centuries are often difficult to interpret, not the least problem being the inadequacy of the testimonies. The twentieth century provides many rich pickings of manic-depressive poets. Many are North American; their mood disorders often seem to be entwined with personality disorders or alcohol abuse (or both). They invariably knew, admired, loved, or feared one another; and several committed suicide. Some, including Robert Lowell, belonged to the so-called confessional school of poetry, creating public poetry out of their private lives. A considerable part of Lowell's biography is constructed from his own autobiography and from the contents of his poetry.[7]

Not very distinguished at school, Lowell earned himself the nickname Cal, from Caliban but also, in part, from Caligula. He was argumentative and unpopular. His relationship with his father was uneasy and physically intense.[8]

His first major breakdown was in 1949, when he was thirty-two, and the pattern was similar to most of the succeeding ones: a manic upswing, alcohol abuse, religiosity, and the investiture of another muse. Robert Fitzgerald has observed that

> our friend labored under the strain and exaltation of religious experience . . . There were times when everything he saw that happened, seemed miraculous to him; when his steps were directed and his eyes opened; when he felt that God spoke through him and that his impulses were inspired . . . At the end of the week he visited a priest for absolution and then went off to make a week's retreat for absolution and counsel with the Trappists in Rhode Island.

One morning, Lowell "filled his bathtub with cold water, and went in first on his hands and knees, then arching on his back, and prayed thus to Therese of Lisieux in gasps. All his motions that morning were 'lapidary,' and he felt a steel coming into him that made him walk very erect." He went to mass and communion, and then into a Protestant church, and then a Jesuit Church, and then finally to the Church of Saint Francis.[9]

Three weeks later Lowell was floridly psychotic, shouting profanities and obscenities, and he was arrested by the police. He was diagnosed as having a psychotic reaction, paranoid type.

Lowell described his manic spells thus:

Seven years ago I had an attack of pathological enthusiasm. The night before I was locked up I ran about the streets of Bloomington Indiana crying out against devils and homosexuals. I believed I could stop cars and paralyse their forces by merely standing in the middle of the highway with my arms spread. Each car carried a long rod above its tail-light, and the rods were adorned with diabolic Indian or Voodoo signs. Bloomington stood for Joyce's hero and Christian generation. Indiana stood for evil, unexorcised, aboriginal Indians. I suspected I was a reincarnation of the Holy Ghost, and had become homicidally hallucinated.[10]

After this episode he became depressed and was admitted and treated at the Payne Whitney Clinic, in New York, where he was diagnosed as manic-depressive. After some four months of psychotherapy, Lowell improved, and gradually he began writing poetry again.

His second breakdown was some three years later, and the third attack after another two years. Further manic episodes followed, with hospitalizations and attachments to muses: in 1957 (hospitalized at Boston Psychopathic, where he fell in love with Ann Adden, a nurse), 1958 (at McLean Hospital, Boston), 1959 and 1961 (at the Neurological Institute of Columbia-Presbyterian Medical Center, while in love with Sandra Hochman, a poet), 1962 (hospitalized at the Clinica Bethlehem, Argentina, then transferred to the Institute for Living, Hartford, Connecticut), 1963 (again at the Institute for Living), 1965 (again at the Institute for Living, this time in love with Vija Vetra, a dancer), a second time in 1965 (at McLean Hospital, infatuated with Jacqueline Kennedy), and in 1966 (again, at McLean).

It was on the last occasion, in 1966, that he was given the newly introduced drug lithium carbonate.[11] The medication contained him for a while; his next bout of illness was not until 1970, while in England, when, infatuated and living with Lady Caroline Blackwood, he was taken to Greenways Nursing Home, London.[12] Further attacks of his illness were recorded in 1971 and in 1975. He died in a New York taxi on September 12, 1977.

There can be no doubt about the diagnosis. Lowell was clearly manic-depressive, and he had regular bouts of mania, with increasing frequency, from 1949 until the time he was prescribed lithium. Lithium quelled his wilder swings. Often, the manic episodes were followed by depressions, recriminations, and feelings of self-debasement. The attacks of mania were often violent, associated with extravagant spending, passion for a new muse, and religiosity. Indeed, his involvement with religion was lifelong. At school he was to feel God as an infinite power, trying to perfect man, which he felt was the only duty of art. His first published verse was entitled *Madonna*. In 1941 he was baptized in the Catholic Church. Although at various stages of his illness he gave up on his religion (and his poetry), the inspiration always returned, fueled by his manic intensity, as the above quotes reveal.

Lowell seems to have recognized the difference between his sane poetry and that of his madness: "Unrealism can degenerate into meaningless clinical hallucinations or rhetorical machinery, but the true unreal is about something, and eats from the abundance of reality."[13] Indeed, while ill he was usually unproductive.

For months
My madness gathered strength
To roll all sweetness to a ball
In color, tropical . . .
Now I am frizzled, stale and small.[14]

Anne Sexton

Anne Sexton was also one of the confessional poets, although her confessions became notorious, not only through her poetry but also through the exposures of her psychiatrist. Her well-publicized illness and suicide fuelled the creativity-madness debate, Anne Sexton herself belonging, literally, to the school of poetry as therapy.

She came from a family with a considerable tendency toward mental illness. Her maternal great aunt and paternal grandfather were hospitalized for psychiatric illness, her father was an alcoholic, and an aunt and a sister committed suicide.

Although Sexton had suffered some depressive mood swings as a teenager, her first depressive breakdown was postpartum, following the birth of her second child in 1956. She had loss of appetite, tearfulness, listlessness, and panic attacks, and she feared being alone with her babies. She threatened suicide and was admitted to Westwood Lodge, where she stayed for three weeks. There she met Dr. Martin Orne. In therapy, she would report that she could not recall the contents of the previous session, and therefore Dr. Orne encouraged her to write down what she did remember. This having failed, he then tried audiotaping the sessions, letting her retrace them later, noting any discrepancies between what she could remember and what actually happened. These tapes were saved by Dr.

Orne, and after her death they were released to Sexton's biographer, Diane Middlebrook.[15]

Sexton's developing symptoms included violent mood swings, anorexia, prolonged episodes of euphoria and exhilaration, and auditory hallucinations in which "Ugly angels spoke to me. The blame, / I heard them say, was mine. They tattled / like green witches in my head, letting doom / leak like a broken faucet."[16]

She began writing poetry as a teenager, but the impulse later went dormant, being awakened in the therapeutic setting; thus she began writing poetry again at the behest of Dr. Orne. In her first book of poetry, *To Bedlam and Part Way Back* (1960), she presented the experience of madness, whereas in her second, *All My Pretty Ones* (1962), she concerned herself more with the possible causes of mental illness.

Sexton referred to her moods as manic, and others also used this descriptively about her. She experienced constant rhyming inside her head. Her attacks, sometimes with hallucinations, sometimes coming over her as blackouts, were frequent, and from about 1970 her mental health deteriorated. Depressions outweighed elations, although the latter were still there, especially if she was off medication. She reported fugues, which were so frequent that she was investigated for possible temporal lobe epilepsy.

When drugs became available she was prescribed chlorpromazine, imipramine, and later lithium, although it is unclear whether she ever benefited from these therapies. She acknowledged that the chlorpromazine steadied her mania, but she feared its effect on her productivity and was noncompliant because of this worry.[17]

Her alcohol intake accelerated, and she took several overdoses of drugs. However, this did not prevent the flow of poetry, which again seems to have been the main source of her therapy. In 1974 she overdosed, remained undiscovered for a day, and it was feared she had been left with some brain damage. A short time later another suicide attempt was made. Sexton "took a cab to Cambridge and got out a short distance from Linda's dormitory, and then strolled down to the Charles river and danced her way along the embankment, wading in and out of the water . . . and then began taking handfuls of pills, washing them down with milk from a thermos bottle she had taken along."[18] She was again rescued, but on October 4th, after a busy but not extraordinary day, she went home, sat in the seat of her car, turned on the ignition, and killed herself.

Religion was always important in Sexton's life, and her later poems were increasingly religiose in content. She is often referred to as a religious poet. Religious sentiments become most apparent in the last three books of poems, written between 1972 and 1975, *The Book of Folly, The Death Notebooks,* and *The Awful Rowing toward God.* She shared these religious beliefs with friends and apparently used to chat for hours about Jesus, as if he were in the next room.

Anne Sexton, about whom there is much recent and detailed testimony at hand, displayed evidence of a personality disorder, and almost certainly the contents of her mental state were altered by the years of psychotherapy that she had with several psychiatrists.[19] However, a good case for a bipolar disorder can be made. She was hospitalized at least eight times, generally following suicidal gestures or with expressed suicidal ideas, often at Westwood but also at Massachusetts General Hospital. She had moods of elation, associated with an abundance of energy, a lessened need for sleep, extravagant behavior, and often sexual promiscuity. These moods were calmed by a major tranquillizer (chlorpromazine) and were linked to profound depressions. She took impulsive overdoses of drugs, but her final suicide seemed the more intentional, a reflection, perhaps, of her addiction to death rather than to drugs.

> Sleepmonger,
> deathmonger,
> with capsules in my palms each night,
> eight at a time, from sweet pharmaceutical bottles
> I make arrangements for a pint-sized journey.
> I'm the queen of this condition.
> I'm an expert on making the trip
> And now they say I'm an addict.
> Now they ask why.
> Why!
>
> Don't they know
> I promised to die![20]

To what extent the mood swings aided Sexton's creation of poetry is unclear, but she claimed it did. When asked about the creative moments, she said, "Those moments before a poem comes, when the heightened awareness comes over you, you prepare yourself. I run around, you know, kind of skipping around the house, marvelous elation. It's as though I could fly, almost."[21]

Anne Sexton was awarded the Pulitzer Prize for poetry in 1967.

Some Other Examples

The experiences of Cowper, Lowell, and Sexton highlight several important aspects of the alteration of language that comes with psychiatric illness. First, manic-depressives write poetry and do so until their last years. Their poetic abilities seem interlinked with some phases of the illness, but while floridly manic their powers fail, as they do in the depths of depression. All three had strong religious sentiments, which were expressed in their personal behavior and in their poetry and were associated with their bouts of manic-depressive illness. They were all suicidal at times, and in Sexton's case this was her chosen way to die.

Images of melancholy and suicide pervade poetry, especially of certain eras: from the poet and physician Mark Akenside (1721–70) to Coleridge and through to the modern icons such as Sylvia Plath (1932–63) and John Berryman (1914–72). The writings of the latter two correlate with their ultimate suicidal fates, Plath by placing her head in a gas oven, Berryman by jumping off a bridge into the ice of the Mississippi River. Berryman had suffered drug dependency for more than twenty years and was diagnosed in his midfifties with chronic severe alcoholism with associated alcoholic peripheral neuropathy.

Others have taken a similar way out of life. Hart Crane (1899–1932) leaped into the Caribbean some three hundred miles north of Havana, an act possibly aided, as was Berryman's suicide, by alcohol. Hereditary psychiatric illness, alcoholism, and affective disorder afflicted Elizabeth Bishop (1911–79), whose poetic output declined when her drinking was excessive. This is in contrast to the claim of many artists that drugs actually aid their inspiration.

Delmore Schwartz (1913–66) suffered from affective disorder and paranoia, although he died of a heart attack. Theodore Roethke (1908–63), for whom Lowell had a special affection but whom he also saw as a rival, had a manic-depressive psychosis, and Randall Jarrell (1914–65) was killed by a motor car on a bypass, an accident that was assumed to be a suicide.[22] Weldon Keys (1914–55), curiously, just disappeared.

Some Notable Religious Poets

John Skelton (1464–1529) took religious orders in 1498. Although much poetry of the Elizabethan era was secular rather than religious, for some, Sir Philip Sidney (1554–86), for example, religious poetry was a special form of poetry, the poet being God's prophet and the referents being the Bible, the psalms, and hymns. Some view *The Faerie Queene* of Edmund Spenser (1552/53–99) as a most important religious poem, but his work also includes such poems as *An Hymne of Heavenly Beauty* and *An Hymne of Heavenly Love*. However, the *Oxford Book of Christian Verse* gives relatively little space to this epoch compared with the large number of inclusions from the seventeenth century.[1]

The metaphysical poets and John Milton (1608–74) dominated that period. John Donne (1572–1631), George Herbert (1593–1633), Richard Crawshaw (1613?–49), and Thomas Traherne (1637–74) were all ordained ministers. Donne switched from Catholicism to Anglicanism and became dean of Saint Paul's. Crawshaw went the other way. His friend Herbert wrote religious poetry almost exclusively, freely using prayers, hymns, and the Bible as material and patterning some of his verse in religious symbolism. Henry Vaughan (1622–95), too, was deeply influenced by the Bible and by the poems of Herbert. He wrote openly about his religious conversion. He published his chief collection of poems, *Silex Scintilans*, after the death of his brother, in July 1648, after which bereavement he entered a prolonged melancholy. Others included within the Elizabethan and metaphysical penumbra with distinctly religious leanings are William Drummond (1585–1649), Sir Henry Wotton (1568–1639), Fulke Greville (1554–1628), Robert Herrick (1591–1674), Giles Fletcher (1585?–1623), and Robert Southwell (1561?–95).[2]

The metaphysical poets were not alone in the seventeenth century in espousing the virtues of religion in and for poetry, and the Bible was seen as a source of extreme value but above all as a source of revealed truth. Milton and Abraham Cowley (1618–67), among others, noted the importance of biblical themes as opposed to fables as the proper sources for verse: poetry, they felt, had been stolen by the devil and was in urgent need of restoration to God. Milton, who at an early age dedicated himself to writing religious poetry, believed in the plain simple Protestant truth of the Scriptures and in the Puritan cause. He chose as the topic for his great epic the fall of man and the loss of Paradise, which were for him historical fact rather than allegory.

John Dryden (1631–1700) and Alexander Pope (1688–1744) were both devout Catholics. Dryden, who underwent a conversion, wrote "So pale grows Reason at Religion's sight / So dyes, and so dissolves in Supernatural Light" as an affirmation of the limits of reason in a rationalistic age and of the essential nature of revelation.[3] Isaac Watts (1674–1748) was a preacher and writer of hymns who also wrote devotional verse. Joseph Addison (1672–1719) wrote popular religious papers and divine poetry. The poet and physician Mark Akenside (1721–70) and James Thomson (1700–48) both wrote Miltonic poems infused with deism. Edward Taylor (1645?–1729) was a pastor who on his death left a four-hundred-page compendium of religious poems, and even the playful, lusty, atheist Rochester (John Wilmot, 1647–80) is said to have undergone a late-life religious conversion. George Crabbe (1754–1832) was ordained in 1781. William Blake (1757–1827) was a visionary mystic who could see angels and prophets. Blake created a whole religious system of his own, best developed in *The Four Zoas,* in which fear, love, and apocalypse are central themes. The case of Cowper has already been noted in chapter 5 and extended in appendix 1.

The romantic era was filled with mysticism and religiosity, Samuel Taylor Coleridge being an excellent example. He came from a Christian family, and his father was a vicar. Coleridge himself developed a secure Christian orthodoxy, combining the romantic necessity for oneness with nature with the development of his philosophy of mind and the importance of reason, which knows the *Ding-an-sich,* and God:

> And what if all of animated nature
> Be but organic Harps diversely fram'd
> That tremble into thought, as o'er them sweeps
> Plastic and vast, one intellectual breeze,
> At once the Soul of each, and God of all?

Coleridge was interested in philosophy from an early age, and many of his best-known poems are metaphysical. However, as his poetic genius waned, in part on a tide of laudanum, his philosophical writings became more intense. The revelation of Kant's a priori knowledge gave him a vehicle for the development of his own philosophical system in which reason, independent of understanding, justified the existence of God and was an expression of God's power.[4]

The spirituality of William Wordsworth (1770–1850), in contrast to that of Coleridge, was more bound into his poetry:

> A meditation rose in me that night
> Upon the lonely Mountain when the scene
> Had passed away, and it appeared to me
> The perfect image of a mighty Mind,
> Of one that feeds upon infinity,
> That is exalted by an underpresence,
> The sense of God, or whatso'er is dim
> Or vast in its own being . . .[5]

Charles Wesley (1707–88) is best known for his hymns, but he was a religious poet whose works emphasized the individual's religious struggle and the immutability of God.

The nineteenth century provided many more examples. John Keble (1792–1866), Matthew Arnold (1822–88), John (Cardinal) Newman (1801–90), Ralph Waldo Emerson (1803–82), Robert Browning (1812–89), Coventry Patmore (1823–96), Christina Rossetti (1830–94), Emily Dickinson (1830–86), Robert Bridges (1844–1930), and Gerard Manley Hopkins (1844–89) were all Christian poets who adopted Christian themes for some or most of their work and had deep religious convictions. Some, such as Keble, Newman, Emerson, and Hopkins, were ordained. The poetry of Hopkins reflects a response to the wonderful spiritual "inscape" of nature, either indirectly through symbolism, such as in his famous *Windhover* or, more directly, in *God's Grandeur*. For others, such as Patmore and Rossetti ("If I might only love my God and die!"), it was a more personal quest.[6]

In the twentieth century, Siegfried Sassoon (1886–1967), David Jones (1895–1974), T. S. Eliot (1888–1965), and W. H. Auden (1907–73) are good examples. Sassoon took refuge in the Catholic Church, and religion was a source of inspiration for much of his later poetry. Jones, like Sassoon, was engaged in active war service and also underwent a conversion to Catholicism. Eliot did not doubt that there was a relationship between mysticism and some kinds of poetry, although he was cautious to extend it too far. He adopted Anglo-Catholicism in 1927, Christianity becoming a counter to his pessimism. His family was strongly Unitarian, but his earlier poems contain, in addition to their pessimism, overt attacks on the church. However, poems of the style of *The Waste Land* and *Prufrock*, later gave way to those such as *Ash Wednesday* and *The Four Quartets*, reflecting his change of orientation and religious philosophy.

Wystan Hugh Auden was born to a religious family, but in his younger life he adopted different views, including, for a time, Marxism. But his poetry became increasingly Christian, especially after the outbreak of the Second World War. Grappling with the apparent evil of Hitler and the failure of liberal thought to accommodate faith, he began reading theology, attending church, and taking communion. Later in life he thought he came to accept the actual existence of the devil and said he had on a couple of occasions "heard God."[7]

Edith Sitwell (1887–1964) converted to Catholicism late in life. Robert Fitzgerald (1910–85), the translator of *The Iliad, The Odyssey,* and *The Aeneid,* described "moments of vision" and commented that he was brought to the church with "a terrific bump."[8] Many of Robert Lowell's early poems were religious, with references to Christ and God, and the later ones remained religious in orientation but without the symbolism.

Charles Causley (1917–2003) is referred to as a religious poet, as are the two Thomases, R. S. (1913–2000) and Edward (1878–1917). R. S. Thomas, an editor of *The Penguin Book of Religious Verse,* was ordained in 1936, and his poetry often reflects rural and religious imagery. Edward Thomas was killed in the Great War. Roy Campbell (1901–57) was another Catholic convert; Donald Davie (1922–95) and Geoffrey Hill (1932–) became Anglicans. Patricia Beer (1919–1999), born into a Plymouth Brethren family, and Elizabeth Jennings (1926–2001), a Catholic, both wrote much religious poetry.

Allan Ginsberg (1926–98) had a religious conversion, just after the Second World War. He was living alone in New York and had recently been rejected by his lover, Neal Cassidy. He had just masturbated, and he had a book of Blake's works on his lap:

> My eye was idling over the page of "Ah, Sun-flower! Weary of time / who countest the steps of the sun; / Seeking after that sweet golden climb, / Where the traveller's journey is done." . . . While looking at it, suddenly, simultaneously with understanding it, I heard a very deep earthen grave voice in the room, which I immediately assumed, I didn't think twice, was Blake's voice . . . The peculiar quality of the voice was something unforgettable because it was like God had a human voice, with all the infinite tenderness and anciency and moral gravity of a living Creator speaking to his son.

This experience was accompanied by a mystical visual experience and Ginsberg's realization that "the spirit of the universe was what I was born to realize." His body felt light, and he had "a sudden awakening into a totally deeper real universe" than he had previously known.[9]

Introduction

1. Young 1981. A wonderful account of the relationship between brain and behavior, with special emphasis on language and creativity.

2. Elkins 2001.

Chapter 1 · Where Did It All Begin?

1. "To see a World in a Grain of Sand, / And a Heaven in a Wild Flower / Hold Infinity in the palm of your hand / And Eternity in an hour" (Blake 1993, "Auguries of Innocence").

2. *Australopithicans* were walking but not talking great apes. The genus *Homo* evolved some 2.5 million years ago. *Homo habilis* made simple stone tools and may also have discovered fire. *Homo ergaster* was an early bipedal hominid who some suggest used an early form of musical language (Mithen 2005). *Homo erectus*, which closely resembled modern humans, may have evolved around 2 million years ago, made complex tools, and may have been capable of some kind of verbal language (Fischer 1999).

3. The dating of our ancestral past is forever shifting, backward. Neanderthals, who inhabited much of Europe and western Asia, were perhaps the immediate ancestors of modern humans, and their remains have been traced back two hundred thousand years. They buried their dead and wore decorations. *Homo neanderthalensis* is thought to have evolved from *H. erectus* about three hundred thousand years ago. They represented one of at least two lines to evolve from *H. erectus*, the other being *H. sapiens*.

4. *Homo erectus pekingensis* practiced anthropophagy (cannabalism), dating to seven hundred thousand years ago. The further evidence is studied of early hominid behavior, the further back in time the origins of our cultures extends.

5. This is not to imply that grief in some form has not been posited in some animals. What is distinctively human is the realization of that grief in private ritual and public ceremony.

6. For example, the engraved cross has been in use for well over a hundred thousand years and is a common symbol in many developed religions.

7. Joseph 2001.

8. Joseph 2001.

9. Blake 1993, "The Marriage of Heaven and Hell," plate 2.

10. Campbell 2002.

11. This teaching obviously is echoed in Christianity: the evil spirit is called the Lie, and any who follow the Lie are condemned to an equivalent of the Christian concept of hell. Later forms of the religion teach the resurrection of the dead and the renewal of the world. The religion survives in India with the Parsis.

12. Zarathustra revealed two creator gods, the good Ahura Mazda, god of light, truth, and justice, and the evil Angra Mainyu, god of darkness, deception, and malice. In the beginning, Ahura Mazda created the universe, which then became corrupted by Angra Mainyu. Because the first man, Gayomart, was corrupted, and thence fallen, humankind must choose between the ancient way of good or evil; only by seeking the way of virtue can the uncorrupted universe be restored. This quest will be helped by the prophet Zarathustra, born of a virgin. A final battle is prophesized in which goodness, light, and justice, led by a reincarnation (scion of Zarathustra, yet also born of a virgin), overcome darkness. Sound familiar? "Thus a complete new mythology arose, and instead of the ancient Sumero-Babylonian contemplation of the disappearances and reappearances of planets as revelatory of an order of nature with which society was to be held in accord, an idea of good and evil, light and dark, even of life and death as separable took hold" (Campbell 2002, 16).

13. Kant's distinction of phenomena, the world we experience, from the thing-in-itself, the underlying reality behind things, the noumenon, was fundamental. We have no access to the noumena, only to phenomena, a philosophy that has been borne out by neurology. Our brains only interpret and reconstruct reality; we have no direct access to the objects of our external world, nor to ourselves for that matter.

14. Blake 1993, "The Marriage of Heaven and Hell."

15. Nietzsche 1999.

16. Nietzsche 1997.

17. James 1982. The collection was variously greeted as "unique" and "one of the great books of our time." James, a psychologist-philosopher and the brother of Henry the novelist, was a nonpracticing medical doctor. His masterwork was *Principles of Psychology,* a text that is still widely read today by those interested in psychology.

18. James 1982, 31.

19. James 1982, 6, 24. James referred to Fox as a psychopath, or *détraqué,* and a hereditary degenerate.

20. James 1982, 24–25.

21. James himself said that he had no living sense of commerce with a god, though he recognized his own "mystical germ."

22. James 1982, 55.

23. James cites Leo Tolstoy and John Bunyan as examples of religious melancholy. When he was about fifty Tolstoy had an episode of depression: his life lost meaning, and he had suicidal thoughts. After about two years, the "force of life" returned to him, and he came to the idea of God. Bunyan, after years of emotional turmoil, eventually became a minister and the author of *Pilgrim's Progress,* an allegory that tells of a believer traveling toward a new Jerusalem along a spiritual path beset by the temptations of Satan.

24. James 1982, 267, 268.

25. Citing examples, James also notes that counterconversions, to freedom, apostasy, or avarice, were equally plausible.

26. James 1982, 383.

27. Frazer was an English anthropologist, whose text *The Golden Bough* was subtitled *A Study in Magic and Religion* (Frazer 1915).

28. Gods were not, however, a fundamental and permanent aspect of religion in Durkheim's view.

29. Durkheim 1995, 223.

30. Durkheim 1995, 218, 228.

31. Otto 1917.

32. Eliade 1957, 11. The term *hierophany* expresses no more than that something sacred shows itself to us.

33. Eliade 1957, 13, 64.

34. Eliade 1957, 128. Eliade refers to Marxism as one of the great eschatological myths of the Asiatico Mediterranean world. He also notes the religious nature of such movements as those avowing complete sexual freedom, nudism, and the like, characterizing them as having a "nostalgia for Eden." "In short, the majority of men 'without religion' still hold to pseudo religions and degenerated mythologies."

35. Freud 1913. Freud was quoting Goethe's remark from part 1 of *Faust*, "Im Anfang war die Tat." Freud's other main texts on religion are *The Future of an Illusion* (1927), in which he argues that the Oedipus complex was the origin of totemism, rather than of religion per se, although the two were obviously related, and that religious ideas are illusions and fulfillments of the oldest wishes of mankind; and *Moses and Monotheism*, which was published in 1938.

36. Silk and Stern 1981, 373.

37. Jung 1970, 50.

38. Wilson 1978, 169–93.

39. Armstrong 1993, xix–xx. She continues, "Other rabbis, priests and Sufis would have taken me to task for assuming that God was—in any sense—a reality 'out there'; they would have warned me not to expect to experience him as an objective fact that could be discovered by the ordinary process of rational thought. They would have told me that in an important sense God was a product of the creative imagination, like the poetry and music that I found so inspiring" (xx).

40. Feuerbach 1845. All Bible quotations are from the Saint James edition.

41. There are many speculations in this approximate story. The interested reader is referred to Armstrong 1993, Seydel 2001, Byrne 2002, and Boyer 2001.

42. Actually a goddess; see Joseph 2001. The earliest religions were matriarchal, linked to fertility and fecundity—and thereby to Mother Earth.

43. The evolution of ideas about God in Western culture can be followed to some extent from the Bible. The vengeful God of the Patriarchs, Jehovah ("You shall have no other Gods before me . . . I the Lord your God am a jealous God" [Exod. 20:3]), the God of Abraham, Isaac, Jacob, and Moses, was preeminent from about 4000 BC for about three millenniums. Then, until the end of the Old Testament for about six hundred years, reigned

the God of the Prophets, less a tribal god and apparently less vengeful. The Father God ("Our Father, who art in Heaven, hallowed be thy name") was revealed in the New Testament (Seydel 2001). The monotheistic religions, with ideas of a personal God, are, of course, only a part of the story, since even today most of the world's people come from polytheistic cultures. (All Bible quotations are from the St. James edition.)

44. Pseudo-Dionysus, quoted by Byrne 2002, 48.

45. Spinoza, the seventeenth-century philosopher, conceptualized God and the world as one, neither one being reducible to the other. His influence on Einstein is clear. Einstein quoted in Byrne 2002, 129.

46. Byrne 2002, 135. For more about Einstein's beliefs and lambda, see Powell 2002. "Lambda is often called a fudge factor, but it is much more than that. It carries the charge of Einstein's cosmic spirit. It stands for the unknown, spiritual element that the scientist desperately hopes will make each cosmological model more beautiful, more complete, more true. It stands for the insane optimism that the universe is knowable. It stands for Einstein's inspiring belief that science and reason can edge ever closer to the true, divine reality, the mystical secrets of the Old One. By the time Einstein abandoned Lambda, many of his disciples were lining up to devote themselves to it" (Powell 2002, 144).

47. Boyer 2001, 357, 230.

48. In other words, God, for Kant, was a transcendental ideal and could never be empirically known.

49. Wagner 1994, 213.

Chapter 2 • The Neuroanatomy of Emotion

1. Crick 1994, 1.

2. Quoted in Simon 1978, 220.

3. Hollander's (1920) *In Search of the Soul and the Mechanism of Thought, Emotion, and Conduct*, a two-volume text devoted to the history of the neurological basis of the soul and the intellect, is a tour-de-force review of the literature summarizing the views of apparently everyone who has written on the subject since time immemorial.

4. Snell 1982.

5. Achilles prefers to die young and achieve immortality rather than live long but remain unsung. Immortality was conveyed in the songs sung to a hero after his death (singing tales of men's glory); for the early Greeks, there was no clear conception of an afterlife or a Christian equivalent of a heaven. Death was an integral part of the human condition. There are the gods and humans; when the gods fall out it is not so desperate, and all may end in laughter; when humans fall out, the end is tragedy.

6. Bruyn 1982.

7. Shakespeare, *The Merchant of Venice*, act 3, scene 2, line 63.

8. The ventricles, referred to as the lateral ventricles and the third and fourth ventricles, are fluid-filled spaces within the brain. The fluid is called the cerebrospinal fluid.

9. Bruyn 1982.

10. Christianity became established in the fourth century, incorporating Gnostic and Greek myths into its doctrines, including that of the immaterial unembodied soul.

11. Willis's *Cerebri Anatome* was the most complete description of the nervous system to appear by its time (1664). He identified the arteries at the base of the brain (known since as the circle of Willis) and nine of the twelve paired cranial nerves. The word *neurologie* was used for the first time in this text. For an extended discussion of Willis's ideas, see Zimmer 2004.

12. In Descartes's view, the pineal alone in the brain was not paired but was a single structure, hence its relevance as the seat of the soul. Von Haller, considered one of the most important synthesizers of medical knowledge of all time, distinguished irritability (of muscle) from sensibility (of nerves). The medulla oblongata is that portion of the rhombencephalon (hindbrain) below the pons and is continuous with the cervical spinal cord. Within it are the nuclei and emerging roots of the lower cranial nerves.

13. Quoted in Norrving and Sourander 1989, 69. Emanuel Swedenborg, who probably had epilepsy, was a scientist and mystic seer who founded a religious sect. In 1735, he suddenly began studying the brain, in an attempt to understand its relation to mental activities and to prove the immortality of the soul. He is discussed again in chapter 7.

14. The latter is brilliantly explored in Richardson 2001, from which much of this section is quoted.

15. Gall worked on his theories with Spurzheim in Vienna. They examined the brain by cutting horizontal slices, as Willis had done. Gall's theories were highly controversial and, according to Lawrence McHenry (1969), forced him to leave Vienna, but eventually two medals were struck in his honor in Berlin. Gall died rich in Paris. Phrenology was soon exploited by quacks and became discredited. Gall's works were disapproved of by the church and received an interdiction from the Emperor Francis I. Spurzheim later became an evangelist.

16. For an extended discussion of Gall's work, see Hollander 1920.

17. Descartes, seeking the irrefutable basis of certain knowledge, concluded that the one thing that could not be doubted was the fact of his own doubting—I think, therefore I am. In fact, he turned the theological world upside-down, since he proved the existence of God through reason, whereas traditional dogma had asserted that human reason was given to man by God. Locke was a physician who discarded traditional dualism in favor of empiricism, a philosophy that rejected the existence of innate ideas; there was no knowledge, he asserted, without experience. Locke had little to say about emotions, however, and for him, feeling and moral principles came from understanding.

18. Note that the appetite and the emotions were relegated to the *res extensa*.

19. Coleridge, while antagonistic to philosophical dualism, was ambivalent toward the materialists and maintained a Christian, Platonic view of the mind. He was opposed to phrenology, insisting on a holistic view of the mind. His addiction to opiates, however, revealed to him the way the mind is affected by drugs. As Richardson (2001) has noted, Coleridge's poem "Kubla Khan," written after taking opium and famously being only partially written down after Coleridge was disturbed by a man from Porlock, reveals the effects of drugs on the poet's mind, and did so also for Coleridge. Coleridge speculated on dreams

and the power of unconscious forces, and he is credited with first using the term *psychoso-matic*.

20. At this time poet-philosophers such as Coleridge were well acquainted with the sciences, and scientists such as Erasmus Darwin (1731–1802)—the grandfather of Charles—often wrote of their theories in verse; see, for example, his *Zoonomia*.

21. Coleridge 1971, 55–71.

22. Bell was the first to clearly demonstrate the motor function of the anterior roots of the spinal cord, but also, in his anatomical dissections, he revealed the muscles of facial expression in considerable detail. He anticipated some twentieth-century views on emotion when he urged attention be paid to the interrelations between the mental operations and the physiological condition of the body. Cabanis was a French philosopher and physiologist who approached the mind-brain problem as a materialist: life reflects an organization of physical forces, and thought emerges as secretions from the brain, analogous to bile coming from the liver.

23. Richardson 2001, 22.

24. Hughlings Jackson was a physician and neurologist at the London Hospital and the National Hospital for the Paralysed and the Epileptic, now the National Hospital for Neurology and Neurosurgery, at Queen Square, London.

25. The correct pronunciation of *Papez* is "papes" (rhymes with *tapes*), not "pap-pez." It is easy to remember, according to Paul MacLean, since his family stemmed from Papists. MacLean was inspired by Papez's paper, on the proposed mechanism of emotion, to visit him. Papez himself was influenced by the comparative neuroanatomist J. B. Johnson and published a volume of poems called *Fragments of Verse* in 1957. Papez's own text on comparative anatomy was published in 1929, and his most admired works were his comparative studies of the diencephalon and the basal ganglia (MacLean 1976). Yakovlev qualified in medicine at the Military Medical Academy in Saint Petersburg and at one time considered psychiatry as a career. A student of Paul Flechig (1847–1929), he became a research fellow in neurology at Harvard in 1926 and had a considerable interest in epilepsy. He established the Yakovlev collection of brains (more than nine hundred), which became a national resource of histoanatomical documentation. He published his paper, "Motility, Behaviour, and the Brain," in 1948. Apparently written without knowledge of Papez's publication, the paper produced a theory similar to those of Papez and MacLean. For further details, see Lautin 2001. MacLean, who did the most to integrate comparative neuroanatomy with clinical knowledge, is still active in intellectual neurobiological pursuits.

26. The glial cells play a much more active part in brain activity than has been acknowledged until recently. There are several kinds, referred to as oligodendrogia, microglia, and astrocytes. In the human brain, these cells outnumber neurons by at least a factor of two.

27. For more extensive descriptions of the neurons and their transmitters and synapses, see LeDoux 2002 and Trimble 1996. LeDoux's view of things is that the synapse is the key to understanding how we tick: "You are your synapses" (324).

28. A preferred neuroanatomical term is the *isocortex*. This refers to the six-layered cortex, in contrast to the nonisocortex or allocortex, the two- or three-layered, or transitional, cortex.

29. There were many problems, actually, which are beyond the scope of this book to discuss further. How neurons in different parts of the brain bind together to allow an identifiable image is but one; how those percepts are revealed to us as qualia is another.

30. Papez 1937, 743.

31. MacLean 1990. The unfolding of this story and the elegant work of Paul MacLean are fully documented in his book *The Triune Brain in Evolution*, which is the main reference to his papers quoted here.

32. It was Broca who emphasized the connections between the olfactory apparatus and what he referred to as the limbic lobe and speculated that the latter was involved in olfactory functions. Olfaction, while interesting, was of little interest to neuroscientists; hence a general lack of research for nearly a century after Broca on the limbic lobe, especially as the olfactory bulbs in humans are relatively so small.

33. The names for various cortical components relate to their phylogenetic age. Thus the archicortex and paleocortex refer to the earliest forms of cortex, the mesocortex or proisocortex refers to an intermediate form of cortex, with a structure between the paleocortex and the neocortex (isocortex). The hippocampus is archicortical, two- and three-layered, while the neocortex characteristically has six layers. Another way of expressing this is to say that the isocortex has six layers and the term *allocortex* denotes all cortex that is not isocortex. Some refer to the transitional cortex as the paralimbic cortex. For an excellent discussion of this difficult area, see Lautin 2001.

34. MacLean 1990, 247.

35. MacLean 1990, 578.

36. Both give generous credit to those who worked with them to develop their ideas and help with their research.

37. The remark was probably made by Fred Gibbs, a neurophysiologist and epileptologist. The Sylvian fissure is one of the major landmarks on the surface of the brain, seen when viewed from the lateral side. It seemingly separates the temporal lobe below from the frontal and parietal cortices above.

38. There are other examples in other languages: in Latin, *ex movere* (*movere*, to move), and in German, *bewegt* (*bewegen*, to move).

39. Lennart Heimer, personal communication.

40. Scott Young, Alheid, and Heimer 1984.

41. Nauta 1986.

42. The autonomic nervous system is made up of those nerves that coordinate the functions of the internal body organs, essential for survival. It is usual to refer to sympathetic and parasympathetic divisions, and alteration of activity in this system reflects emotional states. The limbic outputs through the amygdala and hypothalamus directly influence autonomic function.

43. Heimer et al. 1991.

44. For a succinct view of these ideas, see Heimer 2003.

45. These so-called parallel segregated reentrant circuits have become an anatomical basis for explaining several neuropsychiatric disorders. However, it is often not appreciated that there is a limbic circuit, outlined by Heimer and his colleagues, as well as the better-known motor circuits, described by DeLong and Georgopoulos (1981).

46. The existence of the extended amygdala is not acknowledged by all neuroanatomists but is currently receiving a lot of attention as a possible neuroanatomical circuit for an understanding of the behavioral changes associated with several neuropsychiatric disorders, from drug addiction to schizophrenia.

47. Dolan 2002.

48. Dolan 2002.

49. Cox 2003.

50. Damasio 1999.

51. Freund 2003.

52. Siegel 2003.

53. Fletcher et al. 1995; Cavanna and Trimble 2006.

54. Colvin, Handy, and Gazzaniga 2003.

55. If its head size were to enlarge too much, the fetus would not be able to travel through the birth canal.

56. Chiron et al. 1997.

57. Vallortigara and Rogers 2005.

58. Vallortigara and Rogers (2005) argue that there is also an advantage at a population level, by conferring a predictability of behavior, and that "there are social constraints that force individuals to align their asymmetries with those of other individuals in the group"— this is referred to as an evolutionary stable strategy.

59. Vallortigara and Rogers 2005. Interestingly, the bias of the right hemisphere for the expression of these vocalizations seems to be present in adults but not infants, suggesting perhaps an environmental adaptation rather than a direct development from a genetic diathesis. There is evidence in other species for a lateralization of the cerebral mechanisms of species-specific vocalizations (left encephalon), for right-sided brain preferences for tasks of spatial orientation in some bird species, and for preferences of the right hemisphere for face recognition in some sheep and monkey species. These data are controversial in the overall context of the debate on the meaning of the laterality of functions in the brain. However, the point is that the biasing of the brain to laterality of function is not a new evolutionary trait that has emerged with *Homo sapiens*, and the evolutionary advantages of such plasticity must have conferred some species advantages. Whether or not there exists a laterality gene, which in *H. sapiens* has driven speciation, is a hotly argued debate; see Crow 2002.

60. Gloor 1997; Hermann and Chhambria 1980.

61. Leutmezer et al. 2003; Blok, Willemsen, and Holstege 1997.

62. Shelley and Trimble 2004.

63. Tucker and Williamson 1984; Glick, Alan, and Hough 1982; Amaducci et al. 1981.

64. It is the case that the first words of the first known poetry, Homer's *Iliad*, contain the translated word *anger* (the anger of Achilles). It is a poem and a song ("Sing, goddess, of the anger of Achilles").

65. Coleridge 1971, 109.

66. MacLean 1990, 578.

Chapter 3 · *Language and the Human Brain*

1. Some assert that it is even later, with *Homo erectus,* about 1.5 million years ago. The interested reader should refer to Pinker 1994 and Crow 2002. There is also a useful review in *Scientific American,* "New Look at Human Evolution," 2004.

2. There is continuing debate about this, with occasional claims that chimpanzees have attained the status of language use akin to human language (Deacon 1997, 124–25; also see Pinker 1994, 340).

3. Goethe suggests the same; see "Im Anfang war die Tat," *Faust,* part 1, line 1237.

4. For a detailed discussion, see Corballis 2003. The picture is slowly changing as new data, especially genetic analyses, become available. The details are less relevant than the fact that it seems likely that a protolanguage developed before language as we know it, and that language did not suddenly appear in the form we recognize today. Furthermore, language as we know it is a relatively recent evolutionary development. For some dissent and discussion, see also Crow 2002.

5. The so-called theory of mind is relevant both to concepts of cooperation and to the development of language and religion; Baron-Cohen 1999.

6. Cited in Piattelli-Palmarini 1980. While Chomsky seems to have many detractors, it is difficult to counter his arguments when it comes to observing the stunning skill with which children of all cultures acquire so effortlessly such complex grammars as are necessary for language.

7. Chomsky 2002.

8. The central tenet of the behavioralists was essentially the rejection of the existence of specific mental events, a standpoint quite incompatible with developments in cognitive neuroscience, let alone anyone's personal experience.

9. Ogden and Richards 1985, 12.

10. Leach 1976. A *metonym* is a figure of speech in which the name of one thing is used for something else, which it suggests—for example, "the crown" to mean the monarchy. A sign such as an arrow pointing upward can only refer to one direction.

11. Critchley 1970, 138.

12. Orwell's book *1984,* published in 1949, has to be one of the most important books ever written in the English language, serving as a warning about the dehumanization of *Homo sapiens* through the relentless power of governments and their abuse of language. Winston Smith's search for truth comes up against the constructed opacities of government, with tissues of lies and contradictions; eventually he is discovered and reeducated to political correctness, and all his human feeling and inspiration are extinguished.

13. Flexibility also allows for a third, propaganda.

14. Quoted in Critchley 1970, 159; Coleridge 1971, 85.

15. The term *mentalese* was first introduced in Fodor 1975.

16. Corballis 2003.

17. Quoted in Riese 1977, 20.

18. Critchley 1970, 75–91.

19. Nietzsche 1974, 179; also see Nietzsche 1997, 159.

20. McEwan 2005, 81.

21. Pinker 1994, 81.

22. This may not at first seem obvious, and there will always be highly articulate people who are exceptions. Nevertheless, a writer has the time to consult dictionaries, thesauruses, and even rhyming manuals. It is also possible in written texts, notably in poetry, to use a more flexible grammar than is demanded by spoken language.

23. The interested reader can consult Critchley 1970, Benson 1979, and Kirshner 1994.

24. *Aphasia* is an acquired loss of language. Earlier authors used such terms as *alalia* and *aphemia*, and a commonly used variant is *dysphasia*. Aphasia has little or nothing to do with mutism, and most aphasic patients have some speech, though it is, by definition, aberrant.

25. After Broca's presentations, M. Dax complained that his father Gustave Dax (1771–1837) had made similar observations in 1836.

26. Wernicke was a German neurologist who attempted to develop a comprehensive account of cerebral localization.

27. A *paraphasia* is a replacement word that is a fragment of jargon or a word other than the one intended for use, therefore given inappropriately. Sometimes a new word is given, with no apparent meaning; this is referred to as a *neologism*. *Paragraphia* is the written equivalent of paraphasia.

28. Lesser et al. 1986.

29. Because Broca's area lies adjacent to areas of the brain that modulate the motor movements of the face, lips, and tongue, it has been suggested that much of the language deficit after damage to this area is an articulatory, as opposed to an aphasic, problem. A good review of some of the latest imaging work on the role of the left hemisphere in language function is Price 2000.

30. Ojeman 1991.

31. There is some evidence that in epilepsy the representation of language in the brain is altered, see Abou-Khalil 1995, 234–35.

32. In the words of John Hughlings Jackson, "To locate the damage which destroys speech and to locate speech are two different things" (quoted in Taylor 1958, 130). The development of neurology as a clinical discipline arose from the successes of the physicians of the latter part of the nineteenth century identifying from clinical signs where in the brain a patient's lesion was located. However, the idea that because a certain function is put out of order by a lesion the function itself somehow resides in that part of the brain was misleading, and yet it dominated neurological thinking for most of the twentieth century. Even the concept of a function was unclear, and it remains so today.

33. Apraxia is one consequence of damage to the left hemisphere. Different varieties have been described, but the essential clinical problem is the failure of the patient to execute coordinated motor tasks (for example, "Show me how you would salute," or "Show me how you would take a cigarette out of a packet, put it in your mouth, and light it") in the presence of intact comprehension and an otherwise intact motor system.

34. Taylor 1958, 121–28, 129–45.

35. "But here we must mention that this distinction is not absolute; there are nowhere in the body absolute demarcations betwixt voluntary and automatic movements; and there

are in health all gradations from the most automatic use of words to their most voluntary use" (quoted in Taylor 1958, 133).

36. Quoted in Taylor 1958, 165.

37. Psychopathology is that branch of medicine that studies abnormal mental states; neuropathology, in that time and in this context, was essentially the art of postmortem brain examination.

38. The standard classification systems are those presented in the *Diagnostic and Statistical Manual of Mental Disorders* of the American Psychiatric Association (APA 1994), the latest edition of which is referred to as *DSM IV TR*, and the European equivalent, the World Health Organization's *International Classification of Diseases* (WHO 1992). The *DSM IV* allows for more than two thousand designations of affective disorder.

39. Freud, it should be noted, was first and foremost a neurologist. He developed his own scheme and school of psychology based on his observations in that capacity, but he had no formal psychiatric training. Wagner Juregg was said to have noted at the 1899 Board for Professional Candidates that "Dr. Freud is only *Dozent* for neuropathology and has never really worked in Psychiatry" (personal correspondence, Professor Pierre Pichot).

40. Most neurologists held no interest in the mind, and most psychiatrists had no interest in the brain. There were notable exceptions, however, who kept alive the traditions of neuropsychiatry and paved the way for the development of biological psychiatry and a revamped neuropsychiatry (see Trimble 1988).

41. Henrik Ibsen's play *Ghosts* is but one example of this theme. However, French authors, such as Émile Zola, and even Charles Dickens echo the same sentiments.

42. See Schachter and Devinsky 1997.

43. Sacks 1985. Cases of fascinating, abnormal behavior following neurological lesions to the parietal lobes of the brain have been described for years. The bizarre presentations of right parietal lesions seem the more dramatic, perhaps because of the intact verbal abilities of patients, which allows them to discuss their seemingly strange (psychotic?) behavior apparently rationally.

44. Cutting 1990.

45. Monrad-Krohn 1947.

46. Critchley 1970, 248–61.

47. Quoted in Alajouanine and L'hermitte 1964, 617–18. ("The incapacity to maintain the caesura and the appropriate rhythm, as well as some other faults, but with a good arrangement of rhymes.")

48. Ross 1997.

49. Ross 1997.

Chapter 4 · The Other Way of Using Language

1. Jonson, *Song to Celia*.

2. Rousseau 1986, 11, 51. Rousseau (1712–78) was a Romantic philosopher. His "Essay on the Origin of Languages" was first published in 1852.

3. Aristotle 1970. Plato (ca. 428–348 BC) is best known for his theory of forms, which states that the true reality of an object is to be found in its rational form, or structure, and

not in its material appearance. To seek the truth, reason, unhindered by the emotions, is alone necessary.

4. Aristotle 1970, 23. An *iambus* is a foot consisting of one short or unstressed syllable followed by one long or stressed one. Iambic verse is that composed with iambic feet. Aristotle refers to the original use of the term *iambic,* related to *iambize,* or lampoon. This was "back and forth" speech. Iambe was the daughter of Pan and Echo and is credited as the founder of iambic verse.

5. Aristotle 1970, 59–61.

6. Ascham 1570, 30. Roger Ascham (1515–68) was known for his lucid prose style.

7. Puttenham 1967, 8.

8. Dr. Samuel Johnson is best known for his *Dictionary of the English Language,* published in 1755.

9. Wordsworth and Coleridge 1963; Coleridge 1971.

10. Wordsworth and Coleridge 1963, 1.

11. Coleridge 1971, 3, 172. For Coleridge's discussion on meter and poetry, see 196–205.

12. This brilliant development of philosophical ideas by Coleridge anticipated developments in neurology regarding brain function that are even today only just becoming appreciated (and are noted in chapter 2). The influence of continental philosophy on British neuropsychiatry remains negligible. Coleridge wanted to "make the senses out of the mind—not the mind out of the senses" (Coleridge 1971, 167).

13. "A more than usual state of emotion with more than usual order" (quoted in Holmes 1998, 388).

14. Shelley 1888b, 38, 4–7.

15. Housman 1989, 47. Fanny Brawne was Keats's muse.

16. Frye 1971, 78, 251.

17. Eliot 1933, 111.

18. Eliot, "Burnt Norton."

19. Eliot 1933, 148.

20. Pottle 1941, 57–79, 74.

21. Quoted in Hamburger 1996, 4 ("La poésie ne peut pas, sous peine de mort ou de déchéance, s'assimilier á la science ou á la morale; elle n'a pas la vérité pour objet, elle n'a qu'Elle-méme"; Hamburger's translation).

22. Pottle 1941, 113.

23. This is particularly true of French, Spanish, Italian, and Japanese poetry, whereas German poetry, like English, was mainly stressed.

24. Thomas Gray, "Elegy Written in a Country Churchyard."

25. Shakespeare, "Ariel's Song," from *The Tempest.*

26. *New Encyclopaedia Britannica,* 15th ed., s.v. "Poetry."

27. The root of the word is *meta* (to carry) and *pherin* (over). For an excellent review of the whole topic, see Hawkes 1972. The following account owes much to Hawkes's analysis.

28. Jaspers 1959.

29. Thomas Campion (1567–1620), from *The Third and Forth Booke of Ayres,* 1617.

30. Emily Dickinson, "Poem."

31. Johnson 1905, 14–15. He refers here to the conceits of the metaphysical poets, whose poetry he considered contrived.

32. Hawkes 1972, 77.

33. "C'est par et à travers la poésie que l'ame entrevoit les splendeurs situées derrière le tombeau"; quoted in Chadwick 1971, 3.

34. T. S. Eliot, *The Love Song of J. Alfred Prufrock.*

35. Empson 1991, 3. The book was first published in 1930.

36. This is not to suggest that these are all present in all written texts referred to as poetry. These are merely linguistic components noted over time by various critics as important in poetry.

37. Winston Churchill is credited with saying that ambiguity caused the outbreak of two world wars.

38. W. H. Auden, quoted in Fuller 1989, 30.

39. Luys 1881.

40. Gainotti 1972, 53.

41. Starkstein and Robinson 1993. The term *subcortical* refers to the nuclei of the brain that lie beneath the cerebral cortex but are intimately connected with the cortex. They include the large basal ganglia, which have a role in emotional and motor expression, as discussed in chapter 2.

42. Temporal lobectomy is being done in increasing numbers at the present time. With good patient selection, some 70 percent will be seizure free, with lasting benefit. The operation is widely underperformed, and many thousands of patients could benefit from the procedure.

43. Terzian 1964, 233, 235.

44. Rosadini and Rossi 1967.

45. A more recent replication of these results has been published by Gregory Lee and colleagues (1990). They observed the emotional responses of forty-four patients with temporal lobe epilepsy awaiting surgery and were able to confirm that laughter and elated mood were statistically recorded more frequently following right-hemisphere injections of amylobarbitone and crying more frequently with left-sided injections. In their discussion of the findings they draw attention to the admittedly variable data on hemisphere inactivation in the literature but point out the consistency among observers with regard to results of injections to the right side. Euphoria is constantly seen (60–100 percent), but in their series, in keeping with the other studies, it was observed as the effects of the amylobarbitone were wearing off.

46. Bryden and Ley 1983.

47. Functional magnetic resonance imaging has the advantage of being noninvasive and of not requiring the medium of radioactivity. It is based on the principle of magnetic imaging, in which signals from the brain are analyzed and converted into tomographic images.

48. Price 2000.

49. Cutting 1997, 453.

50. Gardner et al. 1975.

51. Wapner, Hamby, and Gardner 1981.

52. Winner and Gardner 1977.

53. Brownell et al. 1994.

54. Bottini et al. 1994.

55. By way of replication is the study using fMRI conducted by Peter Liddle and colleagues (Kiehl et al. 1999). They noted that during verbal processing, there was bilateral activation of the temporal, frontal, and parietal regions, but that abstract words activated preferentially the right temporal cortex, and concrete words the left temporal cortex.

56. Shallice et al. 1994. This has been replicated by Tulving et al. 1994.

57. In a further exploration of episodic memory using PET, Nancy Andreasen and colleagues compared the brain areas activated by random episodic silent thinking with those affected by focused episodic memories and semantic memory. The first type of thinking was thought to be representative of free thinking, or free association during silent introspection. Again, right hemisphere changes predominated, and the main areas involved included the frontal and temporal cortex, the insula, and the precuneus (Andreasen et al. 1995).

58. This is not to embark on a discussion of the cerebral basis of consciousness, which is now a considerable industry in its own right. However, the split-brain experiments reveal the importance of the left hemisphere for the revelation and expression of conscious experience.

59. Cook 2002, 169.

60. The title of the book by Corballis (1991) is *The Lopsided Ape*.

61. This was determined by assessment from endocasts. The interested reader is referred to Corballis 2003 and Fischer 1999.

62. *Homo erectus* did not have sufficient control over breathing to control exhalation.

63. For further discussion and dating, see Tattersall 2003.

64. It is now accepted that asymmetry is not a feature only of human brains, as discussed in chapter 2, but the clarity of the lateralization is distinctive of the human brain (Corballis 2003).

65. By this I am referring to the now known fact that during the early life of an infant, the developing brain undergoes considerable pruning of not only neuronal numbers but also synaptic connectivity. Perhaps this process, allowing for more neuronal reorganization and greater environmental influences on the developing brain, also allowed for some cerebral talents to emerge, which had immediate survival significance. In some individuals it may allow for extraordinary talents to flourish (which may not have been so advantageous from an evolutionary point of view), and a Mozart develops. However, the process left *Homo sapiens* with a smaller but more efficient brain than some predecessors.

66. So with loss of function of the right hemisphere, the patient attends only to the space attended to by the left hemisphere, but with loss of left hemisphere function, both sides are still attended to.

67. Corballis 2003, 175.

68. Hécaen and Angelergues 1963.

69. Glezerman and Balkoski 1999, 55.

70. Cutting 1990, 107.

Chapter 5 · The Breakdown of Language

1. It is not proposed here to visit the tiresome argument about what is normal and what abnormal. Neither will the equally tiresome quarrel about whether psychiatric illness even exists be considered. It is enough to respect the fact that some people find it hard to live in the world because of communication problems, that such problems are often the result of abnormal cerebral function, and that one reflection of the latter is represented through language.

2. Aretaeus, a physician from Cappadocia, was a follower of the Hippocratic school of medicine.

3. Cullen 1800. Cullen was a professor of physics at Edinburgh. The term *nervous diseases* was applied to those disorders of the brain that provoked nervous symptoms. It failed to survive the division of nineteenth-century neuropsychiatry into twentieth-century neurology and psychiatry. Until 1988 the National Hospital for Neurology and Neurosurgery in London was called the National Hospital for Nervous Diseases. The name had been changed in 1948 from the National Hospital for the Paralysed and the Epileptic.

4. That someone can become mentally ill in association with an acute brain disorder such as an infection, or following a head injury, and that the illness will be accompanied by confusion and hence disturbed thinking is an old idea, and readily understandable, even by those with no medical knowledge. That someone can be mentally ill and not confused is much more difficult for lay people to grasp. That the latter picture may also be the outcome of disturbed, pathological brain action has not fully penetrated through to the medical profession (though it is readily denied by people with no medical knowledge whatsoever).

5. Pinel, a physician to the Bicétre and Salpêtrière, was most famous for his supposed call to free the insane from repression and for his enlightened methods of treating psychiatric patients without chains. Falret was also a physician to the Salpêtrière. Griesinger was professor of mental science at the University of Berlin.

6. For a full review of this fascinating topic, see Temkin 1971.

7. Symptoms are complaints patients make to friends, relatives, doctors, or others. Signs are observed, mostly by the physician, but the signs of many behavior disorders become apparent first to relatives. It is the job of the physician to assemble signs and symptoms into (for the doctor) a recognizable Gestalt, referred to as a syndrome. Syndromes are classified and are the clinical representatives of illness.

8. Kraepelin's fundamental division of psychiatric illness into manic-depressive illness and schizophrenia has had continuing influence on psychiatric thinking. He was the founder of the Research Institute in Munich, which attracted many famous neuroscientists of the early twentieth century. Bleuler was a Zurich psychiatrist who reworked Kraepelin's concepts of dementia praecox.

9. The rubric *personality disorder* occasions much controversy. However, if we all have a personality, there is presumably a statistically defined population that is "normal" as well as variants from that. One definition, given by Kurt Schneider (1887–1967), is that people

with abnormal personalities are those who suffer from their abnormality or through whose personality society suffers (Schneider 1959).

10. Jaspers 1963, 428.

11. For a review, see Trimble 1988.

12. The terms *bipolar disorder* and *manic-depressive disorder* refer to the same clinical presentations. As used in this text, the two terms follow closely the ideas embodied in later editions of the World Health Organization's *International Classification of Diseases* (WHO 1992) and the American Psychiatric Association's *Diagnostic and Statistical Manual of Mental Disorders* (APA 1994). Older authors cited in the text often used terms not found in those manuals, and some highly recognizable neuropsychiatric disorders such as Gastaut-Geschwind syndrome do not appear at all.

13. This is not the appropriate place to describe all the categories of the mental dispositions under discussion, nor is it intended to list the various diagnostic requirements for the disorders. There are many places to find all this, but reference to the original manuals can be helpful.

14. A delusion is a false belief, out of keeping with a patient's cultural milieu and unshakable.

15. In clinical terms, hypomania is a milder variety of mania.

16. Fish 1974, 35.

17. There are many different diagnostic schemas, but all emphasize non-mood-congruent hallucinations and delusions and various thought and speech abnormalities. Gesture is also disturbed, and abnormalities of movement are often observed (Trimble 1996).

18. Morice and McNicol 1985, 59.

19. It is a sad fact that many writers who pronounce on schizophrenia seem to have little contact with patients, other than, perhaps, by way of an academic case conference. No one should pronounce on the subject who has not treated psychotic patients and listened to their woeful stories—except, that is, for schizophrenics themselves.

20. Cutting 1990, 491, 487. In contrast to many writers, Cutting notes the failure of the right hemisphere in schizophrenia.

21. Sims 1988, 135–36. *Clang* refers to when similar words clumsily reverberate together, such as *clang* and *bang*.

22. These terms are for the most part self-explanatory, but for further definitions, see Fish 1974, 48–51.

23. Fish 1974, 36.

24. Cutting 1997.

25. Pies 1985, 14.

26. Seizures and epilepsy are not the same thing. Epilepsy is the liability to have recurrent epileptic seizures, the latter being the outward manifestation (sign) of epilepsy (syndrome). The latest classifications have been developed by the International League Against Epilepsy; a review can be found in Trimble 1991.

27. It is estimated that 60–70 percent of patients with epilepsy can be successfully treated or will go into remission, but the remainder become treatment challenges. The investigation and management of this group is beyond the scope of this chapter, but the importance of the data is that temporal lobe epilepsy is found in a substantial number of the

patients who have continuing seizures and hence ongoing disturbance of cerebral function.

28. A review of the historical developments of these concepts and the literature on the various forms of psychosis associated with epilepsy can be found in Trimble 1991.

29. For reasons that are not always clear, these behavioral syndromes found in patients with epilepsy have occasioned much controversy. For a full review, see Trimble 1988, 1991.

30. For discussion of the relationship between epilepsy and affective disorders, see Robertson 1988.

31. Fish 1974, 36.

32. Waxman and Geschwind 1974.

33. For a fuller review see Trimble 1986.

34. Only a minority of patients develop these syndromes, and the full syndrome is not necessarily found in all patients. Some exhibit only some of the features. Some patients display hypergraphia more in association with their seizures (postictally); in others, it waxes and wanes. Hypergraphia is probably an all-or-nothing phenomenon, rather than some graded trait, and, as such, is easily missed in small groups of patients.

35. Roberts, Robertson, and Trimble 1982. Of fifteen published cases, none had a localized left-sided focus; they were all unilateral right or bilateral.

36. Van Vugt et al. 1996. Utilization behavior is seen in many patients with lesions of the frontal lobes of the brain. They simply use objects placed in front of them, irrespective of a need to use them. The classic example is the patient who will put on spectacles if presented with them, even if he or she is already wearing a pair. A related frontal lobe sign is imitation behavior, in which patients imitate the gestures of those examining them, regardless of how silly the gestures may be.

37. Okamura, Motomura, and Asaba 1989.

38. Kraepelin 1919, 99.

39. Critchley 1970, 355.

40. The Prinzhorn collection is discussed later in the chapter. See note 49.

41. Penfield and Perot 1963.

42. Roberts, Robertson, and Trimble 1982.

43. Temkin 1971.

44. Jamison 1993; Winokur and Tsuang 1996.

45. Slater 1979, 97–98. Slater later examines the biographies of the composers Robert Schumann and Hugo Wolf, both of whom had manic-depressive illness. He quotes others with similar diagnoses, including Peter Cornelius, George Friederic Handel, Heinrich Marschner, Max Reger, Franz Schubert, and Johann Strauss.

46. Slater 1979, 98.

47. Michael Trimble, "Schizophrenia and Poetry," unpublished paper.

48. One contemporary commentator referred to "Song to David" as a "fine piece of Ruins." The "Jubilate" was written during his confinement, and its contents have been discussed endlessly. To a psychopathologist, it reflects the breakdown of his linguistic skills as his illness progresses.

49. J. H. Plokker (1964, 70), in his book on art and psychosis, writes of artists who "become affected by the schizophrenic process and whose productivity—often after an initial

rise—either rapidly ceased completely or showed a rapid qualitative deterioration until there finally remained nothing but senseless bungling." To support his view he quotes the biographies of various schizophrenic painters such as Carl Frederik Hill (1851–1906) and Ernst Josephson (1841–1911)—both Swedish artists—as well as Vincent van Gogh, the playwright August Strindberg, and the poet Hölderlin. It may well be the case that some schizophrenic patients are capable of generating good art, and, as noted, there has been much discussion of schizophrenic painting. The Prinzhorn collection brought together more than five thousand art pieces. However, to what extent the individual patients can be deemed great or even good artists is debatable, and few of them are renowned for their work. August Natterer, Otto Stuss, and Carl Lange, three important patients whose work is in the collection, are hardly well-known artists. See Brugger, Gorsen, and Schröder 1997. There are other well-known collections of psychotic, possibly schizophrenic paintings, for example, the one at the Bethlem Hospital, in south London. Certainly, some of the work displayed there is of considerable standard, including that of Richard Dadd (1817–86) and Louis Wain (1860–1938). Of further interest, Hartmut Kraft, in his recent book *Grenz-gänger Zwischen Kunst und Psychiatrie*, discusses a host of schizophrenic painters, includ-ing, in addition to those already mentioned, Adolf Wölfli and Alfred Kubin. His section de-voted to mania and depression, however, is brief, and he discusses only one painter. Kraft (1998) commented that only about 2 percent of psychiatric patients spontaneously begin to create paintings or sculpture during their illnesses.

50. Post 1994, 30.

51. Bleuler 1951, 88–89.

52. Hallowell and Smith 1983, 138.

53. Critchley 1970, 362.

54. Bleuler 1951.

55. It is estimated that in industrialized nations, the prevalence of epilepsy is 4–8 per 1,000.

56. Burton 1621. This was destined to become the most popular psychiatric text for gen-erations, and it went through five editions in Burton's lifetime (1577–1640). The phenom-enon of Elizabethan melancholy, its relationship with politics and religion, and its reflec-tion through literature is discussed in Harrison's (1929) edition of Nicholas Breton's *Melancholic Humours*.

57. Another popular medical text was Sir Richard Blakemore's *A treatise of the Spleen and Vapors; or, hypocondriacal and hysterical affections*. Blakemore (1653–1729) was also a poet.

58. Jamison 1993. It is not clear why these names appear in Jamison's list. Critical re-view of their work unveils the development of schizophrenia, although it is often the case that, during the development of the illness, affective and even manic symptoms are pres-ent. This may lead the unwary to miss the later evolution of the schizophrenia.

59. Walters 1988.

60. Ellis 1926.

61. Juda 1949. Juda's classification owes much to the philosopher Arthur Schopen-hauer (1995), who identified an intermediate group, between geniuses and the vast ma-

jority, of dull education and average intellect. The mission of the intermediates, according to Juda (1949, 302), is to lead the lower classes.

62. Post 1994. Post felt that including poets would have given an unacceptably strong bias toward English and German subjects.

63. Ludwig 1995, 5.

64. Brain 1960, 20.

65. Andreasen 1987.

66. Ludwig 1994.

67. Jamison 1993.

68. Brain 1960. Harold Nicholson (1886–1968) was a journalist and writer, married to Vita Sackville-West. Nicholson used Shelley as an example of a writer with both problems: Shelley not unreasonably had a fear of catching consumption, but on at least two occasions he had visions. In one, which happened in Pisa, a man in a cloak and hood approached him; when the man then raised his hood, Shelley realized it was himself. The vision asked him, in Italian, if he was satisfied, then vanished (Nicholson 1947).

69. Jamison 1989; Jamison 1993, 63–71. The poets listed with manic-depressive illness are William Collins (1721–59), Christopher Smart (1722–71), William Cowper (1731–1800), Robert Fergusson (1750–74), Thomas Chatterton (1752–70), William Blake (1757–1827), Robert Burns (1759–96), S. T. Coleridge (1772–1834), Walter Savage Landor (1775–1864), Thomas Campbell (1777–1844), Lord Byron (1788–1824), Percy Bysshe Shelley (1792–1822), John Clare (1793–1864), John Keats (1795–1821), George Darley (1795–1846), Hartley Coleridge (1796–1849), Thomas Lovell Beddoes (1803–49), Robert Stephen Hawker (1803–75), and James Clarence Mangan (1803–49).

70. Ludwig 1995.

71. Post 1996.

72. The details of the neuroanatomy of these area of the brain is discussed in chapter 2.

73. Various authors have noted abnormalities in such areas in schizophrenia; see Trimble 1996.

74. Cutting (1997) has made the best and most substantial claim to date of the role of the right hemisphere in schizophrenia. This has also been recently reviewed by Mitchell and Crow (2005).

75. McGuire et al. 1998.

76. Franck et al. 2002.

77. For an excellent update on the neurophysiological and neuropsychological bases of hallucinations, see Spence and David 2004.

78. Crow 1998.

79. Mellers et al. (1998) have shown that the same area of the left temporal cortex that is involved in schizophrenia, the speech-related superior temporal gyrus, functions abnormally in patients with epilepsy who develop a schizophrenia-like psychosis.

80. This is not in harmony with some of the blood-flow studies noted above. To some extent the results of such studies depend on the state of the patient at the time of the study, the length of the patient's illness, and what medications he or she is taking. It is important

to recognize the progressive nature of schizophrenia, as originally described by Kraepelin, since the changes in bipolar patients are much less obvious between episodes, and in most sufferers intellectual decline is not a feature of the latter disorder.

81. For reviews, see Trimble 1996 and George et al. 1998.

82. For review see Trimble 1996 and George et al. 1998.

83. George et al. 1998, 220.

84. Migliorelli et al. 1993; Starkstein et al. 1990.

85. George et al. 1998, 227.

Chapter 6 · Music and the Brain

1. Novalis (Friedrich von Hardenberg, 1772–1801) was a German Romantic poet. Like a number before and after him, he fell in love with a young girl (Sophie von Kuehn was fourteen), who died soon afterward and inspired his poetry.

2. Richards 1976, 103–12.

3. The word *ballad* derives from the French "ballet," for a song that was danced.

4. Gibbon 1930, 196.

5. Quoted in Gibbon 1930, 196.

6. Quoted in Makin 1999, 35, 36.

7. Stephen Pinker (1997), for example, has suggested that if music disappeared from the earth, it would make no difference to the rest of our life style at all; music is biologically useless.

8. Pinker (1997, 534) refers to music as "auditory cheesecake."

9. Jason Warren, personal communication.

10. Kivy 2002.

11. Darwin 1871. In one interesting recent study, the testosterone levels of a group of students were monitored before and after listening to music of various types. In males, the testosterone levels went down, in females they went up. Since in females testosterone is closely linked to libido, and in males to aggression, the evolutionary and contemporary advantage of listening to late-night music might extend beyond holding hands.

12. Mithen 2005. The term *musilanguage* is attributed to the musicologist Stephen Brown.

13. Quoted in Storr 1992, 16.

14. Storr 1992.

15. Corballis 1991, 269; Makin 1999.

16. Cooke 1959, 33.

17. Bernstein 1976, 29.

18. Bernstein 1976, 79.

19. Scruton 1997, 171–210. For other views on the relationships between spoken language and music, see Cooke 1959 and Lehrdahl and Jackendoff 1983. Scruton himself is skeptical of the overall thesis of a strict analogy. "Music has a quasi-syntactic structure; it also has a kind of meaning. But unless the first articulates the second, and is interpreted in terms of it, there is no reason to believe that the structure is genuinely syntactical, or that the *structure* is the vehicle of meaning" (Scruton 1997, 198). "We have no means of

proving that the 'deep structure' read into music by this or that analytic theory really does have a generative function; no way of showing that the surface is derived from the structure, rather than the structure from the surface" (323). He concludes that musical syntax is essentially a metaphor.

20. Bernstein 1976, 125, 109, 149. "These intrinsic musical meanings are generated by a constant stream of metaphors, all of which are forms of poetic transformations" (131). *Anaphora* is the device of beginning lines or stanzas with the same initial words or phrase. *Chiasmus* is the reversal of the elements of a line or phrase, such as President Kennedy's "Ask not what your country can do for you, but what you can do for your country."

21. Meyer 1956.

22. Bernstein 1976, 51.

23. Meyer 1956, 187. "The practiced listener has learned to direct his attention in particular ways . . . hence he not only tends to improve articulation in general, but tends to favour certain types of (musical) organizations over others."

24. Meyer (1956, 62) points out that certain musical relationships are universal, such as the octave and the fifth or fourth, which are stable focal tones toward which other terms of the system tend to move. Furthermore, almost all the tonal systems that have been used in music are essentially diatonic.

25. Meyer 1956, 81; Meyer attributes the remark to James Mursell, who reviewed the literature on this subject.

26. Meyer 1956, 256, 258.

27. Brust 1999. The first report was in 1745; the patient could say only one word, yes, but could sing hymns if someone else sang along.

28. Alajouanine 1948.

29. I am grateful to Jason Warren for these observations.

30. Luria 1977, 139–44, 144.

31. Yamadori et al. 1977; Signoret et al. 1987; Basso and Capitini 1985.

32. Gardner et al. 1977, 343.

33. Brust 1999.

34. For example, a recent study of patients with either left or right hemisphere aneurysms suggests that the right hemisphere is essential for the recognition of music. Patients with lesions on that side had an apperceptive musical agnosia and a failure to appreciate melodic contour. Those with left-sided aneurysms had poor long-term memory representations of music, but they also had verbal memory deficits, suggesting that the loss may be related to the inability to use verbal mediation in the task. However, the right side was seen as "essential in mediating access to these stored representations" (Ayotte et al. 2000, 1935).

35. For some of the literature on this topic, see Trehub 2001.

36. Storr 1992, 8.

37. Storr 1992, 36.

38. Bertoncini et al. 1989; Trehub 2001; Sloboda 1985.

39. Penfield and Perot 1963.

40. Wieser et al. 1997.

41. See, for example, the review by Kaplan (2003).

42. Ley and Bryden 1982.

43. Milner 1962.

44. Kester et al. 1991; Liégeios-Chauvel et al. 1998.

45. Zatorre and Halpern 1993; Halpern and Zatorre 1999.

46. Zatorre 2001; Samson, Zatorre, and Ramsey 2002. Timbre is the quality given to sound by its overtones. Different instruments, as well as different speaking voices, are distinguished by their particular timbre. Pitch relates to vibration frequency of the source.

47. Parsons 1999.

48. Among nonmusicians, significant activations of the cerebellum were noted in a range of musical tasks. Rather in the same way that the right hemisphere of the brain has been relatively ignored from the point of view of function, the cerebellum is now attracting a lot of interest. Previously thought of as a purely motor-related structure, it is now being investigated for a role in a spectrum of cognitive activities, including music, and it may play a role in a number of neuropsychiatric disorders, including schizophrenia and autism.

49. Altenmüller 1999. One explanation given was that professionals used a covert inner speech, as during the tasks given they named the intervals and harmonies that were presented to them.

50. The anterior part of the corpus callosum contains fibers connecting mainly motor areas of the brain and the prefrontal cortices. The planum temporale is located in the superior temporal gyrus and is bounded anteriorly by Heschl's gyrus. The planum temporale is larger on the left side in right-handed humans and is part of Wernicke's area. Heschl's gyrus contains the primary auditory cortex.

51. Schlaug 1999.

52. Schneider et al. 2002.

53. Patel 2003.

54. Anderson, Outhern, and Powers 1999; Hutsler and Gazzaniga 1996.

55. Lerdahl 1999, 353.

56. Sloboda 1991.

57. Blood et al. 1999; Blood and Zatorre 2001.

58. Blood et al. 1999; Blood and Zatorre 2001.

59. Storr 1992, 52. This is not to say that the adoption of equal temperament and the diatonic scale, in which the octave is divided into twelve equal semitones, is derived from acoustic laws, but that the harmonic series itself is based on "invariant acoustic phenomena, which can be mathematically described and measured" (57).

60. Quoted in Storr 1992.

Chapter 7 • Neurotheology I: Epilepsy

1. Much of the history of epilepsy is to be found in the study by Temkin (1971), *The Falling Sickness*.

2. Adams 1939. These ideas suggested a somatic rather than a psychological basis for human ills and diseases, and they associated disease with an imbalance of humors. In the more fully developed scheme of Galen (129–ca. 199), the four basic humors were phlegm,

blood, black bile, and yellow bile. The melancholic condition was related to black bile. Hippocrates quoted in Simon 1978, 220.

3. Mark 9:17–22, 26–27, with additions in italics from Matthew's and Luke's versions of the same incident.

4. Shakespeare, *Othello*, act 4, scene 1, lines 51–57.

5. The writings of such authors as Jules Falret (1824–1902), Benedict Morel (1809–73), and Jean-Etienne-Dominique Esquirol (1772–1840), from France, and Wilhelm Griesinger (1817–68) and Paul Samt (1844–75), from Germany, were seminal. The interested reader is referred to Trimble 1991 for further information on these early writers.

6. Trimble 1991; Lambert et al. 2003.

7. For a review of this whole area, see Trimble 1991.

8. Gallhofer et al. 1985; Maier et al. 2000.

9. The second form, the psychoses that are associated with nonconvulsive status epilepticus, especially arising from the temporal lobes, may also present as a schizophrenia-like psychotic state.

10. It was the original observations of these relationships that led to investigations into laterality differences in the brains of schizophrenic patients. In recent years, considerable evidence has accumulated to show that, whatever else is going on in the schizophrenic brain, left-sided pathology, especially in the left medial temporal areas, is often found. The literature is reviewed in Trimble 1996. See also pp. 114–115 of this book.

11. Quoted in Temkin 1971, 150.

12. Agrippa's full name was Heinrich Cornelius Agrippa von Nettesheim. He was physician and court secretary to Charles V of France. His philosophical interest was in cabalistic analyses of past texts as a method to get to know the nature of God. For Agrippa, rapture was an illumination of the soul that originated in God and was caused by a supreme contemplation on sublime things.

13. Samt 1876, 147 ("die armen Epileptischen, wie sie wohl in jeder Anstalt zu treffen sind, welche Gebetbuch in der Tasche, die lieben Gott auf der Zunge").

14. Temkin 1971, 363. Krafft-Ebing was a German neuropsychiatrist.

15. Henry Maudsley was one of the pillars of nineteenth-century neuropsychiatry. His *Physiology and Pathology of the Mind* was widely read and translated and is now one of the classics of British psychiatry. He was no lover of metaphysical speculation but lamented the lack of understanding that at that time neuroscientists had about the brain and its fine structure. He advocated for more research and education about mental illness, and in 1907 he offered thirty thousand pounds to the London County Council to establish a hospital exclusively for early and acute cases of mental illness, with provision for a pathological and research laboratory. The hospital was opened in 1923, and to this day, with its associated Institute of Psychiatry, is at the forefront of biological research in psychiatry.

16. Quoted in Foote-Smith and Smith 1996, 212.

17. Maudsley 1869; Johnson 1994.

18. Howden 1873. The church was founded in 1780, in London. There is still a Swedenborg Society, whose premises are in Holborn, London, and he still has his followers.

19. Quoted in Temkin 1971, 368. Lombroso was one of the unsung heroes but also a

bête noire of neuropsychiatry. His last position in Turin was as professor of criminal anthropology. Influenced by the evolutionary theories of Darwin and by German materialism, he was interested in biological and anthropological studies of criminals and delinquents. He famously set out to test his hypothesis about the pathology of genius by paying a visit to Leo Tolstoy. He went to Yasnaya Polyana, Tolstoy's home, imagining the writer to be cretinous and degenerate. He found himself face to face with an elderly gentleman with no obvious stigmata of degeneration. They argued over the concept of the born delinquent, which Tolstoy would have none of, and in his diary, Tolstoy noted Lombroso to be an ingenious but limited old man. The outcome of the discussions on the scientific basis of hereditary and criminality found its way into Tolstoy's *Resurrection*.

20. Emil Kraepelin, quoted in Cutting 1997, 183.

21. Lombroso 1891, 336; Nisbet 1891.

22. Lombroso 1891, 338. The whole area of epileptic equivalents is tricky. In the past century, some patients with epilepsy developed, in the course of their illness, acute behavior problems. In some, the seizures stopped, and because the behavioral outburst had a sudden onset, was characterized by overactivity, and was of rapid offset, it seemed to follow the general pattern of an epileptic seizure. This clinical observation was referred to by authors at that time by several terms, including *transformed epilepsy* and *epileptic equivalent*. It was not such a great leap to then suggest that when these behavior patterns occurred, even in the absence of a history of a seizure, they could represent epilepsy. These issues are still controversial and with us today, episodes of aggressive behavior with such characteristics being referred to as the episodic dyscontrol syndrome.

23. Dostoyevsky, in *Besi*, quoted in Lombrosos 1891, 339.

24. Lombroso 1891, 347. The evidence that any of these people, other than Dostoyevsky, had epilepsy is slender indeed, and can only forever remain a matter of speculation. Muhammad's alleged epilepsy was always denied by Islamic tradition and is thought by Temkin (1971, 154) to have "all the earmarks of religious and political propaganda." Dostoyevsky was diagnosed with epilepsy in 1848, and although Freud thought that his attacks were psychogenic, most authors who have considered the subject believe him to have had epilepsy.

25. Trimble 1991; Saver and Rabin 1997.

26. Saver and Rabin 1997.

27. Dewhurst and Beard 1970, 498.

28. Kanemoto, Kawasaki, and Kawai 1996.

29. Penfield and Perot 1963. In déjà vu, the person has an experience, which is experienced as a reexperience, of events that are about to happen and that seem to have happened before in exactly the same way. It occurs as an aura of epilepsy in about 7 percent of patients with epilepsy. Strictly speaking, the term refers to a visual experience, *déjà vécu* referring to the experience.

30. Roberts, Robertson, and Trimble 1982.

31. Bear 1986, 24.

32. Trimble and Freeman 2006.

33. In patients with other forms of epilepsy, it is often difficult to rule out temporal lobe

involvement in the seizure process, although the question can now be better resolved with high-resolution brain-imaging studies.

34. Kass et al. 1991
35. Hood 1975.
36. Csernansky et al. 1990. For further reviews of the small literature in this area, the interested viewer is referred to Trimble 1991; also see Devinsky 2003 and Csernansky et al. 1990. Often the numbers of patients studied is small; in the Csernansky paper, for example, there were only five with a right-sided focus and seventeen with left or bilateral abnormalities.
37. Devinsky 2003, 77.
38. Ogata and Miyakawa 1998.
39. For example, Lombroso 1891.
40. Lennox and Lennox 1960.
41. Gastaut 1956; Trimble 1991; Jamison 1993.
42. Quoted in Trimble 1991, 186.
43. Impey and Mellanby 1992.
44. The biographical notes on Kierkegaard are from "Kierkegaard's Epilepsy," by Heidi Hansen and Lief Bork Hansen. At the time of this writing it is unpublished.
45. Lennox and Lennox 1960.
46. Lennox and Lennox 1960; Grosskurth 1997, 25. When, as a child, Byron was scolded by his mother, who called him a "lame brat," he replied, "I was born so, mother" (Bett 1952, 149). He had a deformed right foot and required specially built-up shoes. The problem was a clubfoot, of the varus type, turning inward. Edward Trewlawny (1792–1881), Byron's friend and a member of the Shelley-Byron circle in Italy, uncovered Byron's corpse and recorded that both Byron's feet were clubbed, and his legs withered to the knee. He had, Trewlawny remarked, "the form and features of an Apollo, with the feet of a sylvan satyr" (quoted in Jenkyns 1998, 26).
47. Pseudoseizures are well known to those who study epilepsy. Patients have episodes that resemble epileptic seizures, but the attacks have psychogenic and not neurological causes. During the attack, which to the tutored eye has some distinguishing features from epilepsy, no abnormal electroencephalographic changes are seen.
48. Jamison 1993, 163; Grosskurth 1997, 459.
49. Swinburne became particularly absorbed in the works of Dante Gabriel Rossetti (1828–82), William Morris (1834–96), and Edward Burne-Jones (1833–98). Milnes was a Victorian poet whose patronage of other writers was well known. He not only championed Swinburne, he also made the American poet Ralph Waldo Emerson known in England.
50. Gosse 1989, 178.
51. Quoted in Richardson 1965, 9.
52. Quoted in Noakes 1968, 330; quoted in Levi 1995, 233.
53. Chitty 1988, 192. Whether this refers to an attempt to control the seizures by psychological mechanisms is unclear. Some people with epilepsy can learn to suppress their attacks by such self-willed mechanisms. However, Vivien Noakes (1968, 21, 330) comments that Lear believed, as did many others at that time, that there was a connection between

epilepsy and masturbation, and that as an adult he blamed the epilepsy on a lack of will power.

54. Lear first published his *Book of Nonsense* in 1846; this and the next edition of 1855 were published under the pseudonym "Old Derry down Derry."

55. Levi 1991, 13, 169. Levi notes that by the end of his life, Lear was prouder of his poems than of his paintings, presumably because of their success with the public.

56. Edward Lear, "How Pleasant to Know Mr. Lear."

Chapter 8 • *Neurotheology II: Other Neurological Conditions*

1. Wilson 1978.

2. Joseph 2002, 7. The more famous quotation about the death of God comes from *Also Sprach Zarathustra*, written some two years later. Nietzsche's point must be that we have killed God with our intellectual insights; as our minds created Him, we have also killed Him as a tenable intellectual construct. Nietzsche struggled against decadent religion and metaphysical untruths. "That God became man only indicates that man should not search for his blissfulness in infinity, but establish his heaven on earth; the delusion of an extraterrestrial world has brought man's spirituality to a false position regarding the earthly world" (quoted in Thiele 1990, 146). Nietzsche, as Zarathustra, wanted people to celebrate life here on the earth.

3. Nietzsche was brought up in a deeply religious family. His father and both grandfathers were pastors. His mother, the daughter of a pastor, was deeply religious. At school Nietzsche was nicknamed "the little pastor."

4. Saver and Rabin 1997.

5. The cause or causes of these forms of dementia, as with Alzheimer disease, are unknown. They have a genetic basis, and they tend to present earlier in life than the Alzheimer form. Memory is not affected early on. If the left frontal area is involved, then speech disorder is prominent, and a condition called primary progressive aphasia is seen. For a review, see Cummings and Trimble 2002.

6. Edwards-Lee et al. 1997. In another patient, artistic skills were kindled: patient RTLV 4 reported that colors reverberated in his head, and over a ten-year period his painting skills steadily improved.

7. Lynch et al. 1994, 1878.

8. Edwards Lee et al. 1997, 1039.

9. Kroll and Sheehan 1989.

10. For a review, if somewhat dated, see Bateson and Ventis 1982.

11. Tek and Ulug 2001. Freud refers to these links in his essay "Obsessive Actions and Religious Practices" (Freud 1961) but also in *Totem and Taboo* (Freud 1913). See also Fiske and Haslam 1997.

12. For a review, see Trimble 1996. Of all the neuroses, obsessive compulsive disorder seems to be the most "neurological," and increased obsessionality accompanied by abnormal motor behaviors is a feature of several neurological disorders, including Parkinson disease, Sydenham's chorea, Gilles de la Tourette syndrome, and encephalitis lethargica.

13. Azari et al. 2001.

14. For a summary of his work, see Persinger 2001; also see Persinger 1984a, 1984b; Cook and Persinger 1997; Persinger and Valliant 1985.

15. Persinger 2001, 515.

16. Makarec and Persinger 1985.

17. Persinger 1984a.

18. Persinger 2001, 517. Persinger monitored such fluctuations in various settings, for example, in the house of someone who experienced apparitions in the bedroom and was able to detect complex magnetic fields in the strength range of 15 to 30 microteslas coinciding with the apparitions.

19. These observations were initially made in the nineteenth century, when effective treatments for epilepsy were not available. There was a debate about what was happening in the brain and how the transformation took place. Some contested that in reality the acute behavior problems were actually postictal but the preceding seizure had simply not been witnessed. Others considered that a transformation of the manifestations of the underlying disease had occurred. In the twentieth century, with the development of effective treatments for epilepsy, it was observed that some patients with chronic epilepsy could respond well to antiepileptic drugs, become seizure free, and lose the EEG abnormalities that had earlier been present. The Swiss epileptologist Heinrich Landolt (1917–71) called this phenomenon "forced normalization" (*forcierte Normalizierung*). See also chapter 7, note 22.

20. This was all part of the work that led to the extensive use of antiepileptic drugs in the management of patients with bipolar disorders. See Post and Udhe 1986.

21. Persinger 1993b, 923. Persinger is here referring to the psychoanalyst R. D. Laing.

22. Wuerfel et al. 2004.

23. Murai et al. 1998.

24. See Joseph 2002, Joseph 2001, and Alper 2001. Certainly, these are not the only writers on these topics of interest, and others, including collaborators of these authors, have contributed to these interesting debates. However, these authors in particular have developed a coherent view of the way they see the data and expressed them in their books. The four books cited are all from this new millennium; neurotheology has arrived.

25. D'Aquili and Newberg 2002; Newberg and Iversen 2002; also see Newberg et al. 2001. These results have many difficulties with regard to methods and conclusions. As noted, SPECT scans have very poor resolution, and it is difficult with some machines to view subcortical structures. An acceptance of the authors' interpretation of the functions of the parietal lobes, and their suggestion that what they call absolute unitary being, in which there is no space or time, relates to the total failure of afferent inputs to the orientation association area, requires considerable caution.

26. Joseph 2001; also see Joseph 2002.

27. Joseph 2001, 67–68, 66. It must be pointed out that the evidence he generously includes in this and many other texts is indirect. There is a considerable amount of neuromythology generated in his and related writings. No doubt the present author will fall under the same criticism.

28. Joseph 2001, 187, 265.

29. Atran 2001, 166.

30. Alper 2001.

31. Persinger 1993a; Lazar et al. 2000; Herzog et al. 1990.

32. Austin 1998, 591.

33. Waller et al. 1990.

34. Hamer 2004.

35. See Pasnau 2002, 309. Aquinas was a theologian and scholasticist.

36. Galileo Galilei (1564–1642) fell out with the established church and was under house arrest for supporting the Copernican view of the solar system—namely, the "astonishing" idea that the planets revolve around the sun.

37. Alexander Pope's "An Essay on Man"; the poem continues:

He hangs between; in doubt to act or rest;
In doubt to dream himself a god, or beast;
In doubt his mind or body to prefer;
Born to die, and reas'ning but to err.

Chapter 9 · God, Music, and the Poetry of the Brain

1. Gallup and Lindsay 1999; Spilka et al. 2003, 150, 209.

2. Gallup and Newport 1996; Barna 1996; Pugh Research Center, *San Francisco Chronicle*, December 22, 1997.

3. Wheen 2004. The book is a marvelous account of the irrationality of human beliefs, many supported by gimcrack politicians with little understanding of human nature and even less of the scientific method.

4. For a full exposition, see Lampert 2001.

5. Otto Rank (1884–1939), a close intimate of Freud, had a particular interest in the psychology of myths. He was ultimately expelled from the inner circle, and he was manic-depressive.

6. Rank 1932, 15.

7. Frye 1971.

8. Santayana 1900, 24, 289. Santayana was a Spanish philosopher and poet whose contributions to aesthetics included consideration of the workings of the mind and the relationship between poetry and philosophy.

9. Boccaccio was an Italian poet best known for *The Decameron*. Alfred Austin became a poet laureate.

10. It goes without saying that much art has been inspired by religion, and in many times and places, religious authorities have been wealthy patrons.

11. "When my work does not advance, I retire into the oratory with my rosary and say an *ave;* immediately ideas come to me" (quoted in Lombroso 1891, 19).

12. Blake 1993, "Songs of Experience: Introduction."

13. Beatrice Portinari (1266–90) was Dante's lifelong muse to whom and for whom he wrote most of his poetry. In *The Divine Comedy* he describes his journey through hell and his redemption in paradise with the guidance of Beatrice.

14. Graves 1946, 444.

15. Santayana 1900, 261.

16. Richards 1976, 220.

17. John Keats (1795–1821), "Ode on a Grecian Urn." The full quote is as follows:

"Beauty is truth, truth beauty"—that is all
Ye know on earth, and all ye need to know.

18. Richards 1976, 225–26.

19. Frye 1971, 125.

20. Brown 1983.

21. The root *steno* comes from the Greek for closed or restricted; Brown 1983, 19.

22. Brown 1983, 15. Brown points out that the logical positivists, whose view it was that the meaning of a statement lay in its method of verification, could therefore ascribe to poetry only a purely "meaningless" emotional role. Wheelwright's "depth language" has had to yield to the great dictator of science and its language (Brown 1983, 186).

23. This contradicts the view of the logical positivists.

24. Brown 1983, 171–74.

25. Quoted in Ghiselin 1952, 125.

26. Buckley 1968, 25 (quoting from Eliade 1961, 24).

27. The first term is from Paul Tillich, the second from Gerard Manley Hopkins, the third from George Santayana.

28. Kris 1953. The "primary process" refers to an id-bound process of hallucinatory wish fulfillment. In psychoanalytic theory it is distinguished from the secondary process, which is an ego function and, in contrast to the former, is characterized by logical thinking and an ability to delay gratification. It is the process we use to maintain our contacts with reality. The psychoanalyst Silvano Arieti (1916–81) used the term *tertiary process* to express a combination of primary and secondary processes. For him, appropriate matching of the primary and secondary processes led to innovation since the tertiary process, with specific mechanisms and forms, blends the rational with the irrational (Arieti 1976).

29. Ludwig 1995, 5.

30. Jamison 1993.

31. Cited in Richards and Kinney 1990.

32. Richards and Kinney 1990, 213.

33. Jaynes 1990. The term *bicameral,* literally meaning having two chambers, has been used in this book in a somewhat different way. It is here argued that the bicameral brain had essential equipotentiality between the two hemispheres (chambers) before the cerebral skewing that led propositional language to take over so much of the left hemisphere and altered not only the relationship of the right hemisphere to the left but also that between the hemispheres and their monitoring of the environment.

34. Jaynes (1990, 93) goes on to argue that the threshold for hallucinations was much lower than today and that schizophrenics have hallucinations that are "similar to the guidelines of the gods in antiquity."

35. Jaynes 1990, 104, 208. Interestingly, the novelist Sebastian Faulks in his book *Human Traces* plays heavily on Jaynes's theories. The book is a fascinating account of the strug-

gles by two psychiatrists to understand the causes of mental illness in the late nineteenth century and calls upon many of the names quoted in this book.

> Suppose that what had disappeared was the capacity to hear the voice or the voices of the god. Once, all those fishermen would have heard a god; now only Christ could. For early humans separated from their group—the young man, for instance, dispatched to fish upstream—the ability to hear instructions, to produce under the influence of stress or fear the voice of the absent leader or god, had once been a necessary tool of survival; but as the capacity to remember and communicate through words had slowly developed, humans had lost the need for heard instruction and comment. (p. 206)

36. Jaynes 1990, 361.
37. Sagan 1977, 185.
38. The interested reader can refer to Ornstein 1986.
39. MacLean 1990, 545.
40. Deacon 1997, 314.
41. Deacon 1989.
42. The midbrain structures include the periaqueductal gray area, the dorsal tegmental area, and the parabrachial nuclei. For further descriptions of the anatomy, see Deacon 1989.
43. Akinetic mutism is a clinical picture of mutism with lack of spontaneous movements.
44. The view that a reorganization of existing structures and connections in the brain is responsible for the development of human language stands in contrast to an alternative view that new structures, and additional connections with them, are developed. Deacon (1989) supports the former view. Part of the argument for the latter is, for example, that in humans, as opposed to other primates, there are direct connections between the cortex and the nucleus ambiguus. The latter controls movement of the diaphragm and is, therefore, clearly essential for the control of human language.
45. George Crile, quoted in Storr 1991, 201.
46. Chaucer, prologue to "The Monk's Tale."
47. Steiner 1996.
48. For a fuller discussion, see Nutall 1996 and House 1980.
49. For others, the essence of tragedy is a conflict between humankind as a part of nature and at the same time above nature, mortal and immortal, or between the individual and the forces (the gods, fate, later, in modern tragedy, society) that destroy him. For a fuller discussion of the conflicts inherent in tragedy, see Gardner 1971, 13–37.
50. Joyce 1991.
51. The word *religion* stems from the Latin *ligare,* to bind.
52. Nietzsche 1993. For more on Nietzsche's illness, see Orth and Trimble 2006. It is argued that Nietzsche had a frontotemporal dementia, a condition described in chapter 8. This would explain the early onset of his disorder and his extraordinary literary output in the last year of his productive life (1888).

53. For much more on the work of Nietzsche and theories of tragedy, see Silk and Stern 1981.

54. Dionysus was driven mad by the goddess Hera. The cult of Dionysus came to Greece from earlier civilizations and can be traced back to at least the thirteenth century BC.

55. Dalby 2003, 123; "Self-knowledge emerges through violence and destruction" (Feder 1980, 43).

56. In Euripides' *Bacchae*, wisdom (Tiresias) and control (Pentheus) are set alongside Dionysus.

57. Nietzsche 1993, 16.

58. Nietzsche 1993, 43.

59. Nietzsche 1993, 8.

60. "While in all productive people instinct is the power of creativity and affirmation, in Socrates instinct becomes the critic, consciousness the creator—a monstrosity *per defectum!*" (66). Nietzsche expected that the operas of Wagner would give birth to a regeneration of true art in Germany.

61. Nietzsche 1993, 89.

62. The Socratic view that for a thing to be good it must be conscious represented a repudiation of the creative unconscious; the will to obtain knowledge overtook myth, art, and religion.

63. If God is dead, there can be no ultimate validation. For Nietzsche, what was needed, since contemporary values were decadent, was the revaluation of all values (*die Umwertung aller Werte*). He abused Kant for implying that morality emerges as a set of rules—a categorical imperative, a kind of moral rule of thumb, universally applicable. Philosophers, he felt, should place themselves "beyond good and evil." Nietzsche opined that the categorical imperative smelt of cruelty.

64. Booker 2004. Sir James Frazer, in *The Golden Bough*, makes similar observations with regard to myth, as does Joseph Cambell (Frazer 1915; Campbell 2002). The seven basic plots are: overcoming the monster; rags to riches; the quest; voyage and return; comedy; tragedy; and rebirth and the dark power (from shadow into light).

65. Quoted in Safranski 2002, 200.

66. Reed 1974, 364.

67. For example, Narcissus says to Goldmund, "Natures of your kind, those with strong and delicate senses, the inspired, the dreamers, poets, lovers, are almost always superior to us men of intellect. Your origin is maternal . . . Your kind live life to the full . . . We intellectuals live a parched existence" (Hesse 1957, 41).

68. For example, *Hedda Gabler.*

69. Paglia 1990, 96.

70. Flaherty 2004, 220.

71. Cavanna and Trimble 2006.

72. Coleridge 1868, 2:463.

73. Nietzsche 1986, 65.

74. This has been shown through the EEG.

75. The feeling generated in the artist during an act of creation is not, of course, the same as the feeling engendered in the observer. For both, however, the experience is different from those feelings that daily permeate their lives. For many people, this is an often unrevealed emotion; and for biological or cultural reasons, it is perhaps not accessible to everyone.

76. For exposition and criticism of Nietzsche's views, see, for example, Young 1992 and Jaspers 1997. The concepts of the Dionysian and the Apollonian are not to be taken too literally; rather, they represent a highly imaginative way of viewing two kinds of cognition that interact with the world.

77. Nietzsche 1993 (quoted in Young 1992, 45).

78. See Homer, *Odyssey*, book 8, lines 70ff. (Chapman 2000). Odysseus drew his cloak across his face to hide his tears from his companions.

79. Arroyo et al. 1993.

80. Luciano, Devinsky, and Perrine 1993.

81. In other words, crying in response to an unresolved domestic argument is not likely to lead to the same effects.

82. Laughter, on the other hand, involves mainly expiration (Deacon 1997, 419).

83. Walt Whitman, *Leaves of Grass*.

Epilogue

1. German: *kennen* as opposed to *wissen*.

2. The neuroscientist and philosopher John Smythies has pointed out to me that much modern philosophy is focused almost entirely on reason, logic, and mechanical linguistics and pays little attention to emotion, myth, and the unconscious—and even less to modern neuroscience. It is, as he remarked, Apollonian.

3. Lord Byron, *Manfred*, scene 1, lines 10–12.

4. Nietzsche 1997.

5. James 1982, 73, 74.

6. Kant asked what kinds of knowledge we have and gave two broad categories, a priori (deductive) and a posteriori (inductive). Furthermore, knowledge is either analytic (*b* is contained in *a*) or synthetic (*b* contains more than *a*). The faculty of reason supplies the principles of knowledge a priori. *Synthesis* refers to synthesis of the manifold into time and space. Kant opines that what objects may be in themselves remains completely unknown to us and that synthesis is the result of the power of the imagination, a process about which we are scarcely ever conscious. Kant's own view was not one of perspectivism.

7. Magee 1995, 32; Camus 2000, 24, 49.

8. See, for example, "Gore Vidal: American Novelist at Home," in Haught 1996; and Dawkins 2003: "Let's call a spade a spade. The Emperor has no clothes. It is time to stop the mealy-mouthed euphemisms: 'Nationalists,' 'Loyalists,' 'Communities,' 'Ethnic groups,' 'Cultures,' 'Civilisations.' *Religions* is the word you need. Religions is the word you are struggling to avoid" (158).

9. Whitehead 1926, 37; Pullman 1995, 1997, 2000.

10. "Queen Mab," in Shelley 1888a, 1:131. The following is also worthy of consideration in this regard:

> 1978: In Jonestown, Guyana, 638 adults and 276 children died after drinking cyanide at the People's Temple commune, led by the self-proclaimed messiah, Jim Jones.
>
> 1993: In Waco, Texas, 59 adults and 21 children of the Branch Davidian sect died in a conflagration; all were under the influence of their religious leader, David Koresh.
>
> 1994: In Switzerland, 48 members of the Order of the Solar Temple were either shot or burned alive; they were followers of Luc Jouret, who claimed to be a member of a fourteenth-century order of Christian Knights; followers were told they would go to the star Sirius after death.
>
> 1995: In the French Alps, 16 members of the Order of the Solar Temple were found dead in a burned-out house.
>
> 1997: In San Diego, 39 members of the Heaven's Gate cult committed suicide (after the men had castrated themselves). With their leader, Marshall Applewhite, they believed they were going to a higher level on a divine spaceship towed by the Hale-Bopp comet.
>
> 1997: In Quebec, Canada, five members of the Order of the Solar Temple burned themselves alive.

11. Brown 2003, 451.

12. Perspectivism asserts that there are no objective truths, only perspectives on reality.

13. Nietzsche 1999. Life needs something to hold onto.

14. "Neither man nor beast would be able to live without the extraordinary security provided by belief" (Jaspers 1997, 196).

15. Quotes are from *Thus Spake Zarathustra* (Nietzsche 1999, 23). Many animals dream, so the ancestors of modern man would have been no exception. There is some debate about the relationship between hemisphere laterality and dreaming, case histories of both right and left hemisphere damage leading to loss of dreaming; Cutting (1997) favors the left. Curiously, Nietzsche placed dreams in the Apollonian camp.

16. The earliest known cave drawings are about forty thousand years old. Artifacts for personal decoration have been found that are about the same age. The famous paintings at Lescaux are about seventeen thousand years old. The evolution of the kind of intelligence required for artistic achievement must have gone on over a period of sixty thousand to eighty thousand years, presumably encouraged by the huge evolutionary advantages that came with the development of language, social communication, and effective tool making.

17. Dryden 1687, "A Song for St. Cecelia's Day," quoted in Tillyard 1998, 109.

18. Nietzsche 1986, 99.

19. Descartes thought that through doubt he had reached the truth, but Nietzsche, through an analysis of the truth, reaches only doubt.

20. In *Human, All Too Human* (Nietzsche 1986), the title of Nietzsche's book published in 1878, dedicated to Voltaire, the illusion of life is explored largely through aphorisms.

21. Steiner 1996, 315.
22. Lancker 1991.
23. Wagner 1994, 213.
24. The first quote is from Friedrich Schiller, the second from Wagner. Both are cited in Hartwich 1996.
25. "Lying" here refers to the use of metaphor.
26. Cutting, personal communication.
27. Emily Dickinson, "This World Is Not Conclusion," in Dickinson 1960, no. 501.

Appendix 1: Brief Biographies of Some Poets with Bipolar Disorder

1. Cowper wrote more than thirty biographies and five volumes of letters. Cowper's mother, Anne Donne, was thought to be a distant relation of John Donne. His grief after her death left a lifelong impression on his works and lifestyle.

I heard the bell toll'd on thy burial day,
I saw the hearse that bore thee slow away,
And, turning from my nurs'ry window, drew
A long, long sigh, and wept a last adieu!

Interestingly, many poets have early bereavements, with loss of a parent in childhood. This is known to predispose to later affective disturbances and may be relevant for the development of poetic creativity.

2. Cowper left his own much-quoted autobiography, in which he described the onset and quality of these experiences. Entitled *Adelphi* (The brothers), it was written in two parts, the first in 1767, the second in 1770.

3. He believed that he was referred to in the newspapers and that people would laugh at him.

4. Cowper's account of his attempts to kill himself is discussed in some detail in his autobiography (Quinlan 1953). Like many other doctors in this era, Cotton, himself a poet, owned his own private madhouse.

5. Cowper, *Jehovah-Jesus, Jehovah Our Righteousness.*

6. Cowper, letter to Lady Hesketh, 1792, in Claridge, Pryor, and Watkins 1990, 107.

7. Much of the following comes from Hamilton 1982. Lowell's autobiography, written between 1955 and 1957, exists in draft form in the Houghton Library. The published version is "91 Revere Street," in Lowell 1959. Part 1 consists of poems; part 2, "91 Revere Street," recounts his childhood between 1925 and 1928 and contains essays about friends and literary figures.

8. Lowell writes:

In the Marlborough Street Parlor,
where oatmeal roughened
the ceiling blue as the ocean,
I torpedoed my Father to the floor—

9. Cited in Hamilton 1958, 149–50.

10. Hamilton 1958, 157.

11. This drug dramatically altered psychiatric practice, especially in the United States. It was shown to be effective in the long-term prophylaxis of bipolar disorder, and hence there was a need to identify that condition more effectively. Until its introduction, many patients who would have been diagnosed as manic-depressive in the United Kingdom were called schizophrenic in the United States. The introduction of a successful treatment often leads to increased identification of the index disorder. Thereafter, the number of patients with a diagnosis of schizophrenia in the United States declined, and the diagnostic practice of the American psychiatrists became more European.

12. At one time Lady Caroline was married to Lucien Freud, at another to a musician. She had Lowell's child, and in 1972 they married.

13. Cited in Reed 1974, 95.

14. Robert Lowell, *Home after Three Months Away.*

15. This unconventional maneuver created considerable controversy, mainly related to the issue of patient confidentiality. One of Dr. Orne's rationales for releasing the material was that he felt Sexton would have wanted them used in a biography. He claimed that he had her permission to do what he wanted with the tapes, although no written evidence of this was ever presented.

16. Anne Sexton, *The Double Image.*

17. Chlorpromazine certainly affected any pleasure she might have derived from sitting in the sun, as she developed one of its well-known side effects, light sensitivity. "I am not going to take any more Thorazine. I want to write poems!" (quoted in Middlebrook 1991, 236).

18. Quoted in Middlebrook 1991, 392–93. Linda is Sexton's daughter.

19. Sexton had about eight psychiatrists in her lifetime and an affair with at least one of them.

20. Anne Sexton, *The Addict.*

21. Quoted in Plimpton 1989, 272.

22. Roethke died of a heart attack while playing tennis at the age of fifty-five.

Appendix 2: Some Notable Religious Poets

1. Cecil 1940. The anthology includes work by many more poets than I have named here.

2. See Woodhouse 1965, 42–89. Some others are William Alabaster (1567–1640), William Cartwright (1611–43), Thomas Heyrick (1649–94), Henry King (1592–1669), John Norris of Bemerton (1657–1711), and Francis Quarles (1592–1644).

3. *Religio Laici,* in Dryden 1958.

4. "Reason truly was for Coleridge, nevertheless, a human power to know the absolute" (Wendling 1995, 145). Imagination stood between reason and understanding.

5. William Wordsworth, from *The Prelude,* book 13.

6. Christina Rossetti, "If only," in "The First Day."

7. Cited in Carter 1981, 282–99.

8. Cited in Carter 1981, 434.

9. Quoted in Plimpton 1989, 210–12.

Abou-Khalil B. 1995. Insights into language mechanisms derived from the evaluation of epilepsy. In *Handbook of Neurological Speech and Language Disorders*, ed. Kirshner HS, 213–75. Dekker, New York.

Adams F. 1939. *The Genuine Works of Hippocrates*. Williams & Wilkins, Baltimore.

Alajouanine T. 1948. Aphasia and artistic realisation. *Brain* 71, 229–41.

Alajouanine T, L'hermitte F. 1964. Essai d'introspection de l'aphasie. *Revue Neurologique* 110, 609–21.

Alper M. 2001. *The "God" Part of the Brain*. Rogue, New York.

Altenmüler EO. 1999. How many music centres are there in the brain? In *The Biological Foundations of Music*, ed. Zatorre RJ, Peretz I, 273–80. New York Academy of Sciences, vol. 930.

Amaducci L, Sorbi S, Albanese A, Gainotti G. 1981. Choline acetyltransferase activity differs in right and left human temporal lobes. *Neurology* 31, 799–805.

Amaral DG, Avendano C, Benoit R. 1989. Distribution of somatostatin-like immunoreactivity in the monkey amygdala. *Journal of Comparative Neurology* 284, 295–313.

American Psychiatric Association (APA). 1994. *Diagnostic and Statistical Manual of Mental Disorders*, 4th ed. APA Press, Washington, D.C.

Anderson B, Southern BD, Powers RE. 1999. Anatomic asymmetries of the posterior superior temporal lobes: a post-mortem study. *Neuropsychiatry, Neuropsychology, and Behavioural Neurology* 12, 247–54.

Andreasen N. 1987. Creativity and mental illness: prevalence rate in writers and their first-degree relatives. *American Journal of Psychiatry* 144, 1288–92.

Andreasen N, O'Leary DS, Cizadlo T, Arndt S, et al. 1995. Remembering the past: two facets of episodic memory explored with positron emission tomography. *American Journal of Psychiatry* 152, 1576–85.

Arieti S. 1976. *Creativity, the Magic Synthesis*. Diane Publishing.

Aristotle. 1970. *Poetics*. Trans. Else GF. University of Michigan Press, Ann Arbor.

Armstrong K. 1993. *A History of God*. Ballantine Books, New York.

Arroyo S, Lesser RP, Gordon B, et al. 1993. Mirth, laughter, and gelastic seizures. *Brain* 116, 757–80.

Ascham R. 1570. Of imitation. In *Elizabethan Critical Essays*, ed. Smith CG, 1:1–45. Oxford University Press, Oxford, U.K.

Atran S. 2001. The neuropsychology of religion. In *NeuroTheology: Brain, Science, Spirituality, Religious Experience,* ed. Joseph R, 147–66. University of California Press, Berkeley.

Austin J. 1998. *Zen and the Brain: Toward an Understanding of Meditation and Consciousness.* MIT Press, Cambridge, Mass.

Ayotte J, Peretz I, Rousseau I, Bard C, Bojanowski M. 2000. Patterns of music agnosia associated with middle cerebral infarcts. *Brain* 123, 1926–38.

Azari NP, Nickel J, Wunderlich G, et al. 2001. Neural correlates of religious experience. *European Journal of Neuroscience* 13, 1649–52.

Barna G. 1996. *Index of Leading Spiritual Indicators.* Word Publishing, Dallas.

Baron-Cohen S. 1999. The evolution of a theory of mind. In *The Descent of the Mind,* ed. Corballis MC, Lea SE, 261–77. Oxford University Press, Oxford, U.K.

Basso A, Capitini E. 1985. Spared musical abilities in a conductor with global aphasia and ideomotor apraxia. *Journal of Neurology, Neurosurgery, and Psychiatry* 48, 407–12.

Bateson CD, Ventis WL. 1982. *The Religious Experience: A Social-Psychological Perspective.* Oxford University Press, Oxford, U.K.

Bear D. 1986. Behavioural changes in temporal lobe epilepsy: conflict, confusion, challenge. In *Aspects of Epilepsy and Psychiatry,* ed. Trimble MR, Bolwig T, 19–29. Wiley and Sons, Chichester, U.K.

Benson DF. 1979. *Aphasia, Alexia, and Agraphia.* Churchill Livingstone, New York.

Bernstein L. *The Unanswered Question: Six Talks at Harvard.* Harvard University Press, Cambridge, Mass.

Bertoncini J, Morais J, Bileljac-Babic R, et al. 1989. Dichotic perception and laterality in neonates. *Brain and Language* 37, 591–605.

Bett WR. 1952. *The Infirmities of Genius.* Christopher Johnson, London.

Blake W. 1993. *Selected Poems.* Everyman, London.

Bleuler E. 1951. *Textbook of Psychiatry.* Ed. AA Brill. Dover Publications, New York.

Blok BFM, Willemsen ATM, Holstege G. 1997. A PET study on brain control of micturition in humans. *Brain* 120, 111–21.

Blood AJ, Zatorre RJ. 2001. Intensely pleasurable responses to music correlates with activity in brain regions implicated with reward and emotion. *Proceedings of the National Academy of Sciences* 98, 1818–23.

Blood AJ, Zatorre RJ, Bermidez P, Evans AC. 1999. Emotional responses to pleasant and unpleasant music correlate with activity in paralimbic brain regions. *Nature Neuroscience* 2, 382–87.

Booker C. 2004. *The Seven Basic Plots: Why We Tell Stories.* Continuum, London.

Bottini G, Corcoran R, Sterzi R, Paulesu E, et al. 1994. The role of the right hemisphere in the interpretation of figurative aspects of language: a positron emission tomography activation study. *Brain* 117, 1241–53.

Boyer P. 2001. *Religion Explained.* Heinemann, London.

Brain WR. 1960. *Some Reflections on Genius, and Other Essays.* Pitman, London.

Brown D. 2003. *The Da Vinci Code.* Corgi, London.

Brown FB. 1983. *Transfiguration.* University of North Carolina Press, Chapel Hill.

Brownell H, Gardner H, Prather P, Martino G. 1994. Language, communication, and the right hemisphere. In *Handbook of Neurological Speech and Language Disorders,* ed. Kirshner H, 325–49. Marcel Dekker, New York.

Brugger I, Gorsen P, Schröder KA. 1997. *Kunst und Wahn.* Kunstforum Wien und DuMont, Köln, Ger.

Brust JCM. 1999. Music and the neurologist. In *The Biological Foundations of Music,* ed. Zatorre RJ, Peretz I, 143–52. New York Academy of Sciences, vol. 930.

Bruyn GW. 1982. The seat of the soul. In *Historical Aspects of the Neurosciences,* ed. Clifford Rose F, Bynum WE, 55–81. Raven, New York.

Bryden MP, Ley RG. 1983. Right hemisphere involvement in the expression and perception of emotion in normal humans. In *Neuropsychology of Human Emotion,* ed. Heilman KM, Satz P, 6–44. Guilford, New York.

Buckley V. 1968. *Poetry and the Sacred.* Chatto and Windus, London.

Burton R. 1621. *The Anatomy of Melancholy.* Published as Democritus Junior, *The Anatomy of Melancholy.* 1849. William Tegg, London.

Byrne J. 2002. *God.* Continuum, London.

Campbell, J. 2002. *The Inner Reaches of Outer Space: Metaphor as Myth and as Religion.* New World Library, California. (Orig. pub. 1986.)

Camus A. 2000. *The Myth of Sisyphus.* Penguin Books, London. (Orig. pub. 1955.)

Carter H. 1981. *W. H. Auden: A Biography.* George Allen and Unwin, London.

Cavanna AE, Trimble MR. 2006. The precuneus: a review of its functional anatomy and behavioural correlates. *Brain* 129, 564–83.

Cecil D. 1940. *The Oxford Book of Christian Verse.* Oxford University Press, Oxford, U.K.

Chadwick C. 1971. *Symbolism.* Routledge, London.

Chapman G. 2000. *Homer.* Wordsworth Editions, Ware, U.K. (Orig. pub. 1598.)

Chiron C, Jambaque I, Nabbout R, et al. 1997. The right brain hemisphere is dominant in human infants. *Brain* 120, 1057–65.

Chitty S. 1988. *That Singular Person Called Lear.* Weidenfeld and Nicholson, London.

Chomsky N. 2002. *On the Nature of Language.* Cambridge University Press, Cambridge, U.K.

Claridge G, Pryor R, Watkins G. 1990. *Sounds from the Bell Jar.* Macmillan, London.

Coleridge ST. 1868. The Friend. In *The Complete Works.* Harper, New York.

———. 1971. *Biographia Literaria.* JM Dent and Sons, London. (Orig. pub. 1817.)

Colvin MK, Handy TC, Gazzaniga MS. 2003. Hemispheric asymmetries in the parietal lobes. In *The Parietal Lobes,* ed. Siegel AM, Andersen RA, Freund H-J, Spenser DD, 321–34. Lippincott Williams & Wilkins, New York.

Cook CM, Persinger MA. 1997. Experimental induction of the "sensed presence" in normal subjects and an exceptional subject. *Perceptual and Motor Skills* 85, 683–93.

Cook ND. 2002. Bihemispheric language: how the two hemispheres collaborate in the processing of language. In *The Speciation of Modern* Homo Sapiens, ed. Crow TJ, 169–96. Oxford University Press, Oxford, U.K.

Cooke D. 1959. *The Language of Music.* Oxford University Press, Oxford, U.K.

Corballis MC. 1991. *The Lopsided Ape.* Oxford University Press, New York.

————. 2003. *From Hand to Mouth*. Princeton University Press, Princeton, N.J.

Cox MLC. 2003. Learning to like: functional neuroimaging of conditioned reward in humans. *Journal of Psychopharmacology* 17, Suppl., A 81.

Crick F. 1994. *The Astonishing Hypothesis*. Simon & Schuster, London.

Critchley M. 1970. *Aphasiology and Other Aspects of Language*. Edward Arnold, London.

————. 1979. *The Divine Banquet of the Brain*. Raven, New York.

Crow TJ. 1998. Why cerebral asymmetry is the key to the origin of *Homo Sapiens:* how to find the gene or eliminate the theory. *Current Psychology of Cognition* 17, 1237–77.

————, ed. 2002. *The Speciation of Modern* Homo Sapiens. Oxford University Press, Oxford, U.K.

Csernansky J, Leiderman, Mandabach M, Moses JA. 1990. Psychopathology and limbic epilepsy: relationship to seizure variables and neuropsychological function. *Epilepsia* 31, 275–80.

Cullen W. 1800. *Nosology*. Creech, Edinburgh.

Cummings JL. 1993. Frontal-subcortical circuits and human behaviour. *Archives of Neurology* 50, 873–80.

Cummings JL, Trimble MR. 2002. *A Concise Guide to Neuropsychiatry and Behavioral Neurology*. 2d ed. APA Press, Washington, D.C.

Cutting J. 1990. *The Right Cerebral Hemisphere and Psychiatric Disorders*. Oxford University Press, Oxford, U.K.

————. 1997. *Principles of Psychopathology*. Oxford Medical Publications, Oxford, U.K.

Dalby A. 2003. *Bacchus: A Biography*. British Museum Press, London.

Damasio A. 1999. *The Feeling of What Happens*. Heinemann, London.

D'Aquili E, Newberg AB. 2002. The neuropsychology of aesthetic, spiritual, and mystical states. In *NeuroTheology: Brain, Science, Spirituality, Religious Experience,* ed. Joseph R, 243–50. University Press of California, Berkeley.

Darwin C. 1871. *The Descent of Man*. Murray, London.

Dawkins R. 2003. *A Devil's Chaplain*. Weidenfeld and Nicholson, London.

Deacon TW. 1989. The neural circuitry underlying primate calls and human language. *Human Evolution* 4, 367–401.

————. 1997. *The Symbolic Species*. Allan Lane, Penguin, London.

DeLong MR, Georgopoulos AP. 1981. Motor functions of the basal ganglia. In *Handbook of Physiology*, vol. 2, ed. Mountcastle VB, Brooks VB, sec. 1, 1017–61. American Physiological Society, Bethesda, Md.

Devinsky O. 2003. Religious experiences and epilepsy. *Epilepsy and Behavior* 4, 76–77.

Dewhurst K, Beard AW. 1970. Sudden religious conversions in temporal lobe epilepsy. *British Journal of Psychiatry* 117, 497–507.

Dickinson E. 1960. *The Complete Poems of Emily Dickinson*. Ed. Johnson TH. Little Brown, Boston.

Dolan RJ. 2002. Emotion, cognition, and behaviour. *Science* 298, 1191–94.

Dryden J. 1958. *Poems of John Dryden*. Ed. Kinsley J. Clarendon, Oxford, U.K.

Durkheim E. 1995. *The Elementary Forms of Religious Life*. Free Press, New York. (Orig. pub. 1912.)

Edwards-Lee T, Miller B, Benson DF, Cummings J, Russell GL. 1997. The temporal variant of frontotemporal dementia. *Brain* 120, 1027–40.

Eliade M. 1957. *The Sacred and the Profane.* Harcourt, Brace, and World, New York.

———. 1961. *The Sacred and the Profane.* Harper Torchbook, New York.

Eliot TS. 1933. *The Use of Poetry and the Use of Criticism.* Harvard University Press, Cambridge, Mass.

Elkins J. 2001. *Pictures and Tears: A History of People Who Have Cried in Front of Paintings.* Routledge, London.

Ellis HA. 1926. *Study of British Genius.* Houghton-Mifflin, Boston.

Empson W. 1991. *Seven Types of Ambiguity.* Hogarth, London.

Faulkes S. 2005. *Human Traces.* Hutchinson, London.

Feder L. 1980. *Madness in Literature.* Princeton University Press, Princeton, N.J.

Feuerbach L. 1845. *The Essence of Christianity.* O. Wigland, Leipzig.

Fischer SR. 1999. *A History of Language.* Reaktion Books, London.

Fish F. 1974. *Fish's Clinical Psychopathology.* Ed. Hamilton M. John Wright and Sons, Bristol, U.K.

Fiske AP, Haslam N. 1997. Is obsessive compulsive disorder a pathology of the human disposition to perform socially meaningful rituals? *Journal of Nervous and Mental Disease* 185, 211–22.

Flaherty AW. 2004. *The Midnight Disease: The Drive to Write, Writer's Block, and the Creative Brain.* Houghton Mifflin, Boston.

Fletcher PC, Frith CD, Baker SC, et al. 1995. The mind's eye: precuneus activation in memory related imagery. *Neuroimage* 2, 195–200.

Fodor JA. 1975. *The Language of Thought.* Crowell, New York.

Foote-Smith E, Smith TJ. 1996. Emanuel Swedenborg. *Epilepsia* 37, 211–18.

Franck N, O'Leary DS, Flaum M, Hichwa RD, Andreasen NC. 2002. Cerebral blood flow changes associated with Schneiderian first rank symptoms in schizophrenia. *Journal of Neuropsychiatry and Clinical Neuroscience* 14, 277–82.

Frazer JG. 1915. *The Golden Bough.* Macmillan, London.

Freud S. 1913. *Totem and Taboo.* Trans. Strachey J. Hogarth, London.

———. 1927. *The Future of an Illusion.* Trans. Strachey J. Hogarth, London.

———. 1961. Obsessive actions and religious practices. In *The Standard Edition of the Complete Psychological Works of Sigmund Freud,* ed. Strachey J. Hogarth, London. (Orig. pub. 1907.)

Freund H-J. 2003. Somatosensory and motor disturbances in patients with parietal lobe lesions. In *The Parietal Lobes,* ed. Siegel AM, Andersen RA, Freund H-J, Spenser DD, 179–93. Lippincott Williams & Wilkins, New York.

Frye N. 1971. *Anatomy of Criticism.* Princeton University Press, Princeton, N.J.

Fuller R. 1989. *Agenda,* 3.

Gainotti G. 1972. Emotional behaviour and hemisphere side of lesion. *Cortex* 8, 41–45.

Gallhofer B, Trimble MR, Frackowiak, R, Gibbs J, Jones TA. 1985. A study of cerebral blood flow and metabolism in epileptic psychosis using PET and O-15. *Journal of Neurology, Neurosurgery, and Psychiatry* 48, 201–6.

Gallup G, Lindsay DM. 1999. *Surveying the Religious Landscape: Trends in U.S. Beliefs.* Morehouse, Harrisburg, Pa.

Gallup GH, Newport F. 1996. Gallup poll of American religious beliefs. *Wall Street Journal,* January 30.

Gardner H. 1971. *Religion and Literature.* Faber and Faber, London.

Gardner H, Ling PK, Flamm L, Silverman J. 1975. Comprehension and appreciation of humourous material following brain damage. *Brain* 98, 399–412.

Gardner H, Silverman J, Denes G, et al. 1977. Sensitivity to musical denotation and connotation in organic patients. *Cortex* 13, 242–56.

Gastaut H. 1956. La maladie de Vincent van Gogh. *Annales Médico Psychologiques* 114, 196–238.

George MS, Ketter TA, Kimbrell TA, Post RM. 1998. Brain imaging. In *Mania: Clinical and Research Perspectives,* ed. Goodnick PJ, 191–238. American Psychiatric Press, Washington, D.C.

Ghiselin B. 1952. *The Creative Process.* University of California Press, Berkeley.

Gibbon JM. 1930. *Melody and the Lyric from Chaucer to the Cavaliers.* JM Dent, London.

Glezerman T, Balkoski V. 1999. *Language, Thought, and Brain.* Plenum, New York.

Glick SD, Alan D, Hough LB. 1982. Lateral asymmetry of neurotransmitters in human brain. *Brain Research* 234, 53–63.

Gloor P. 1997. *The Temporal Lobe and the Limbic System.* Oxford University Press, Oxford, U.K.

Gosse E. 1989. *Aspects and Impressions.* Russell, London.

Graves R. 1946. *The White Goddess.* Faber and Faber, London.

Grosskurth P. 1997. *Byron, the Flawed Angel.* Hodder and Stoughton, London.

Hallowell EM, Smith HF. 1983. Communication through poetry in the therapy of a schizophrenic patient. *Journal of the American Academy of Psychoanalysis* 11, 133–58.

Halpern AR, Zatorre RJ. 1999. When the tune runs through your head: a PET investigation of auditory imaging for familiar melodies. *Cerebral Cortex* 9, 697–704.

Hamburger M. 1996. *The Truth of Poetry.* Anvil, London.

Hamer D. 2004. *The God Gene: How Faith Is Hardwired into Our Genes.* Doubleday, New York.

Hamilton I. 1982. *Robert Lowell: A Biography.* Random House, New York.

Harrison GB, ed. 1929. *Melancholic Humours,* by Nicholas Breton (1600). Scholastic, London.

Hartwich WD. 1996. Religion and art in Wagner's later years. In German. *Jahrbuch der deutschen Schillergesellschaft* 40, 297–323.

Haught JA, ed. 1996. *2000 Years of Disbelief: Famous People with the Courage to Doubt.* Prometheus, New York.

Hawkes T. 1972. *Metaphor.* Routledge, London.

Hécaen H, Angelergues R. 1963. *La Cécité Psychique.* Masson, Paris.

Heimer L. 2003. A new anatomical framework for neuropsychiatric disorders and drug abuse. *American Journal of Psychiatry* 160, 1726–39.

Heimer L, de Olmos J, Alheid GJ, Zaborszky L. 1991. Perestroika in the basal forebrain;

opening the borders between neurology and psychiatry. *Progress in Brain Research* 87, 109–65 (Elsevier, Holland).

Heimer L, Van Hoesen G. 2006. The limbic lobe and its output channels: implications for emotional functions and adaptive behavior. *Neuroscience and Biobehavioral Reviews* 30, 126–47.

Hermann B, Chhambria S. 1980. Interictal psychopathology in patients with ictal fear. *Archives of Neurology* 37, 667–68.

Herzog H, Lele VR, Kuwert T, et al. 1990. Changed pattern of regional glucose metabolism during Yoga meditative relaxation. *Neuropsychobiology* 23, 182–87.

Hesse H. 1957. *Narcissus and Goldmund.* Peter Owen, London.

Hollander B. 1920. *In Search of the Soul and the Mechanism of Thought, Emotion, and Conduct.* 2 vols. Kegan Paul, Trench, Trubner, New York.

Holmes R. 1998. *Coleridge: Darker Reflections.* HarperCollins, London.

Hood RW. 1975. The construction and preliminary validation of a measure of reported mystical experience. *Journal for the Scientific Study of Religion* 14, 29–41.

House H. 1980. Catharsis and the emotions. In *Tragedy: Developments in Criticism,* ed. Draper RP, 50–57. Macmillan, London.

Housman AE. 1989. *The Name and Nature of Poetry and Other Selected Prose.* Ed. John Carter. New Amsterdam Books, Amsterdam, Holland. (Orig. pub. 1933.)

Howden JC. 1873. The religious sentiment of epileptics. *Journal of Mental Science* 18, 491–97.

Hutsler J, Gazzaniga M. 1996. Acetyl cholinesterase staining in human auditory and language cortices: regional variation of structural features. *Cerebral Cortex* 6, 260–70.

Impey M, Mellanby J. 1992. Epileptic phenomena as a source of creativity: the work of Alfred Kubin. *International Journal of Moral and Social Studies* 7, 153–71.

James W. 1982. *The Varieties of Religious Experience.* Penguin Books, New York. (Orig. pub. 1902.)

Jamison K. 1989. Mood disorders and pattern of creativity in British writers and artists. *Psychiatry* 52, 125–34.

———. 1993. *Touched with Fire.* Free Press, New York.

Jaspers K. 1959. *Truth and Symbol.* College and University Press, New Haven, Conn.

———. 1963. *General Psychopathology.* Trans. Hoenig J and Hamilton MW. Manchester University Press, Manchester, U.K. (Orig. pub. 1913.)

———. 1997. *Nietzsche: An Introduction to the Understanding of His Philosophical Activity.* Trans. Wallraff CF, Schmitz FJ. Johns Hopkins University Press, Baltimore. Md. (Orig. pub. 1936.)

Jaynes J. 1990. *The Origin of Consciousness in the Breakdown of the Bicameral Mind.* Penguin Books, London.

Jenkyns R. 1998. *London Review of Books* (November), 26, 11.

Johnson J. 1994. Henry Maudsley on Swedenborg's messianic psychosis. *British Journal of Psychiatry* 165, 690–91.

Johnson S. 1905. *Lives of the English Poets.* Ed. Birkbeck G. Hill, Oxford, U.K.

Joseph R. 2001. *The Transmitter to God.* University Press of California, Berkeley.

———. 2002. *NeuroTheology: Brain, Science, Spirituality, Religious Experience.* University Press of California, Berkeley.

Joyce J. 1991. *A Portrait of the Artist as a Young Man.* Signet Classics, New York. (Orig. pub. 1916.)

Juda A. 1949. The relationship between highest mental capacity and psychic abnormalities. *American Journal of Psychiatry* 106, 296–307.

Jung CG. 1970. *Psychology and Religion.* Vol. 2 in *Collected Works,* 2d ed. Routledge and Kegan Paul, London.

Kanemoto K, Kawasaki J, Kawai I. 1996. Post-ictal psychosis: comparison with acute interictal and chronic psychoses. *Epilepsia* 37, 551–56.

Kaplan P. 2003. Musicogenic epilepsy and epileptic music: a seizure's song. *Epilepsy and Behaviour* 4, 464–73.

Kass JD, Friedman R, Leserman J, et al. 1991. Health outcomes and a new index of spiritual experience. *Journal of the Scientific Study of Religion* 30, 203–11.

Kester DB, Saykin AJ, Sperling MR, et al. 1991. Acute effect of anterior temporal lobectomy on musical processing. *Neuropsychologia* 29, 703–8.

Kiehl KA, Liddle PF, Smith AM, Mendrek A, Forster BB, Hare RD. 1999. Neural pathways involved in the processing of concrete and abstract words. *Human Brain Mapping* 7, 225–33.

Kirshner HS. 1994. *Handbook of Neurological Speech and Language Disorders.* Marcel Dekker, New York.

Kivy P. 2002. *Introduction to a Philosophy of Music.* Clarendon, Oxford, U.K.

Kraepelin E. 1919. *Dementia Praecox.* E.S. Livingstone, Edinburgh.

Kraft H. 1998. *Grenzgänger zwischen Kunst und Psychiatrie.* Dumont, Köln, Ger.

Kris E. 1953. *Psychoanalytic Explorations in Art.* Allen and Unwin, London.

Kroll J, Sheehan W. 1989. Religious beliefs and practices among 52 psychiatric in-patients in Minnesota. *American Journal of Psychiatry* 146, 67–72.

Lambert MV, Schmitz B, Ring H, Trimble MR. 2003. Neuropsychiatric aspects of epilepsy. In *Neuropsychiatry,* ed. Schiffer RB, Rao SM, Fogel BS, 1071–131. Lippincott Williams & Wilkins, New York.

Lampert L. 2001. *Nietzsche's Task: An Interpretation of Beyond Good and Evil.* Yale University Press, New Haven, Conn.

Lancker D van. 1991. Personal relevance and the human right hemisphere. *Brain and Cognition* 17, 64–92.

Lautin A. 2001. *The Limbic Brain.* Kluwer Academic, New York.

Lazar SW, Bush G, Gollub RL, et al. 2000. Functional brain mapping of the relaxation response and meditation. *Neuroreport* 11, 1581–85.

Leach E. 1976. *Culture and Communication.* Cambridge University Press, Cambridge, U.K.

LeDoux J. 2002. *Synaptic Self.* Viking Penguin, New York.

Lee GP, Loring DW, Meador KJ, Brooks BB. 1990. Hemisphere specialisation for emotional expression. *Brain and Cognition* 12, 267–80.

Lehrdahl, F. 1999. The sounds of poetry viewed as music. In *The Biological Foundations of Music,* ed. Zatorre RJ, Peretz I, 337–54. New York Academy of Sciences, vol. 930.

Lehrdahl F, Jackendoff R. 1983. *A Generative Theory of Tonal Music.* MIT Press, Cambridge, Mass.

Lennox WG, Lennox MA. 1960. *Epilepsy and Related Disorders.* J and A Churchill, London.

Lesser RP, Luders H, Morris HH, Dinner DS, et al. 1986. Electrical stimulation of Wernicke's area interferes with comprehension. *Neurology* 36, 658–63.

Leutmezer F, Schernthaner C, Lurger S, et al. 2003. ECG changes at the onset of epileptic seizures. *Epilepsia* 44, 348–54.

Levi P. 1991. *The Art of Poetry.* Yale University Press, New Haven, Conn.

———. 1995. *Edward Lear: A Biography.* Macmillan, London.

Ley RG, Bryden MP. 1982. A dissociation of right and left hemisphere effects for recognising tone and emotional content. *Brain and Cognition* 1, 3–9.

Liégeios-Chauval C, Peretz I, Babaï M, et al. 1998. Contribution of different cortical areas in the temporal lobes to musical processing. *Brain* 121, 1853–67.

Lombroso C. 1891. *The Man of Genius.* Walter Scott, London.

Lowell R. 1959. *Life Studies.* Farrar, Straus and Cudahy, New York.

Luciano D, Devinsky O, Perrine K. 1993. Crying seizures. *Neurology* 43, 2113–17.

Ludwig AM. 1994. Mental illness and creative activity in female writers. *American Journal of Psychiatry* 151, 1650–56.

———. 1995. *The Price of Greatness.* Guilford, New York.

Luria AR. 1977. *Neuropsychological Studies in Aphasia.* Swets and Zeitlinger, Amsterdam.

Luys JB. 1881. Recherches nouvelles sur les hemiplegies emotives. *Encephalé* 1, 644–46.

Lynch T, Sano KS, Marder KL, Bell LL, et al. 1994. Clinical characteristics of a family with chromosome 17 link disinhibition dementia Parkinsonism amyotrophy complex. *Neurology* 44, 1878–84.

MacLean PD. 1976. Challenges of the Papez heritage. In *Limbic Mechanisms: The Continuing Evolution of the Limbic System Concept,* ed. Livingston KE, Hornykiewicz O, 1–16. Plenum, New York.

———. 1990. *The Triune Brain in Evolution.* Plenum, New York.

Magee B. 1995. *Sight Unseen.* Oxford University Press, Oxford, U.K.

Maier M, Mellers J, Toone B, Trimble MR, Ron MA. 2000. Schizophrenia, temporal lobe epilepsy, and psychosis: an in vivo magnetic resonance spectroscopy and imaging study of the hippocampus/amygdala complex. *Psychological Medicine* 30, 571–81.

Makarec K, Persinger MA. 1985. Temporal lobe signs: electroencephalographic validity and enhanced scores in special populations. *Perceptual and Motor Skills* 60, 831–42.

Makin P. 1999. *Basil Bunting on Poetry.* Johns Hopkins University Press, Baltimore, Md.

Maudsley H. 1869. Emanuel Swedenborg. *Journal of Mental Science* 15, 169–98.

McEwan I. 2005. *Saturday.* Cape, London.

McGuire PK, Quested DJ, Spence SA, et al. 1998. Pathophysiology of positive thought disorder in schizophrenia. *Psychological Medicine* 30, 345–57.

McHenry, Lawrence. 1969. *Garrison's History of Neurology.* Charles C. Thomas, Springfield, Ill.

Mellers JD, Adachi N, Takei N, Cluckie A, et al. 1998. SPET study of verbal fluency in schizophrenia and epilepsy. *British Journal of Psychiatry* 173, 69–74.

Mesulam M, Mufson, EJ. 1985. The insula of Reil in man and monkey. In *Cortex*, vol. 4. ed. Peters A, Jones EG, 4:179–228. Plenum, New York.

Meyer LB. 1956. *Emotion and Meaning in Music*. University of Chicago Press, Chicago.

Middlebrook DW. 1991. *Anne Sexton: A Biography*. Virago, London.

Migliorelli R, Starkstein S, Teson A, et al. 1993. SPECT findings in patients with primary mania. *Journal of Neuropsychiatry and Clinical Neurosciences* 5, 379–83.

Milner B. 1962. Laterality effects in audition. In *Interhemispheric Relations and Cerebral Dominance*, ed. Mountcastle VB, 177–95. Johns Hopkins University Press, Baltimore, Md.

Mitchell RLC, Crow TJ. 2005. Right hemisphere language functions and schizophrenia: the forgotten hemisphere. *Brain* 128, 963–78.

Mithen S. 2005. *The Singing Neanderthals*. Weidenfeld and Nicholson, London.

Monrad-Krohn GH. 1947. Dysprosody or altered melody of language. *Brain* 70, 405–15.

Morice R, McNicol D. 1985. The comprehension of complex syntax in schizophrenia. *Cortex* 21, 567–80.

Murai T, Hanakawa T, Sengoku A, et al. 1998. Temporal lobe epilepsy in a genius of natural history: MRI volumetric study of post-mortem brain. *Neurology* 50, 1373–76.

Nauta WJH. 1986. Circuitous connections linking cerebral cortex, limbic system, and corpus striatum. In *The Limbic System: Functional Organization and Clinical Disorders*, ed. Doane BK, Livingston K, 43–54. Raven, New York.

Newberg AB, Alvi A, Baime M, et al. 2001. The measurement of rCBF during the complex cognitive task of meditation. *Psychiatric Research* 106, 113–22.

Newberg AB, Iversen J. 2002. On the neuro in neurotheology. In *NeuroTheology: Brain, Science, Spirituality, Religious Experience*, ed. Joseph R, 251–67. University Press of California, Berkeley.

New look at human evolution. 2004. *Scientific American* 13 (2).

Nicholson H. 1947. The health of authors. *Lancet* (November 15), 709–14.

Nietzsche F. 1974. *The Gay Science*. Random House, New York. (Orig. pub. 1882.)

———. 1986. *Human, All Too Human*. Trans. Hollingdale R. Cambridge University Press, Cambridge, U.K. (Orig. pub. 1878.)

———. 1993. *The Birth of Tragedy*. Penguin Books, London. (Orig. pub. 1872.)

———. 1997. *A Nietzsche Reader*. Penguin Books, London.

———. 1999. *Thus Spake Zarathustra*. Dover Publications, New York. (Orig. pub. 1883–85.)

Nisbet JF. 1891. *The Insanity of Genius*. Ward and Downey, London.

Noakes V. 1968. *Edward Lear: The Life of a Wanderer*. Collins, London.

Norrving B, Sourander P. 1989. Emanuel Swedenborg's theories on the structure and function of the nervous system. In *Neuroscience across the Centuries*, ed. Rose FC, 65–72. Smith-Gordon, London.

Nutall AD. 1996. *Why Does Tragedy Give Pleasure?* Clarendon, Oxford, U.K.

Ogata A, Miyakawa T. 1998. Religious experiences in epileptic patients with a focus on ictus-related episodes. *Psychiatry and Clinical Neurosciences* 52, 321–25.

Ogden CK, Richards IA. 1985. *The Meaning of Meaning*. Ark, London. (Orig. pub. 1923.)

Ojeman G. 1991. Cortical organisation of language. *Journal of Neuroscience* 11, 2281–87.

Okamura T, Motomura N, Asaba H. 1989. Hypergraphia in temporal lobe epilepsy, compared with stroke of the right hemisphere. *Japanese Journal of Psychiatry and Neurology* 43, 524–25.

Ornstein R. 1986. *The Psychology of Consciousness*. Penguin Books, London.

Orth M, Trimble MR. 2006. Friedrich Nietzsche's mental illness: general paralysis of the insane versus frontotemporal dementia. *Acta Psychiatrica Scandanavica*, 439–44.

Otto R. 1917. *Das Helige*. Breslau, Pol.

Paglia C. 1990. *Sexual Personae: Art and Decadence from Nefertiti to Emily Dickinson*. Yale University Press, New Haven, Conn.

Paittelli-Palmarini M, ed. 1980. *Language and Learning: The Debate between Jean Piaget and Noam Chomsky*. Routledge and Kegan Paul, London.

Papez JW. 1937. A proposed mechanism of emotion. *Archives of Neurology and Psychiatry* 38, 725–43.

Parsons LM. 1999. Exploring the functional neuroanatomy of musical performance, perception, and comprehension. In *The Biological Foundations of Music*, ed. Zatorre RJ, Peretz I, 211–31. New York Academy of Sciences, vol. 930.

Pasnau R. 2002. *Thomas Aquinas on Human Nature*. Cambridge University Press, Cambridge, U.K.

Patel AD. 2003. The relationship of melody to the melody of speech and to the syntactic processing disorder in aphasia. *Annals of the New York Academy of Science* 1060, 59–70.

Penfield W, Perot P. 1963. The brain's record of auditory and visual experience: a final summary and discussion. *Brain* 86, 595–696.

Persinger MA. 1984a. People who report religious experiences may also display enhanced temporal-lobe signs. *Perceptual and Motor Skills* 58, 963–75.

———. 1984b. Propensity to report paranormal experiences is correlated with temporal lobe signs. *Perceptual and Motor Skills* 59, 583–86.

———. 1993a. Transcendental meditation and general meditation are associated with enhanced complex partial epileptic-like signs: evidence for "cognitive kindling." *Perceptual and Motor Skills* 76, 80–82.

———. 1993b. Vectoral cerebral hemisphericity as differential sources for the sensed presence, mystical experiences, and religious conversions. *Perceptual and Motor Skills* 76, 915–30.

———. 2001. The neuropsychiatry of paranormal experiences. *Journal of Neuropsychiatry and Clinical Neuroscience* 13, 515–24.

Persinger MA, Valliant PM. 1985. Temporal lobe signs and reports of subjective paranormal experiences in a normal population: a replication. *Perceptual and Motor Skills* 60, 903–9.

Pies RW. 1985. Poetry and schizophrenia. *Literature and Medicine* 4, 13–23.

Pinker S. 1994. *The Language Instinct*. Penguin Books, London.

———. 1997. *How the Mind Works*. Norton, New York.

Pitkänen A. 2000. Connectivity of the rat amygdaloid complex. In *The Amygdala*, 2d ed., ed. Aggleton JP, 98. Oxford University Press, Oxford, U.K.

Plimpton G. 1989. *Poets at Work*. Penguin Books, London.

Plokker JH. 1964. *Artistic Self-expression in Mental Disease*. Charles Skilton, London.

Post F. 1994. Creativity and psychopathology: a study of 291 famous men. *British Journal of Psychiatry* 165, 22–34.

———. 1996. Verbal creativity, depression, and alcoholism: an investigation of 100 American and British writers. *British Journal of Psychiatry* 168, 545–55.

Post RM, Udhe TW. 1986. Anticonvulsants in non-epileptic psychosis. In *Aspects of Epilepsy and Psychiatry*, ed. Trimble MR, Bolwig TG, 177–212. Wiley and Sons, Chichester, U.K.

Pottle FA. 1941. *The Idiom of Poetry*. Cornell University Press, Ithaca, N.Y.

Powell CS. 2002. *God in the Equation*. Free Press, New York.

Price, CJ. 2000. The anatomy of language: contributions from functional neuroimaging. *Journal of Anatomy* 197, 335–59.

Pullman P. 1995. *Northern Lights*. Scholastic, London.

———. 1997. *The Subtle Knife*. Scholastic, London.

———. 2000. *The Amber Spyglass*. Scholastic, London.

Puttenhan G. 1967. The Arte of English Poesie. Reprinted in *Elizabethan Critical Essays*, ed. Smith GG, 2:1–193. Oxford University Press, Oxford, U.K. (Orig. pub. 1589.)

Quinlan MJ, ed. 1953. *William Cowper: A Critical Life*. University of Minnesota Press, Minneapolis.

Rank O. 1932. *Art and Artist*. Agathon, New York.

Reed TJ. 1974. *Thomas Mann: The Uses of Tradition*. Oxford University Press, Oxford, U.K.

Richards IA. 1976. *Principles of Literary Criticism*. Routledge and Kegan Paul, London.

Richards R, Kinney DK. 1990. Mood swings and creativity. *Creativity Research Journal* 3, 202–17.

Richardson A. 2001. *British Romanticism and the Science of the Mind*. Cambridge University Press, Cambridge, U.K.

Richardson J. 1965. *Edward Lear*. Longmans, Green, London.

Riese W. 1977. *Selected Papers on the History of Aphasia*. Swets and Zeitlinger, Amsterdam.

Roberts JKA, Robertson MM, Trimble MR. 1982. The lateralizing significance of hypergraphia in temporal lobe epilepsy. *Journal of Neurology, Neurosurgery, and Psychiatry* 45, 131–38.

Robertson MM. 1988. Depression in patients with epilepsy reconsidered. In *Recent Advances in Epilepsy*, ed. Pedley TA, Meldrum BS, 205–40. Churchill Livingstone, Edinburgh.

Rosadini G, Rossi GF. 1967. On the suggested cerebral dominance for consciousness. *Brain* 90, 101–12.

Ross ED. 1997. Right hemisphere syndromes and the neurology of emotion. In *Behavioral Neurology and the Legacy of Norman Geschwind*, ed. Schachter SC, Devinsky O, 183–91. Lippincott-Raven, Philadelphia, Pa.

Rousseau J-J. 1986. *On the Origin of Language*. Trans. Moran JH, Gode A. University of Chicago Press, Chicago. (Orig. pub. 1781.)

Sacks O. 1985. *The Man Who Mistook His Wife for a Hat*. Duckworth, London.

Safranski R. 2002. *Nietzsche: A Philosophical Biography*. W. W. Norton, New York.

Sagan C. 1977. *The Dragons of Eden: Speculations on the Evolution of Human Intelligence*. Hodder and Stoughton, London.

Samson S, Zatorre RJ, Ramsey JO. 2002. Deficits of music timbre perception after unilateral temporal-lobe lesion revealed with multidimensional scaling. *Brain* 125, 511–23.

Samt P. 1876. Epileptische Irreseinsformen. *Archiv für Psychiatrie und Nervenkrankheiten* 6, 110–216.

Santayana G. 1900. *Interpretations of Poetry and Religion.* Adam and Charles Black, London.

Saver JL, Rabin J. 1997. The neural substrates of religious experience. *Journal of Neuropsychiatry and Clinical Neuroscience* 9, 498–510.

Schachter SC, Devinsky O. 1997. *Behavioral Neurology and the Legacy of Norman Geschwind.* Lippincott-Raven, New York.

Schlaug G. 1999. The brain of musicians. In *The Biological Foundations of Music,* ed. Zatorre RJ, Peretz I, 281–99. New York Academy of Sciences, vol. 930.

Schneider K. 1959. Primary and secondary symptoms in schizophrenia. In *Themes and Variations in European Psychiatry,* ed. Hirsch SR, Shepherd M, 40–46. J. Wright, Bristol, U.K.

Schneider P, Scherg M, Dosch HG, et al. 2002. Morphology of Heschl's gyrus reflects enhanced activation in the auditory cortex of musicians. *Nature Neuroscience* 5, 688–94.

Schopenhauer A. 1995. *The World as Will and Idea.* Everyman, London. (Orig. pub. 1817.)

Scott Young W, Alheid GF, Heimer L. 1984. The ventral pallidum projection to the mediodorsal thalamus. *Journal of Neuroscience* 4, 1626–38.

Scruton R. 1997. *The Aesthetics of Music.* Clarendon, Oxford, U.K.

Seldon H. 1981. Structure of human auditory cortex. *Brain Research* 229, 295–310.

Seydel P. 2001. *The Evolution of God.* Dorrance, Pittsburgh, Pa.

Shallice T, Fletcher P, Frith C, Grasby P, Frackowiak RSJ, Dolan RJ. 1994. Brain regions associated with the acquisition and retrieval of verbal episodic memory. *Nature* 386, 633–35.

Shelley BP, Trimble MR. 2004. The insula lobe of Reil. *World Journal of Biological Psychiatry* 5, 176–200.

Shelley PB. 1888a. *The Poetical Works of Percy Bysshe Shelley.* Chatto and Windus, London.

———. 1888b. *The Prose Works of Percy Bysshe Shelley.* Ed. Shepherd RH. Chatto and Windus, London.

Siegel AM. 2003. Parietal lobe epilepsy. In *The Parietal Lobes,* ed. Siegel AM, Andersen RA, Freund H-J, Spenser DD, 335–43. Lippincott Williams & Wilkins, New York.

Signoret JL, Van Eeckhout P, Poncet M, et al. 1987. Aphasie sans amusie chez un organiste aveugle. *Revue Neurologie* 143, 172–81.

Silk MS, Stern JP. 1981. *Nietzsche on Tragedy.* Cambridge University Press, Cambridge, U.K.

Simon B. 1978. *Mind and Madness in Ancient Greece.* Cornell University Press, Ithaca, N.Y.

Sims A. 1988. *Symptoms of the Mind.* Balliere Tindall, London.

Slater E. 1979. The creative personality. In *Psychiatry, Genetics, and Pathography,* ed. Roth M, Cowie V, 89–103. Gaskell, London.

Sloboda JA. 1985. *The Musical Mind: The Cognitive Psychology of Music.* Oxford University Press, Oxford, U.K.

———. 1991. Musical structure and emotional response: some empirical findings. *Psychology of Music* 19, 110–20.

Snell B. 1982. *The Discovery of the Mind in Greek Philosophy and Literature.* Dover, New York.

Spence SA, David AS. 2004. *Voices in the Brain*. Taylor & Francis, New York.

Spilka B, Hood RW, Hunsberger B, Gorsuch R. 2003. *The Psychology of Religion*, 3d ed. Guilford, New York.

Starkstein SE, Mayberg HS, Berthier ML, et al. 1990. Mania after brain injury: neuroradiological and metabolic findings. *Annals of Neurology* 27, 652–59.

Starkstein S, Robinson RG. 1993. Depression in cerebrovascular disease. In *Depression in Neurologic Disease*, ed. Starkstein S, Robinson RG, 28–49. Johns Hopkins University Press, Baltimore, Md.

Steiner G. 1996. *The Death of Tragedy*. Yale University Press, New Haven, Conn. (Orig. pub. 1961.)

Storr A. 1991. *The Dynamics of Creation*. Penguin, London.

———. 1992. *Music and the Mind*. HarperCollins, London.

Tattersall I. 2003. Out of Africa again, and again. *Scientific American* 13, 38–45.

Taylor J, ed. 1958. *Selected Writings of John Hughlings Jackson*. Vol. 2. Staples, London.

Tek C, Ulug B. 2001. Religiosity and religious obsessions in obsessive-compulsive disorder. *Psychiatry Research* 104, 99–108.

Temkin O. 1971. *The Falling Sickness*. 2d ed. Johns Hopkins University Press, Baltimore, Md.

Terzian H. 1964. Behavioural and EEG effects of intracarotid sodium amytal injection. *Acta Neurochirurgica* 12, 230–39.

Thiele PT. 1990. *Frederich Nietzsche and the Politics of the Soul*. Princeton University Press, Princeton, N.J.

Tillyard, EMW. 1998. *The Elizabethan World Picture*. Pimlico, London. (Orig. pub. 1943.)

Trehub SE. 2001. Musical predispositions in infancy. In *The Biological Foundations of Music*, ed. Zatorre RJ, Peretz I, 1–16. New York Academy of Sciences, vol. 930.

Trimble MR. 1986. Hypergraphia. In *Aspects of Epilepsy and Psychiatry*, ed. Trimble MR, Bolwig TG, 75–88. Wiley and Sons, Chichester, U.K.

———. 1988. *Biological Psychiatry*. Wiley and Sons, Chichester, U.K.

———. 1991. *The Psychoses of Epilepsy*. Raven, New York.

———. 1996. *Biological Psychiatry*. 2d ed. Wiley and Sons, Chichester, U.K.

Trimble MR, Freeman A. 2006. *Epilepsy and Behaviour*, 407–14.

Tucker DM, Williamson PA. 1984. Asymmetric neural control systems in human self-regulation. *Psychological Review* 91, 185–215.

Tulving E, Kapur S, Markowitsch HJ, Craik FIM, Habib R, Houle S. 1994. Neuroanatomical correlates of retrieval in episodic memory. *Proceedings of the National Academy of Sciences* 91, 2012–15.

Vallortigara G, Rogers LJ. 2005. Survival with an asymmetrical brain: advantages and disadvantages of cerebral lateralisation. *Behavioural and Brain Sciences* 28, 575–89.

Van Vugt P, Paquier P, Kees L, Crass P. 1996. Increased writing activity in neurological conditions: a review and a clinical study. *Journal of Neurology, Neurosurgery, and Psychiatry* 61, 510–14.

Wagner R. 1994. *Religion and Art*. Trans. Ellis WA. University of Nebraska Press, Lincoln. (Orig. pub. 1897.)

Waller NG, Kojetin A, Bouchard TJ, Lykken DT, Tellegen A. 1990. Genetic and environmental influences on religious interests, attitudes, and values. *Psychological Science* 1, 138–42.

Walters R. 1988. Keats and cyclothymia. *Keats-Shelley Review,* 70–75.

Wapner W, Hamby S, Gardner H. 1981. The role of the right hemisphere in the appreciation of complex linguistic materials. *Brain and Language* 145, 15–33.

Waxman SG, Geschwind N. 1974. Hypergraphia in temporal lobe epilepsy. *Neurology* 24, 629–36.

Wendling RC. 1995. *Coleridge's Progress to Christianity.* Bucknell University Press, Lewisburg, Pa.

Wheen F. 2004. *How Mumbo-Jumbo Conquered the World: A Short History of Modern Delusions.* Forth Estate, London.

Whitehead AN. 1926. *Religion in the Making.* Macmillan, London.

Wieser HG, Hungerbühler H, Siegel A, Buck A. 1997. Musicogenic epilepsy: review of the literature and a case report with ictal SPECT. *Epilepsia* 38, 200–207.

Wilson EO. 1978. *On Human Nature.* Harvard University Press, Cambridge, Mass.

Winner E, Gardner H. 1977. The comprehension of metaphor in brain-damaged patients. *Brain* 100, 717–29.

Winokur G, Tsuang M. 1996. *The Natural History of Mania, Depression, and Schizophrenia.* American Psychiatric Association, Washington, D.C.

Woodhouse ASP. 1965. *The Poet and His Faith: Religion and Poetry in England from Spenser to Eliot and Auden.* University of Chicago Press, Chicago.

Wordsworth W, Coleridge ST. 1963. *Lyrical Ballads.* Ed. Brett RL, Jones AR. Methuen, London. (Orig. pub. 1798.)

World Health Organization (WHO). 1979. *Schizophrenia: An International Follow-up Study.* Wiley and Sons, Chichester, U.K.

———. 1992. *International Classification of Diseases.* 10th ed. World Health Organization, Geneva.

Wuerfel J, Krishnamoorthy ES, Brown RJ, Lemieux L, et al. 2004. Religiosity is associated with hippocampal but not amygdala volumes in patients with refractory epilepsy. *Journal of Neurology, Neurosurgery, and Psychiatry* 75, 640–42.

Yakovlev. 1948. Motility, behaviour, and the brain. *Journal of Nervous and Mental Disease* 107, 313–35.

Yamadori A, Osumi Y, Masuhara S, Okubo M. 1977. Preservation of singing in Broca's aphasia. *Journal of Neurology, Neurosurgery, and Psychiatry* 40, 221–24.

Young J. 1992. *Nietzsche's Philosophy of Art.* Cambridge University Press, Cambridge, U.K.

Young JZ. 1981. *Programmes of the Brain.* Oxford University Press, Oxford, U.K.

Zatorre RJ. 2001. Neural specializations for tonal processing. In *The Biological Foundations of Music,* ed. Zatorre RJ, Peretz I, 193–210. New York Academy of Sciences, vol. 930.

Zatorre RJ, Halpern AR. 1993. Effect of unilateral temporal-lobe excision on perception and imagery of songs. *Neuropsychologia* 31, 221–32.

Zimmer C. 2004. *Soul Made Flesh: Thomas Willis, the English Civil War, and the Mapping of the Mind.* Heinemann, London.

Page numbers followed by *f* and *t* refer to figures and tables, respectively.

Michael R. Trimble, M.D., F.R.C.P., F.R.C.Psych., is a professor of Behavioral Neurology at the Institute of Neurology, University of London. He received his medical degree from Birmingham University, having first obtained a degree in neuroanatomy. His postgraduate training included general medicine at the Radcliffe Infirmary in Oxford; neurology at the National Hospital for Neurology and Neurosurgery in Queen Square, London; and psychiatry at the Maudsley Hospital in London and Johns Hopkins Hospital in Baltimore. For many years, he was a consultant physician to the Department of Psychological Medicine at the National Hospital for Neurology and Neurosurgery and senior lecturer and then professor of Behavioral Neurology at the Institute of Neurology Queen Square in London.

Dr. Trimble studies the interface between neurology and psychiatry, and he developed a research unit that primarily investigated the behavioral consequences of neurological diseases and their treatments. Of particular relevance in his studies has been his contact with people with epilepsy. Other areas of interest have been movement disorders and the history of neuropsychiatry. Besides medicine, Dr. Trimble enjoys music, especially opera, and poetry, and he has studied the artistic productions of his patients with a variety of neurological and psychiatric disorders.

Dr. Trimble has published more than 120 peer-reviewed articles and has contributed many chapters to academic books. He has edited twenty-six books and written seven, mostly about alterations of behavior in relation to neurological dysfunction.

And that is why all religion is about absence. Because once the gods *were* there. And that is why all poetry and music strike us with this awful longing for what once was ours—because it begins in regions of the brain where once the gods made themselves heard.

—S. Faulkes, *Human Tissue,* 453